Information Markets

Information Markets

A New Way of Making Decisions

Editors

Robert W. Hahn and Paul C. Tetlock

AEI-Brookings Joint Center for Regulatory Studies
WASHINGTON, D.C.

Distributed to the Trade by National Book Network, 15200 NBN Way, Blue Ridge Summit, PA 17214. To order call toll free 1-800-462-6420 or 1-717-794-3800. For all other inquiries please contact the AEI Press, 1150 Seventeenth Street, N.W., Washington, D.C. 20036 or call 1-800-862-5801.

Library of Congress Cataloging-in-Publication Data

Information markets : a new way of making decisions / edited by Robert W. Hahn and Paul C. Tetlock.

p. cm.

Includes index.

ISBN-10 0-8447-4228-7 (pbk : alk. paper)

ISBN-13 978-0-8447-4228-1

1. Forecasting—Congresses. 2. Decision making—Congresses. 3. Economic forecasting—Congresses. I. Hahn, Robert William. II. Tetlock, Paul C.

H61.4.I54 2006
003'.2—dc22

2006005981

11 10 09 08 07 06 1 2 3 4 5 6

The AEI Press
Publisher for the American Enterprise Institute
1150 17th Street, N.W.
Washington, D.C. 20036

Printed in the United States of America

Contents

List of Illustrations

FIGURES

TABLES

Preface

Information markets are markets for contracts that yield payments based on the outcome of an uncertain future event. Now used to predict a wide range of events, from presidential elections to printer sales, these markets have in many cases been shown to forecast outcomes better than experts or opinion polls.

This collection of essays provides a state-of-the-art analysis of the potential impact of information markets on public policy and private decision-making. It is the result of an AEI-Brookings Joint Center conference held on December 10, 2004.

The authors examine a number of fundamental issues in this area. These include assessing what we really know about information markets, in particular how well they forecast the future; examining the potential of information markets to improve policy; laying out a research agenda to help improve our understanding of information markets; and explaining how we might systematically improve the design of such markets.

Like all Joint Center publications, this monograph can be freely downloaded at www.aei-brookings.org. We encourage educators to distribute these materials to their students.

ROBERT W. HAHN, Executive Director
ROBERT E. LITAN, Director
AEI-Brookings Joint Center
for Regulatory Studies

1

Introduction to Information Markets

Robert W. Hahn and Paul C. Tetlock

Back in the late 1980s, a handful of academics at the University of Iowa's business school came up with an idea for giving students hands-on experience in trading markets, such as the stock and commodities markets. Rather than using play money to simulate trading, they created a real market in which anyone could bet modest sums on the outcome of future events—for example, on who would be the next president of the United States. And they convinced government regulators that because the market would be primarily a teaching device, it would not require oversight by the Commodity Futures Trading Commission (CFTC).

Today, the Iowa Electronic Markets (IEM) is a thriving nonprofit enterprise, offering markets in which traders can wager on events ranging from the outcomes of presidential elections to the periodic interest rate decisions of the Federal Reserve's Open Market Committee.

To see how the IEM works, consider the winner-take-all 2004 presidential election market. On October 16, 2004, the price of a $1.00 John F. Kerry contract was $0.39, implying that the market "believed" Kerry had a 39 percent chance of beating George W. Bush. (In previous weeks, the price of a Kerry contract had fluctuated from a high of $0.54 to a low of $0.28.)[1] Thus, on October 16, if you believed Kerry's chances of winning were better than 39 percent, you had the opportunity to put your money where your intuition was.

The authors thank Katrina Kosec and Rohit Malik for research assistance. This paper represents the views of the authors and does not necessarily represent those of the institutions with which they are affiliated.

It is tempting to assume that the IEM is just an entertainment device to make more palatable the sometimes dreary task of learning to be a good securities speculator (or corporate commodities hedger). In fact, so-called information markets are beginning to get respect from the pros—and for good reason. Just as Las Vegas parimutuel betting markets have a better record than professional gamblers in predicting the outcomes of sporting events, prices on the IEM during the past four elections have proved more accurate than pollsters in forecasting elections more than 75 percent of the time.[2]

Why do information markets work as well as they do?[3] We are not completely sure, but we have some strong hunches. No individual expert is likely to know everything there is to know about the probabilities of uncertain events. By allowing experts to trade with one another, markets help to aggregate disparate pieces of information. Moreover, anonymous markets are more likely to process all the available information and to reward and punish bettors in a straightforward fashion. So the market price reflects what *New Yorker* columnist James Surowiecki calls, in his fascinating book of the same name, "the wisdom of crowds."[4]

Another theory of why markets outperform experts relies on how markets weigh trading information. Traders with a lot of valuable information may make bigger bets, and they are the ones who influence prices the most.[5] By contrast, without relying on self-reported confidence judgments, there is no obvious way to bring together the diverse opinions of individual experts, some of whom may not possess much information at all.

But there are some real puzzles. For example, prices of securities in Oscar, Emmy, and Grammy awards are highly correlated with actual award outcomes, and the prices of movie stocks are a good predictor of how a movie will fare at the box office. And other markets appear to work well when the stakes are limited, as they are in the Iowa Electronic Markets.[6] The bottom line is that information markets seem to work reasonably well in a wide variety of settings.

The corporate world is catching on to this insight. Indeed, firms ranging from Hewlett-Packard to Microsoft to Goldman Sachs are experimenting with information markets for making business decisions that increase their profits.

We believe the superior ability of markets to amass and process information in many settings could also be harnessed in the service of public policymaking. They could improve the quality of information on which the government bases decisions, as well as make politicians more accountable to the electorate.

In the process, information markets could make more practical the enlistment of private enterprise in pay-for-performance arrangements to meet societal needs. For example, a school district wanting to raise reading test scores might place the value of a ten-point score increase at $5 per child. The school board can then auction off to the highest bidder the right to introduce a program targeted at reading improvement. That bidder receives $5 for each child whose score improves by a specified date. Essentially, the bidder gets paid on the basis of what he delivers. Such a policy shift could result in a genuine renaissance of government in an era of scarce financial resources, and even scarcer public confidence in the efficiency and benevolence of the political system.

Scholars have suggested that information markets can supply information that could improve the benefit-cost analysis of selected policies. For example, a country wishing to implement a vaccination program could use an information market to estimate the number of vaccinations that would result under current policy. This estimate could then be used with other information to decide whether it was worth introducing a new program.[7] More generally, information markets could be used to help lawmakers decide which programs are worth funding and to help guarantee that they actually deliver results. Provided such markets work well, many applications are possible in both the private and public sectors.

If the idea of using markets to replace experts in predicting the seemingly unpredictable sounds a bit familiar—and just a bit bonkers—go to the head of the class. It would be foolish to introduce a novel way of government decision-making by picking the hardest case first, yet that is exactly what happened: In July 2003, the *New York Post* disclosed that the Pentagon's Defense Advanced Research Projects Agency was planning to create a market in which traders could bet on where and when terrorists would strike.[8]

This is not as crazy as it might look at first glance. We know relatively little about the motives or capacities of terrorists. And we are not inclined to trust experts, who can gain politically from predictions, to amass and process the information that is available. But a market for terrorism may have been unworkable. The prices could inform the government about terrorists' attack plans, but they could also inform terrorists about the government's security plans. What's more, terrorists could profit from inside information, leading to public outrage.

Whatever the merits of the plan, Washington proved unwilling to venture into this brave new world. "There is something very sick about it," concluded Senator Barbara Boxer of California. "I think you ought to end the careers of whoever it was thought that up."[9]

Well, we heartily disagree with this last statement. Indeed, some of the contributors to this book were the architects of markets that could have provided valuable information on terrorism.

This volume assembles essays from many of the world's leading thinkers on information markets. It is the product of a daylong conference held at the AEI-Brookings Joint Center on December 10, 2004, the purpose of which was to explore both the strengths and limitations of information markets in aiding economic decision-making in the public, private, and not-for-profit sectors. A number of important arguments regarding information markets were brought out at the conference. We think it fair to say that most of the participants agreed on the following points:

Information markets have substantial potential. Best-selling author James Surowiecki, who attended this conference, offers a number of examples in *The Wisdom of Crowds*, in which small and large groups of people seem to do better at decision-making than individuals. These include figuring out the weight of an ox, estimating the number of jelly beans in a jar, and locating a lost submarine. In his view, the key challenge is to tap into the wisdom of the crowds, and the potential for doing so appears to be quite large.

Surowiecki is not alone in his thinking. Currently, more than twenty websites offer information market contracts.[10] TradeSports.com, for example, offers information contracts in a number of areas, including sports, politics, finance, law, entertainment, and even the weather. Goldman Sachs supports an over-the-counter market called EconomicDerivatives.com, which hosts auctions for contracts based on economic indices.[11] And the Chicago Mercantile Exchange lists weather derivatives.[12]

Companies are also getting into the act. Hewlett-Packard has experimented with information markets to forecast sales, and Eli Lilly has used them to help predict what drugs will be successful.[13] Microsoft set up an experimental market to forecast sales of software.[14] The trend toward greater experimentation with information markets for different applications shows no signs of abating in the short term.

Robin Hanson, one of the pioneers in this area, has suggested that decision markets (information markets that directly inform a decision, such as whether to implement a specific policy) should be used to assess all kinds of government policies. For example, if information market prices suggest a policy will increase GDP, then it should be adopted.[15] Michael Abramowicz has also noted the potential for such markets. He advocates using information markets that predict the results of a cost-benefit analysis to be conducted in the future by a designated expert.[16] Several scholars have suggested these markets be considered in small-group settings, and two chapters in this volume—one by Abramowicz and the other by Cass Sunstein—discuss some novel applications.

Some critical design issues need to be addressed before information markets should be used widely, especially as decision markets. Prospects for manipulation might be greater if market participants had a large stake in the outcome of the decision itself. As John Ledyard discusses in chapter 3 of this book, such a linkage can make the already challenging problem of designing a market even more difficult. In his examination of several design issues, Ledyard notes that information markets tend to work well where a large number of potential traders with dispersed information are good at updating probabilities on the basis of new information. When markets are illiquid, meaning that it is costly to buy or sell large quantities, traders have trouble updating probabilities. In addition, when information is concentrated in one or two individuals, the prices in information markets may not provide useful information.

There are two important points to note. First, we need to gain a better understanding of the limits of these markets—something that Ledyard does in the experiments discussed in his chapter[17]—asking, for example, what are the costs and benefits of different mechanisms aimed at providing liquidity in markets? Second, we need to consider that even if information markets perform below some hypothetical optimum level, they could still be very valuable as sources of information if they improve upon the status quo.

The regulation of information markets in the United States is likely to stymie innovation. It is currently difficult to set up an information market in the United States. A firm basically has five options:[18]

- Obtain a "no action" letter from the CFTC.[19]
- List the information market on a traditional futures exchange, such as the Chicago Mercantile Exchange.
- Get approval for the firm from relevant regulatory commissions in all the states in which it plans to operate.
- Open up a market outside the United States but run the risk of prosecution.
- Develop a market, as Goldman Sachs does with its EconomicDerivatives.com, that is excluded from CFTC regulation because it involves large, sophisticated investors.

Both the states and the federal government assert jurisdiction over information markets. Frequently, states treat them as a kind of Internet gambling. Firms or researchers who are setting up a market do not want to be subject to a variety of different state laws that are often ambiguous.

At the federal level, the CFTC regulates many kinds of information markets, but its regulations are currently in flux. Only one academic group, the Iowa Electronic Markets, is operating, and that is because its researchers were lucky enough to obtain a letter from the CFTC that permitted them to do so under certain conditions. These letters are no longer being given out.

It is also difficult for firms to get regulatory approval. This may be one of the reasons that TradeSports.com is not located in the United States. Recently, the CFTC allowed HedgeStreet.com to set up information market contracts and claimed regulatory jurisdiction over them.

A key challenge is to design ways of making it easier to introduce information markets that could improve economic welfare. Several scholars have suggested using different kinds of tests to streamline regulation. A basic problem faced by the CFTC is avoiding being seen as an agency that promotes gambling. As a partial solution, some scholars have suggested that information markets be required to pass a kind of economic purpose test.[20] One has suggested that such contracts are better handled using contract law.[21] Although there is not a consensus on the solution, there appears to be a consensus that a problem exists with the way information markets are regulated. Furthermore, there appears to be a consensus that researchers should be allowed to experiment with these markets so they can learn more about their properties and potential.

Plan of This Book

This book addresses a number of cutting-edge topics in the theory of information markets, their design, and their performance to date. Chapter 2, by Justin Wolfers and Eric Zitzewitz, describes five open questions about information markets and gives some background on what we know about them. The authors note that interest in information markets is driven, in part, by the hope that they will improve forecasting, decision-making, and risk management. But to accomplish these things, information and decision markets must confront a number of challenges, including attracting uninformed traders to get informed traders to participate; writing items of interest, such as a policy outcome, into contracts; limiting market manipulation; handling low-probability events; and, finally, separating correlation from causation. On the last issue, the authors suggest a clever way to apply instrumental variables to information markets, a technique often used in econometrics to sort out cause and effect. Although they see promise in this technique for understanding causation, the authors acknowledge that it has limitations when good instrumental variables cannot be identified.

In chapter 3, John Ledyard identifies some key design issues and presents some new data on the limits of information markets. He explains why information markets might and might not work in policy analysis and spells out a research agenda for improving their design. He notes that the many naturally occurring information markets, such as parimutuel betting, have generally performed well. Ledyard uses evidence from theory, experiments, and applications to identify which information market designs will work best. He notes, however, that the theoretical conditions necessary for such markets to work well, such as price-taking and honest revelation, may not apply in many settings. In particular, he suggests that illiquid policy markets, where individuals have a stake in the outcome, may not provide very useful information. Furthermore, he notes that the number of markets needed to address key questions may rise quickly, leading to illiquid markets. Ledyard concludes that policymakers will need to make critical tradeoffs between the number of markets and the value of information.

Chapters 4 and 5 address information markets in small-group settings. Cass Sunstein identifies three possibilities for eliciting and aggregating information in small groups: Groups could use the average of individual judgments; they could deliberate; or they could use information markets. Deliberation, while common, often fails to result in good decisions because some members of the group do not disclose what they know, sometimes due to social pressures. Sunstein argues that information markets may have substantial advantages over deliberation and advocates using them more widely.

In chapter 5, Michael Abramowicz argues that existing information markets offer traders limited incentives to reveal new information. Markets that provide greater incentives might be more accurate and decrease the redundant acquisition of information, especially in small-group settings. To encourage the release of information and analysis, Abramowicz suggests a new approach that rewards participants based on the value of their predictions at intermediate stages in the information market rather than on the ultimate value being predicted. A predictor would, thus, need to convince other market participants of the accuracy of the prediction in order to succeed.

In chapter 6, Robin Hanson tackles the critical issue of the potential for market manipulation in information markets. He notes that the accuracy of these markets, relative to other forecasting tools, has raised interest in their wider application. But before extending the broader application of such markets, he suggests, we need to examine concerns about various forms of "foul play," including lying, manipulation, sabotage, embezzlement, and retribution. Hanson reviews these issues and discusses possible ways to mitigate them. He suggests that foul play seems no worse in information markets than in competing institutions for any given level of participation. Furthermore, allowing wider participation could reduce foul play.

In chapter 7, Joyce Berg and Thomas Rietz review the performance of the Iowa Electronic Markets and identify key areas for future research. Using the 2004 election markets as their primary example, Berg and Rietz argue that prediction markets may provide a viable alternative or addition to traditional forecasting methods. They present several empirical findings associated with the IEM, such as:

- Traders in the IEM are not a random sample of the voting population.
- Traders are biased—for example, Democrats thought Kerry was more likely to win the election than Bush.
- Some trading orders are submitted by robots.
- Large trades can move prices.
- Prices are accurate relative to the polls and in an absolute sense.
- Prices respond quickly to news.

They suggest a number of areas for research, including a theoretical model of the IEM that is consistent with observed trader behavior, and the development of methods to detect price manipulation.

In chapter 8, we offer a new approach to economic development based on performance-based policy. The basic idea is to get better information to implement better development decisions by combining the use of information markets with payments for performance. We argue that performance-based policies have the potential to improve the way aid agencies, foundations, nongovernmental organizations, and the private sector promote economic development. In addition to providing economic benefits, performance-based policies could lead to greater accountability and transparency in economic development. Despite its great potential, the approach has some limitations, particularly in information markets with little trading activity.

Conclusion

This is the place where you might expect economists like us to summarize the virtues of our proposals and leave the field of battle in alleged triumph. But we know the idea of using information markets to revolutionize public- and private-sector decision-making is a stretch. All we ask of readers is to contemplate the notion that such markets could make a difference, and a big one at that. We think this is an important field that deserves attention, and we see this volume as an important first step in better understanding the strengths and limitations of information markets in a number of settings. Despite their great potential to improve decision-making, the test will be in the tasting. The challenge will be to create a regulatory environment that does not artificially impede the introduction of these markets where they can serve a socially useful function.

Notes

1. Iowa Electronic Markets, http://www.biz.uiowa.edu/iem/ (accessed October 16, 2004).

2. Commodity Traders, http://www.commoditytraders.com/online_commodity_trading_analysis_online_commodity_trading_analysis_daytrading_113418.html (accessed December 5, 2005).

3. Information markets have also been referred to as event markets, prediction markets, and policy-futures markets. This book will use the terms interchangeably.

4. James Surowiecki, *The Wisdom of Crowds: Why the Many Are Smarter Than the Few and How Collective Wisdom Shapes Business, Economies, Societies, and Nations* (New York: Doubleday, 2004).

5. See Joyce Berg, Forrest Nelson, and Thomas A. Rietz, "Results from a Dozen Years of Election Futures Markets Research" (working paper, University of Iowa, 2003) for a discussion of how the best-informed agents ("marginal traders") are those driving prices and predictions.

6. Emile Servan-Schreiber, Justin Wolfers, David Pennock, and Brian Galebach, "Prediction Markets: Does Money Matter?" *Electronic Markets* 14, no. 3 (2004): 243–51.

7. Robert Hahn and Paul Tetlock, "Using Information Markets to Improve Public Decision Making," *Harvard Journal of Law and Public Policy* (Fall 2005).

8. Niles Lathem, "Pentagon De-Lists Its 'Terror Market,'" *New York Post*, July 30, 2003.

9. Ken Guggenheim, "Pentagon Says Threat-Bet Program to be Canceled," Associated Press, July 29, 2003.

10. See http://www.aei-brookings.org/policyfutures (accessed December 5, 2005) for a list of active event markets.

11. EconomicDerivatives.com, https://gm-secure.db.com/esa/ (accessed December 5, 2005).

12. Chicago Mercantile Exchange, http://www.cme.com/ (accessed December 5, 2005).

13. Kay-Yut Chen and Charles Plott, "Information Aggregation Mechanisms: Concept, Design and Implementation for a Sales Forecasting Problem" (Working Paper 1131, California Institute of Technology, Pasadena, 2002); Barbara Kiviat, "The End of Management?" *Time*, July 12, 2004.

14. Todd Proebsting, "Tee Time with Admiral Poindexter" (DIMACS Workshop on Information Markets, Piscataway, N.J., February 3, 2005), http://www.financialcryptography.com/mt/archives/000316.html (accessed February 22, 2005).

15. See Robin Hanson, "Shall We Vote on Values, but Bet on Beliefs?" (working paper, George Mason University, 2003), 10: "Therefore, if one is willing to recommend policies that statistical studies suggest will increase (a time average of future) GDP, one should be willing to recommend policies that speculative

markets estimate will increase GDP, and so one should be willing to consider a form of government which relies more on such market estimates in choosing policies."

16. Michael Abramowicz, "Information Markets, Administrative Decision-making, and Predictive Cost-Benefit Analysis," *University of Chicago Law Review* 71 (2004): 940. "This article thus imagines predictive cost-benefit analysis, an information market used to predict a *cost-benefit analysis* that would be performed some time after a decision whether to enact a policy."

17. These experiments were done jointly with Theodore Groves.

18. Michael Gorham and Barnali Biswall, "The Regulatory Outlook for Event Markets: Cool with Patches of Fog" (working paper, IIT Center for Financial Markets, Stuart Graduate School of Business, Illinois Institute of Technology, 2005, on file with authors).

19. A no action letter says that if you do business in the fashion you have indicated in a written request made to the CFTC, then the CFTC's Division of Enforcement will not take action against you.

20. Robert Hahn and Paul Tetlock, "A New Approach for Regulating Information Markets," AEI–Brookings Joint Center for Regulatory Studies, December 2004, http://aei-brookings.org/publications/abstract.php?pid=881 (accessed December 5, 2005), and forthcoming in the *Journal of Regulatory Economics*; Gorham and Biswall, "Regulatory Outlook for Event Markets: Cool with Patches of Fog."

21. See, for example, Thomas Bell, "Gambling for the Good, Trading for the Future: The Legality of Markets in Science Claims," *Chapman Law Review* 5 (2002): 159–80, http://www.tomwbell.com/writings/Gambling4Good.pdf (accessed December 5, 2005). For a different perspective on the need to regulate financial markets, see Bernard Black, "The Legal and Institutional Preconditions for Strong Securities Markets," *UCLA Law Review* 48 (2001): 781–855, http://ssrn.com/abstract=182169 (accessed December 5, 2005).

2

Five Open Questions about Prediction Markets

Justin Wolfers and Eric Zitzewitz

Interest in prediction markets has increased in the past decade among participants, private-sector market operators, policymakers, and academics. Markets on the 2004 U.S. election, for instance, were far more numerous and liquid than they were in 2000. Although past media coverage often treated these markets as curiosities, coverage in the 2004 election cycle was far more frequent and more serious than four years earlier.[1]

Academics are using prediction markets to provide a measure of expectations about an event's probability and then using the co-movement of this measure and financial asset prices to extract information about the expected effects of political decisions,[2] in some cases even before the decisions are made.[3] In the last year, this style of analysis has spread beyond academia, most notably in attempts to analyze the consequences of George W. Bush's reelection. Formal analyses of these markets have tended to conclude that their prices can be useful indicators of likely future outcomes.[4] Interest in new applications of prediction markets is focused in three domains: forecasting, decision-making, and risk management.

The success of corporate prediction markets in forecasting printer sales[5] and project management[6] has stimulated interest in their application to other business problems, and firms such as NewsFutures, Net Exchange,

We would like to thank Brian Elliot, Brian Galebach, and David Pennock for help with data, and Robert Hahn, Marco Ottaviani, Erik Snowberg, and Paul Tetlock for helpful conversations. Wolfers acknowledges the support of a Geewax, Teriker and Co. Research Fellowship, the Mack Center for Technological Research, and the Zull/Lurie Real Estate Center at Wharton.

and Incentive Markets have sprung up to meet this demand. Among the applications being discussed are "decision markets," in which securities are traded that pay off based on an outcome (for example, revenue from a product) if, and only if, a particular decision is made (for example, the decision to launch the product). The idea behind these markets is to elicit knowledge from within an organization that might otherwise be lost.

Similar ideas have been discussed in the policy realm. The Policy Analysis Market of the Defense Advanced Research Projects Agency (DARPA) would have launched securities designed to capture the probability of specific events, along with contingent securities designed to capture the outcome of specific policies. During the 2004 primary season, the Iowa markets ran securities designed to predict the general election success of the Democratic contenders, and, later in the year, TradeSports ran similar contracts designed to capture the effects of geopolitical and economic events on the election.[7] Michael Abramowicz[8] and Robert Hahn and Paul Tetlock[9] envision using prediction markets to assist in policymaking by extracting expert opinion in a credible and objective manner. Robin Hanson goes even further, arguing that policymakers should simply define a "GDP+" measure of social welfare, and base policy decisions entirely on market-based predictions of which policies maximize this measure.[10]

Finally, some envision prediction markets as the first step toward markets where participants could hedge their exposure to political and economic events. For example, an employee in a "Bush industry" (for example, traditional energy) could sell TradeSports's Bush reelection contract to an employee in a "Kerry industry" (for example, alternative energy); both would be hedging their human-capital exposure to the election. The TradeSports Bush reelection contract had trade volume of more than $15 million during the year and a half it traded, and volume of about $3 million on election day.[11] Although this is extremely liquid by prediction-market standards, clearly, more liquidity would be needed to allow for meaningful hedging. HedgeStreet.com, a new CTFC-sanctioned derivatives exchange, is attempting to create markets that individuals can use for such hedging, with a focus more on economic risks such as mortgage rates and real estate prices than on politics.

Will these great expectations for prediction markets be fulfilled? This, we argue, depends in large part on developing answers to five open questions:

1. **How can markets attract uninformed traders?** Counterintuitively, the problem for most prediction markets is attracting sufficient *uninformed* order flow. Markets need uninformed order flow to function; when trading is conducted by rational traders, whose sole motivation is expected returns, the no-trade theorem binds, and the market unravels.[12] Uninformed order flow can have a variety of motivations (entertainment, overconfidence, and hedging, for example), but with the exception of hedging, these are usually noneconomic, putting economists at a comparative disadvantage in predicting which markets will succeed.

2. **How should security design trade off interest and contractibility?** A fundamental problem in mechanism design is that the outcomes of interest are often impossible to write into contracts. Running financial markets on policy outcomes in and of itself does nothing to help with this problem. In fact, using a measure to set payoffs for financial contracts can turn what would otherwise be a good proxy for a policy outcome into a problematic one, as illustrated by the recent experience with the manipulation of cash settlement prices for Standard & Poor's (S&P) and municipal bond futures.

3. **How can markets limit manipulation?** In addition to manipulation of the outcomes on which prediction markets are based, one might worry about manipulation of prediction-market prices themselves, particularly where high-stakes decisions are based on the prices.

4. **Are markets well-calibrated on small probabilities?** Many of the proposed uses of prediction markets will involve the evaluation of small-probability events. A range of behavioral evidence suggests that people are quite poor at distinguishing small probabilities from tiny ones, and even when arbitrage is possible, frictions can cause this miscalibration to carry over into market prices.

5. **How can analysts separate correlation from causation?** Contingent prediction markets allow us to estimate the probability

of an event contingent on another event occurring. Thus, contingent markets provide insight into the correlation of events. Determining whether one event *causes* the probability of another to change is a separate and potentially more important question, however. Many of the proposed uses of decision markets presuppose that the direction of causality can be readily established.

A Framework

Before discussing these questions, we will introduce a simple model that can serve as a common framework for thinking about most of them. We do this by taking the basic setup from the familiar Kyle model[13] and adding transaction costs, which we believe may be an important factor shaping the efficiency of pricing in small-scale prediction markets, and market-maker risk aversion, which allows uninformed order flow to affect prices.

As in Kyle, we consider three types of agents: perfectly informed traders, uninformed (noise or liquidity) traders, and perfectly competitive market-makers. Trade is in a binary prediction-market security that pays $y = \$1$ if an event occurs and $y = \$0$ otherwise.

The probability that the event occurs is given by q; this probability is observed by the market-makers. The perfectly informed traders have inside information and know whether the event will occur. The uninformed traders have a noisy subjective expectation of the event probability given by q plus a noise term η. All traders have log utility and trade to maximize their subjective expected utility. As such, they take positions:

$$x = \frac{w}{p(1-p)}(e-p),$$

where w is their wealth, p is the price of the security, e is their subjective expectation that the event occurs, and these parameters yield demand for x prediction securities.[14]

In addition, we can allow the uninformed traders to derive a direct utility benefit from holding a particular position, perhaps for gambling or entertainment reasons. If this direct benefit has a per-unit certainty equivalent of g, then the uninformed trader will trade as if $e = q + \eta + g$.

Alternatively, if the market price is being used in a decision, traders may have other (external) reasons to trade in order to affect the price. As such, g may represent the gains to market manipulators from their effect on the equilibrium price. Thus, for manipulators, g would be equal to the product of the marginal price impact of their trading and the outside benefit they receive from moving the price.

This framework also lends itself quite naturally to considering a hedging motive for trade. Risk-averse traders have a hedging demand when their wealth depends on whether the event occurs. We can view this as beginning trading with an endowment of contracts, and optimal hedging simply involves deciding how much of this endowment to sell at the market price. In this setup, if the trader's wealth is H lower if the event happens, the trader will trade as if $e = q + \eta + g + H \cdot p \cdot (1-p)/w$.

So, to summarize, traders trade based on the sum of objective probability (q), expectation errors (η), gambling and manipulation motives (g), and a hedging motive related to the risk in the endowment of traders (H). These different beliefs and motives are summarized in the variable e, which is drawn from the distribution $F(e)$.

If traders face a per-contract transaction cost, t, they will buy if $e - t > p$ and sell if $e + t < p$.

A competitive group of market-makers will post bids and offers such that the marginal utility of an additional trade, if made, is zero. These conditions are:

$$P_{bid} = E(y|e + t < P_{bid}) - t_{MM} - cx_{MM}$$

$$P_{ask} = E(y|e - t > P_{ask}) + t_{MM} - cx_{MM}$$

where $c = p\ (1 - p)/w$ captures the risk-averse market-makers' desire to shade prices lower when they built up a large exposure (x_{MM}) in this market.

With no informed traders, the market-makers' *expectations* do not change with the order flow, so $P_{bid} = q - t_{MM} - cx_{MM}$ and $P_{ask} = q + t_{MM} - cx_{MM}$. (Note, however, that due to their desire to limit exposure, market-makers will change *prices* in response to new orders.) Traders only buy or sell when their subjectively held beliefs differ from the market-maker's prices by at least the sum of their own and the market-maker's transaction costs (when $|e - (q - cx_{MM})| >= t + t_{MM}$). The equilibrium bid-ask midpoint must satisfy:

$$p_{mid} = q + c[X_{buy}(p_{mid} + t + t_{MM}) + X_{sell}(p_{mid} - t - t_{MM})]$$

$$X_{buy}(p) = \int_p^1 x(e - p) \cdot dF(e)$$

$$X_{sell}(p) = \int_0^p x(e - p) \cdot dF(e)$$

where X_{buy} and X_{sell} are total demand from buyers and sellers, respectively.

Transaction costs cause trading to be done entirely by the traders with the most noisy observations of the event probability or, alternatively, with the greatest external motivations (gambling, hedging, or manipulation) for holding the securities. The market-maker's observation of the objective probability does help hold market prices close to their efficient levels (q), but market-maker risk aversion, combined with an asymmetry in the distribution of $e - q$, can cause prices to deviate from objective probabilities.[15]

Adding perfectly informed traders has two effects. The perfectly informed traders buy when $y = 1$ and sell when $y = 0$, affecting market-maker inventory in a way that pushes the final bid-ask midpoint toward y. At the same time, these traders force the market-maker to add an adverse-selection component to the bid-ask spread, which causes the uninformed traders to be further restricted to those with extreme values of e.[16] Too much informed trade can cause markets to unravel, and this is especially likely when high transaction costs are already limiting uninformed trade.[17]

The discussion above suggests that low transaction costs are essential to liquid, active, and informative prediction markets. Adding a fixed pool of perfectly informed traders leads these insiders effectively to levy a tax on the trading of market-makers and traders, and greater expected volume can lower the contribution toward this fixed cost required from each trade. High- and low-liquidity equilibria may be simultaneously possible. This brings us to our first open question: Will prediction markets attract necessary uninformed trade?

Attracting Uninformed Traders

An important implication of the model sketched above is that the success of the prediction market in generating trade depends critically on attracting uninformed traders.[18] Prediction markets are too small for meaningful hedging, and are likely to remain so for some time, so the primary motivations for uninformed order flow are likely to be entertainment and overconfidence. Economists may be at a comparative disadvantage in analyzing these motivations, but we can look at what has worked.

Risk-love, or the "thrill of a gamble," provides obvious motives for uninformed traders, and both TradeSports and Betfair have successfully attracted many sports bettors to their markets. TradeSports runs a variety of nonsports markets, but the contracts that attract significant volume on TradeSports are typically those with popular currency (the presidential election, the fates of Saddam Hussein and Martha Stewart, outcomes on *American Idol* and *The Apprentice*), suggesting primarily an entertainment motive for trading. Beyond sports bettors, TradeSports has been quite successful at marketing its platform to those employed in financial markets, a pool of risk-acceptant traders.

At the same time, contracts on more "serious" topics (economic numbers, financial market outcomes, and contingent political contracts) attract volume that compares favorably with volumes on the successful Iowa vote-share markets. These traders may have been attracted more by the substantial free media attention TradeSports has received, and uninformed trading in these contracts may be more of a combination of entertainment and overconfidence motives. As the wonkishness of the contract rises, however, volume and liquidity fall rapidly. The few TradeSports markets of the sort planned by the DARPA Policy Analysis Market (for example, will there be a Palestinian state by 2005?) have not been very successful.

The legal environment has forced onshore prediction markets to make compromises that have limited their attractiveness. The Iowa Electronic Markets agreed to limit positions to $500 in order to receive a "no action" letter from the Commodity Futures Trading Commission (CFTC).[19] This compromise limits the scope and depth of their markets, and possibly their efficiency. For example, the "Will Bush win the popular vote?" contracts on TradeSports and IEM often trade at levels different enough to imply arbitrage opportunities, albeit opportunities to win only small amounts, given the position limits on the Iowa exchange.[20]

Other markets made other compromises. Platforms such as News-Futures, the Hollywood Stock Exchange, and the Foresight Exchange operate using play money, albeit play money that can sometimes be converted into prizes. Many economists may be skeptical that play-money markets solve the cheap-talk problem that prediction markets are meant to solve, and, indeed, play-money and real-money market prices can and do diverge. That said, a comparison of NewsFutures and TradeSports prices for securities predicting NFL victories for the 2003 season found that although the two markets often yielded different predictions, they were about equally well calibrated.[21]

The consulting firms running corporate prediction markets have taken the same approach as experimental economists on campuses: They have subsidized participation, allowing everyone to leave a winner, albeit to varying degrees. The Policy Analysis Market was also supposed to have involved a subsidy for participation. If the information to be generated by the market is important enough to justify the subsidy, and a willing financier can be enlisted, then this approach can work. It is important, however, that subsidies not be designed in such a way that they can be gamed, as one could imagine with per-trade subsidies or with some schemes for subsidization via a money-losing market-maker.

Finally, two markets that we are aware of, Economic Derivatives and HedgeStreet, have obtained regulatory approval to operate as futures exchanges. Both have avoided political contracts and have focused instead on economic events, probably to avoid being considered betting venues as opposed to financial markets. HedgeStreet has only recently started up, but Economic Derivatives, a joint venture by Deutsche Bank and Goldman Sachs that runs markets in economic numbers, has been operating since 2002. Its traders are all institutional, and its markets have attracted volumes of hundreds of millions of dollars. Traders reportedly trade for hedging reasons.[22] In addition, a combination of overconfidence and career concerns may provide a motivation for trading—no self-respecting economic analyst would want to admit that he knows only as much as his average colleague.

Career concerns may conceivably provide a motivation to participate in some of the business and policy applications that are being considered.

If the decision to trade is motivated by career concerns, however, the trading itself may reflect objectives other than maximizing trading profits. For instance, although rank-order tournaments can create efficient incentives in many career models, in the trading context they may lead to "doubling up," or related high-variance strategies.

To summarize, we have suggested that three routes to attracting order flow have been successful thus far: offering sports betting, subsidization, and, possibly, exploiting career concerns. Each has its own drawbacks, however.

Balancing Interest and Contractibility

Observable indicators of contractibility have thus far done little to explain the success of a prediction market. While contracts on the IEM have multipage prospectuses clearly outlining how the market will settle under a number of contingencies, contract "prospectuses" on TradeSports are often limited to the single sentence below the contract name on the trading screen. In some cases, this sentence is supplemented by a short memo announcing the contract, but even then issues that have material effect on event probabilities are only subsequently clarified in response to questions. For example, TradeSports offered a contract on whether Yasser Arafat would depart the Palestinian state by the end of 2005. When he became ill in late 2004, there was mild controversy on the TradeSports forum (http://forum.tradesports.com) about whether seeking medical treatment in Paris or dying was considered departing Palestine. TradeSports tightened the contract definition to include the latter but not the former.

TradeSports traders have thus far been willing to trust the exchange to make a good-faith determination, and this trust is helped because TradeSports does not itself hold positions in any of its contracts, and because it has a clear need to maintain a reputation for fairness among its traders. But as the sums traded become more substantial, traders may begin to worry more about these issues. As the example of the Arafat Security illustrates, in some cases no definition captures the event of interest perfectly.[23]

This issue is likely to become even more salient once contracts start trading on policy outcomes. Many policy outcomes are notoriously difficult to reduce to a simple set of measures. To take one of the less-problematic examples, suppose one runs a prediction market on the crime rate in Baghdad. One presumably cares about the actual crime rate, but a contract is more likely to be written on the reported crime rate. The reported crime rate may have historically been a reasonable proxy for the actual crime rate, but this relationship may not hold up for several reasons. Reported crimes may be an inverted U-shaped function of true crimes—at some point, the reported rate may decline as the true rate rises. Furthermore, if individuals can influence the reported crime rate and have incentives to do so, either arising from, or independent of, the prediction market, the two rates can diverge.

These issues may also arise in business contexts. One might view a tracking stock as analogous to a prediction-market security on the future stream of a business unit's profits. Tracking stocks have been greeted with some skepticism, given the incentive of the parent company to influence the business unit's profits through devices such as transfer pricing.

Managing Manipulation

Just as thinking about the contractibility of the outcomes of interest raises questions about outcome manipulation, the prospect of basing decisions on prediction markets raises questions about the potential for price manipulation.

In some of the applications that have been proposed for prediction markets, one might expect these outside interests to be the dominant determinant of traders' positions. For example, if a market were run among industry participants on which technological standard the industry should adopt, one could imagine that trading would be driven primarily by an interest in influencing the outcome. With no firm-level position limits, one could imagine such a market turning into an auction; with position limits, it could turn into voting. Either mechanism might be a satisfactory way of choosing a standard (ignoring potential antitrust concerns), but, arguably, simply running an auction would be more transparent than (and thus preferable to) running a prediction market that approximates an auction.

Manipulation can be made more expensive by allowing free entry into these markets and by providing a means for entrants to invest in becoming informed.[24] Known attempts to manipulate public prediction markets have largely failed. In 1996, Pat Buchanan's supporters reportedly attempted to bid up his price on the Iowa markets; and in the 2004 election cycle, several large sales of the TradeSports Bush reelection contract temporarily pushed down its price, on September 14 from 63 to 49, and on October 16 from 53 to 10. In these cases, however, the price impact of the trades was reversed within twenty-four hours. Strumpf ran an explicit experiment of randomly placing $500 trades on the Iowa markets and likewise found that the price impact was only temporary.[25]

Although free entry can offset the effects of manipulators, it may be undesirable in corporate contexts where the firm wishes to appropriate returns to the information aggregated in the market. Beyond secrecy concerns, acquiring the information to become an informed trader may be costly enough that free entry does not offset the trading activity of manipulators.

Ensuring Calibration on Small Probabilities

An exception to the generally good predictive track record of betting and prediction markets is their performance on low-probability events. The best-documented example is the favorite/long-shot bias in horse racing.[26] Figures 2-1 and 2-2 on the next page illustrate this point, based on data from a large sample of North American horse races and from the Iowa markets, respectively. Wolfers and Zitzewitz discuss a similar mispricing from S&P 500 index contracts on TradeSports.[27] In both examples, market prices overestimate the probability of unlikely events. In horse racing, the overestimation is greatest for events priced below 5 percent; in the Iowa example, it is present for events priced between 0.2 and 0.3.

A range of experiments by psychologists suggests that the inability to distinguish small from tiny probabilities is not specific to prediction markets. It is, rather, a result of behavioral biases.[28]

A complementary view also suggests that specific types of trading behavior may lead to an overestimation of small probabilities. Charles Manski considered a setting in which prediction-market traders set their bet sizes to maintain a constant downside risk.[29] If this is the case, they

FIGURE 2-1

FAVORITE-LONGSHOT BIAS: RATE OF RETURN AT DIFFERENT ODDS

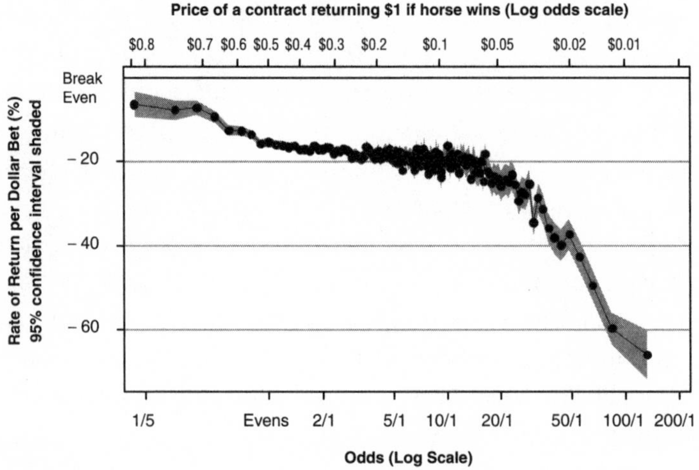

SOURCE: Trackmaster, Inc.

NOTE: Sample is all horse races in the United States, 1992–2002. n=5,067,832 starts in 611,807 races.

FIGURE 2-2

IOWA ELECTRONIC MARKETS: PRICES AND EXPIRY PAYOUTS

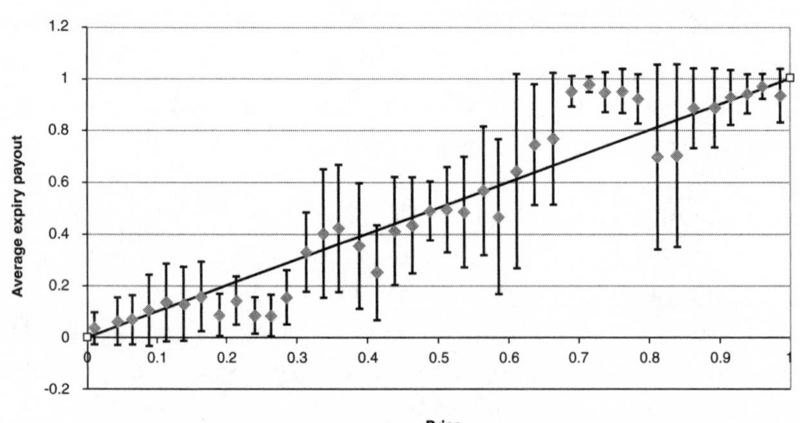

Graph plots the average expiry price of a winner-take-all contract on the Iowa market, conditional on its current price. Data are divided by current price into groups that are 2.5 percentage points wide. Error bars are 95 percent confidence intervals of the estimate of the mean expiry price, calculated from standard errors that are adjusted for sampling the same contract type multiple times. Consecutive groups, however, contain many of the same contracts and thus group means are not indpendent of each other.

SOURCE: Iowa Electronic Markets, http://www.biz.uiowa.edu/iem/.

demand twenty-four times as many contracts when going long at \$0.04 than when shorting the same contract, and, even absent transaction costs, a market price of \$0.04 will reflect the beliefs of traders at the ninety-sixth percentile of the beliefs distribution.[30] Thus, if errors in subjective probability assessments are symmetric, markets may overestimate low probabilities. Wolfers and Zitzewitz analyzed a broader class of models and found these biases to be generally quite small.[31]

The framework discussed earlier suggested a reason these biases could persist in equilibrium. The intuition for the result is that when transaction costs are positive, prices near zero or one are set by those with extreme opinions. To give a concrete example, suppose the objective probability for an event is 3 percent and the market-maker's transaction cost (t_{MM}) is 1 percent. In the absence of informed trading or a net market-maker position, a market-maker will be willing to buy at \$0.02 and sell at \$0.04. If traders also face a transaction cost (t) of \$0.01, then they will buy if their subjective probability is greater than 5 percent and sell if it is less than 1 percent. The former involves an overestimate by a factor of 1.67, the latter an underestimate by a factor of 3. Given these magnitudes, overestimates may be more common than underestimates, leading a risk-averse market-maker to set a bid-ask midpoint greater than the objective probability.

Separating Correlation and Causation

Decision-market securities are designed to allow one to estimate how expectations of policy outcomes vary with the policy chosen. For example, the Iowa markets ran contracts that paid one penny for each percentage point of the two-party vote share won by the Democrats, conditional on the trader also correctly picking the winner of the Democratic nomination race. The ratio of the price of this contract to the price of a contract that pays \$1.00 if the candidate is nominated yields an estimate of the expected vote share of each candidate, conditional on the candidate being nominated (table 2-1 on the next page). In a previous paper, we reported that the expected vote shares on January 29, 2004, were 55 percent for John Edwards, 50 percent for John Kerry, and 46 percent for Howard Dean—if the relevant candidate were to win the nomination.[32]

TABLE 2-1
CONTINGENT MARKETS: 2004 PRESIDENTIAL ELECTION

Contract Pays Conditional on Specific Democratic Candidate	Democratic Candidate Vote Share (Contract price, $) A	Republican Vote Share against This Candidate (Contract price, $) B	Implied Probability This Candidate Wins Nomination (%) $C = A + B$	Expected Share of Popular Vote if Nominated (%) $D = A/C$
John Kerry	0.344	0.342	68.6	50.1
John Edwards	0.082	0.066	14.8	55.4
Howard Dean	0.040	0.047	8.7	46.0
Wesley Clark	0.021	0.025	4.6	45.7
Other Democrats	0.015	0.017	3.2	46.9

SOURCE: Iowa Electronic Markets, closing prices, January 29, 2004.
NOTE: Columns A and B show the prices of contracts that pay $0.01 for each percentage point of the two-party popular vote won by Democrats or Republicans respectively, conditional on picking the winner of the Democratic nomination. (Contracts pay $0.00 if the selected candidate does not win the Democratic nomination.)

It is tempting to draw a causal interpretation from these results: that nominating John Edwards would have produced the highest Democratic vote share. Indeed, as the name "decision markets" implies, this is the inference that we are intended to draw, and, in many circumstances, the most likely source of a correlation will be causal. (Berg and Rietz provide a related account of markets on the 1996 Republican nomination.[33])

But alternative explanations exist. For example, on January 29, Edwards was behind in the delegate count, and only rated a 15 percent probability of winning the nomination. A come-from-behind victory would arguably have required a very good campaigning performance by Edwards or a shift in public sympathies toward his "Two Americas" message, either of which would have boded well for his general election performance. The decision market tells us that in the state of the world in which Edwards wins the nomination, he will also probably do well in the general election. This is not the same as saying that he will do well if, on the basis of the decision market, Democrats nominate Edwards.[34]

A related example of the difficulties of separating correlation from causation comes from the analyses in the financial press of the correlation of

FIGURE 2-3
BUSH'S REELECTION PROSPECTS AND THE STOCK MARKET, 2004

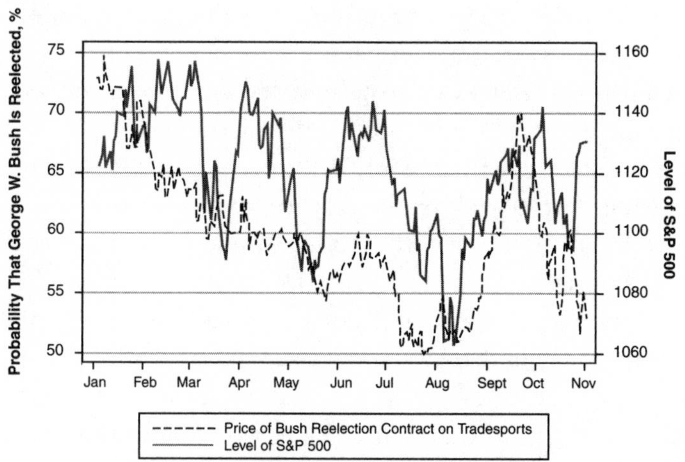

SOURCE: Snowberg, Wolfers, and Zitzewitz, "Partisan Impacts on the Economy: Evidence From Prediction Markets and Close Elections."

President Bush's reelection chances with the performance of the stock market.[35] Figure 2-3, from Snowberg, Wolfers, and Zitzewitz, shows the close relationship between the level of the stock market and the TradeSports contract tied to Bush's reelection.[36] Regressing the (log) level of S&P on the level of Bush price yields a coefficient of 0.204, which led several commentators to infer that Bush's reelection would raise the S&P by 20.4 log percentage points. Difference specifications, which are appropriate given that these are asset prices, yield an estimated effect of 8–16 percentage points.

Only a few careful commentators noted the potential of an endogeneity issue: Bad economic news was hurting both financial markets and Bush's reelection prospects. The disappointing nonfarm payrolls report released three weeks prior to the election provides a stark example of the importance of this omitted causal link: Immediately upon the report's release, the Bush reelection contract fell by 1.5 percentage points (and the S&P 500 future fell by about 0.5 percent).[37]

A common approach to endogeneity issues is to use instrumental variables (IV) estimation. In this context, a valid "instrumental event" must affect Bush's reelection probability, and it affects the stock market only through Bush's reelection probability. The third debate provides one such example.[38] In the three-hour period consisting of the debate and one and a half hours of post-debate spin, the Bush reelection security fell 3 percentage points, and the S&P 500 rallied by 10 basis points. The standard deviation of a three-hour S&P move at that time of day is about 9 basis points, so a 95 percent confidence interval around the estimated market effect of the debate would range from –8 to +28 basis points. Scaling this up to an estimate of the effect of the reelection of President Bush relative to a Kerry counterfactual suggests that the effect of Bush's reelection can be bounded by –9.3 and +2.7 percentage points. Wherever the true causal effect lies in this interval, we can be confident that the naïve inference that a Bush White House would raise the value of U.S. equities by 20 percent was false.

As Snowberg, Wolfers, and Zitzewitz report, an even starker experiment was provided on election night 2004. Figure 2-4 shows the price of the Bush security on TradeSports, sampled every ten minutes, and the S&P 500 (or the December S&P future when the New York markets closed). Clearly, there is strong co-movement in the chart, but the magnitudes are particularly interesting. From 3:00 p.m. to 6:00 p.m., various websites leaked early exit polls that suggested a likely Kerry presidency. These revelations were accompanied by a 1 percent decline in the S&P and roughly a 25-percentage-point decline in the Bush security (from 55 to 30). Later that evening, election returns overturned the exit polls, and from 8:30 p.m. to 1:00 a.m. eastern time, the Bush security rallied from 30 percent to more than 90 percent, and the stock market increased by about 1.5 percent.[39] The former movement scales to an estimated Bush effect of +4 percentage points (= –1/–25), the latter to an estimate of +2.5 percentage points (= 1.5/60).[40] Again, these experiments strongly suggest a different causal effect of a Bush presidency on the stock market than a naïve interpretation of figure 2-3 suggested.

Finally, an instrumental variables approach could potentially be extended to decision markets. For instance, we argued earlier that the price of the "Democrat Vote Share if Edwards" contingent security provided only an estimate of the correlation between Edwards's winning the nomination

FIGURE 2-4

REELECTION PROBABILITY AND THE S&P 500 ON ELECTION NIGHT

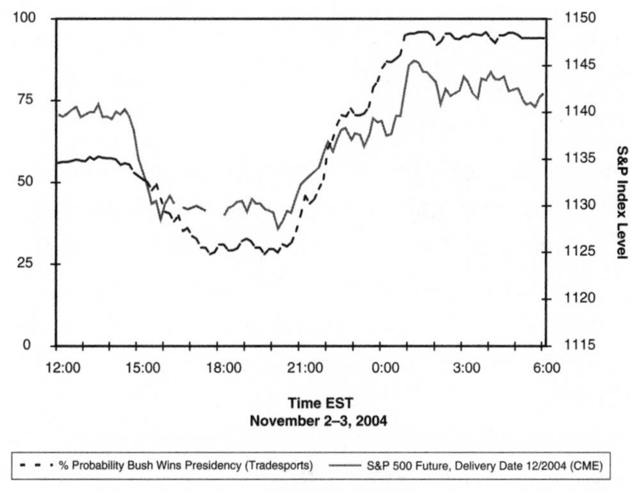

SOURCE: Snowberg, Wolfers, and Zitzewitz, "Partisan Impacts on the Economy: Evidence From Prediction Markets and Close Elections."

and the Democrats' vote share. An ideal instrument for Edwards's receiving the nomination would be an event that affected the likely winner of the Democratic primary, but not Edwards's general election chances. One such event might have been if a sex scandal hurt his only rival.[41] And, indeed, rather than waiting for the event to occur (or, as Matt Drudge did, pretending it did occur), we could run prediction markets to derive the market's expectations of the relevant moments required for an IV estimator. That is, an "IV prediction market" would require five contracts, from which one could derive the two moments required for an IV estimate:

1. A contract paying $1.00 if Edwards is nominated, $P_1 = p(Edwards)$
2. A contract paying $1.00 if Edwards is nominated and a scandal occurs, $P_2 = p(Edwards \,\&\, Scandal)$
3. A contract paying $1.00 if a scandal occurs, $P_3 = p(Scandal)$

4. A contract paying the Democratic vote share if Edwards is nominated and a sex scandal occurs, $P_4 = E[Democrat\ Votes \mid Edwards\ \&\ Scandal] \cdot p(Edwards\ \&\ Scandal)$

5. A contract paying the Democratic vote share if Edwards is nominated, $P_5 = E(Democrat\ Votes \mid Edwards) \cdot p(Edwards)$

The ratio P_2/P_3 yields the probability of Edwards's nomination conditional on a scandal, $p(Edwards|Scandal)$. Furthermore, subtracting the unconditional probability of Edwards winning the nomination (P_1) yields the increase in probability resulting from the scandal: $P_2/P_3 - P_1 = p(Edwards|Scandal) - p(Edwards)$. This difference is analogous to the first-stage regression coefficient in a Wald estimator. Likewise, the ratio P_4/P_3 yields Edwards's expected general election vote-share condition on a scandal: $E\{[E(Democrat\ Votes|Edwards) \cdot p(Edwards)]|Scandal\} \cdot p(Edwards|\ Scandal)$. Subtracting the expected Democratic vote share if Edwards is nominated (P_5) yields the effect of the scandal on Edwards's expected general election vote share: $P_4/P_3 - P_5 = E[Democrat\ Votes \cdot p(Edwards)|Scandal] - E[Democrat\ Votes \cdot p(Edwards)]$. This difference is analogous to the coefficient from the reduced-form regression. The ratio of the reduced-form and the first-stage regression coefficients yields the "prediction IV" Wald estimator, which in this case would be the ratio of the scandal's effect on Edwards's expected general election vote share and its effect on his chances of winning the nomination, or:

$$\beta_{Prediction\ IV} = \frac{P_4/(P_3 - P_5)}{P_2/(P_3 - P_1)}.$$

The numerator of this ratio is the increase in Edwards's expected general election vote share resulting from the scandal, and the denominator is the increase in his probability of being nominated. Given our identifying assumption that the scandal does not affect Edwards's general election chances, this ratio provides an estimate of Edwards's general election performance in states of the world in which he would not have won the nomination but for an exogenous event.[42] It seems plausible that "IV prediction markets" like this better identify causal parameters and hence yield estimates that are more directly applicable for decision-making.[43]

Of course, although we are optimistic that "prediction IVs" are feasible, they run into the same five open questions that we asked earlier in this chapter:

1. **Would traders be willing to trade the relevant securities?** This is particularly problematic, given that few traders have a need to hedge against the types of possible events that make for plausibly exogenous experiments.
2. **Are the relevant outcomes contractible?**
3. **Are these markets manipulation-proof?** Even though the prediction IVs isolate the causal parameter of interest, as is well known, even small changes in the first-stage estimate (or market price) yield large changes in the estimated causal parameter, suggesting that the returns to manipulation may be large.
4. **Would the market be well-calibrated on the small probabilities in these multistate contingent contracts?**
5. **Can we ever fully separate correlation from causation?** As with a lot of other empirical work, it can be difficult to find experiments that truly do identify the causal parameter. The one reason for real optimism on this front is that we no longer need wait for natural experiments, but rather can trade on the likely effects of experiments that may never happen.

Conclusions

In a previous essay, we reviewed much of the accumulated evidence on the operation of prediction markets, concluding on an optimistic note.[44] In this essay, we pose five questions which, we argue, require answers for prediction markets to reach their considerable potential. The research agenda suggested by these questions spans several fields of economics and encroaches significantly on related disciplines.

The first question arguably falls more in the field of marketing than economics: How can one attract uninformed order flow to markets? This question is important because these traders provide the potential profit-motivating informed groups to trade. Lower transaction costs, in both the monetary and the convenience sense, are important, but inherent interest or buzz is clearly an important determinant.

Our second question concerns contractibility: How does one trade off interest with outcome contractibility? Of course, the domain of contracts has expanded considerably over the past few centuries, and there may be lessons in the history of contracts that prediction-market designers would be well-advised to follow.

Third, many of the corporate and policy decision markets that have been proposed raise questions about manipulation, especially in environments where free entry by arbitrageurs cannot eliminate the problem. With position limits, a prediction market may turn into voting; with no position limits, it may turn into an auction. If the markets literally turn into a complicated version of a vote or an auction, presumably we are better off with the simple version. But one might imagine situations in which they turn into a hybrid, and more work on understanding when those hybrids are sensible mechanisms could be productive.

Fourth, as psychologists and insurance salespeople have known for years, most people are badly calibrated when evaluating small probabilities, and some of their difficulties appear to be spilling over into prediction-market pricing. Given the current scale of prediction markets, the relevant limit to arbitrage is probably not the agency problems discussed in Shleifer and Vishny,[45] but rather transaction costs. We are optimistic that both declining transaction costs and carefully framed prediction-market contracts will yield more accurate responses.

Finally, there is the issue of separating causation and correlation, which is a difficult one, but more or less on empirical economists' home turf. For settings where interpretation of correlations is problematic, we propose an "instrumental events" approach for analyses based on time-series movements and an analog in contingent markets—"prediction IVs"—which may help isolate causal parameters.

Notes

1. For example, a Factiva search for mentions of "Iowa Electronic Markets" from January 1 to November 1 yielded twenty-seven hits in 2000 and one hundred in 2004. Adding the largest private-sector market, TradeSports.com (and its politics-only subsidiary Intrade) to the search increases the number of 2004 hits to 237.

2. Joel Slemrod and Timothy Greimel, "Did Steve Forbes Scare the Municipal Bond Market?" *Journal of Public Economics* 74, no. 1 (1999): 81–96; Brian Knight, "Are Policy Platforms Capitalized into Equity Prices? Evidence from Equity Markets during the Bush/Gore 2000 Presidential Election," *Journal of Public Economics* (2006, forthcoming).

3. Andrew Leigh, Justin Wolfers, and Eric Zitzewitz, "What Do Financial Markets Think of War in Iraq?" (Working Paper 9587, National Bureau of Economic Research, Cambridge, Mass., 2003).

4. See, for example, references cited in notes 2 and 3, above.

5. Kay-Yut Chen and Charles Plott, "Information Aggregation Mechanisms: Concept, Design and Implementation for a Sales Forecasting Problem" (Working Paper 1131, California Institute of Technology, Pasadena, 2002)

6. Gerhard Ortner, "Forecasting Markets—An Industrial Application" (mimeo, Technical University of Vienna, 1998).

7. Justin Wolfers and Eric Zitzewitz, "Experimental Political Betting Markets and the 2004 Election," *Economists' Voice* 1, no. 2 (2004) http://www.bepress.com/ev/vol1/iss2/art1/ (last accessed January 26, 2006).

8. Michael Abramowicz, "Information Markets, Administrative Decisionmaking, and Predictive Cost-Benefit Analysis," *University of Chicago Law Review* 71 (2004): 933–1020.

9. Robert W. Hahn and Paul C. Tetlock, "Using Information Markets to Improve Public Decision Making," *Harvard Journal of Law and Public Policy* 29, no. 1 (Fall 2005): 213–89.

10. Robin Hanson, "Shall We Vote on Values, but Bet on Beliefs?" (working paper, George Mason University, 2003).

11. These figures include the trading on a symmetric "Kerry to win" contract.

12. Paul Milgrom and Nancy Stokey, "Information, Trade, and Common Knowledge," *Journal of Economic Theory* 26 (1982): 17–27.

13. Albert Kyle, "Continuous Auctions and Insider Trading," *Econometrica* 53, no. 6 (1985): 1315–36.

14. To derive the above, solve the traders' problem: Set x to maximize subjective expected utility $E[U] = e \cdot ln[w + (1 - p)x] + (1 - e) \cdot ln(w - px)$.

15. For more information, see Justin Wolfers and Eric Zitzewitz, "Interpreting Prediction: Market Prices as Probabilities" (working paper, University of Pennsylvania, Philadelphia, 2005).

16. Suppose that λ traders are informed, each informed trader buys one contract, and $1 - \lambda$ traders are uninformed. Then the market-makers' bids and asks must satisfy

$$P_{ask} = \frac{\lambda q + (1-\lambda)X_{buy}(P_{ask}+t)q}{\lambda q + (1-\lambda)X_{buy}(P_{ask}+t)} + t_{MM} - cx_{MM}$$

and

$$P_{bid} = \frac{-(1-\lambda)X_{sell}(P_{bid}-t)q}{\lambda(1-q) - (1-\lambda)\,X_{sell}(P_{bid}-t)]} - t_{MM} - cx_{MM},$$

where the first term in each expression is the expectation of y conditional on receiving a buy or sell order. With $\lambda = 0$, this first term is always equal to q (the market-maker's unbiased prior), but as λ increases, P_{ask} increases and P_{bid} decreases, leading to wider spreads and less uninformed trading.

17. In the expressions in the above note, it is easy to show that P_{ask} is increasing and P_{bid} is decreasing in t and t_{MM}. It is likewise straightforward to show that when $\lambda > 0$, then for distributions of e that have $min(e) > 0$ and $max(e) < 1$, there will be a level of t that leads to market unraveling, that is, to $P_{ask} = 1$ and $P_{bid} = 0$ being the only values that satisfy the expressions in the above note.

18. The term "uninformed" overstates the requirement, which is that the market must attract traders whose estimate of the true probability is less precise than the market-maker's, or whose hedging demand causes them to trade even when their beliefs coincide with those of the market-maker.

19. The Iowa markets are run as a research project by academics at the Tippie College of Business at the University of Iowa. They are described in Robert Forsythe, Forrest Nelson, George R. Neumann, and Jack Wright, "Anatomy of an Experimental Political Stock Market," *American Economic Review* 82, no. 5 (1992): 1142–61.

20. For example, this contract averaged fifty-two on Iowa during the month of August 2004 and about forty-six on TradeSports.

21. Emile Servan-Schreiber, Justin Wolfers, David Pennock, and Brian Galebach, "Prediction Markets: Does Money Matter?" *Electronic Markets* 14, no. 3 (2004): 243–51.

22. Refet Gürkaynak and Justin Wolfers, "Macroeconomic Derivatives: An Initial Analysis of Market-Based Macro Forecasts, Uncertainty and Risk," in *NBER International Seminar on Macroeconomics*, ed. Christopher Pissarides and Jeffrey Frankel (MIT Press: Cambridge, 2005).

23. Another example of a TradeSports contract whose definition was later clarified is the "Will Bush win the electoral votes of Maine?" contract. One might have supposed this meant all four electoral votes, but the exchange determined after the contract had been trading for several months that three out of four

would suffice. In the same vein as Leigh, Wolfers, and Zitzewitz, "What Do Financial Markets Think of War in Iraq?" we commented on the judgment that would have been required to settle the "Will Saddam Hussein be out of office?" contract had a contract been expiring on April 9, 10, or 11; the active trading on this contract suggests that many traders were comfortable with this possible ambiguity.

24. Robin Hanson and Ryan Oprea, "Manipulators Increase Market Accuracy" (working paper, George Mason University, Fairfax, Va., 2004).

25. Koleman Strumpf, "Manipulating the Iowa Political Stock Market" (working paper, University of North Carolina, Chapel Hill, 2004).

26. Richard H. Thaler and William T. Ziemba, "Anomalies: Parimutuel Betting Markets: Racetracks and Lotteries," *Journal of Economic Perspectives* 2, no. 2 (Spring 1988): 161–74.

27. Justin Wolfers and Eric Zitzewitz, "Prediction Markets," *Journal of Economic Perspectives* 18, no. 2 (2004): 107–26.

28. Daniel Kahneman and Amos Tversky, "Prospect Theory: An Analysis of Decision under Risk," *Econometrica* 47, no. 2 (1979): 263–92.

29. Charles Manski, "Interpreting the Predictions of Prediction Markets" (Working Paper 10359, National Bureau of Economic Research, Cambridge, Mass., 2004).

30. Whether traders use such a budgeting rule is, of course, an empirical question that remains to be answered.

31. Justin Wolfers and Eric Zitzewitz, "Interpreting Prediction Market Prices as Probabilities" (working paper, University of Pennsylvania, Philadelphia, 2005).

32. Wolfers and Zitzewitz, "Prediction Markets."

33. Joyce Berg and Thomas Rietz, "Prediction Markets as Decision Support Systems," *Information Systems Frontiers* 5, no. 1 (2003): 79–93.

34. This issue is referred to as "decision selection bias" in Robin Hanson, "Decision Markets," *IEEE Intelligent Systems* 14, no. 3 (1999): 16–19; Robin Hanson, "Impolite Innovation: The Technology and Politics of 'Terrorism Futures' and Other Decision Markets," in *Promoting the General Welfare: American Democracy and the Political Economy of Government Performance*, ed. Eric Patashnik and Alan Gerber (Washington, D.C.: Brookings Institution Press, 2005).

35. See, for example, E. S. Browning, "As Bush Goes So Goes the Market," *Wall Street Journal*, September 20, 2004, C1.

36. Erik Snowberg, Justin Wolfers, and Eric Zitzewitz, "Partisan Impacts on the Economy: Evidence From Prediction Markets and Close Elections" (working paper, Stanford University, Stanford, Calif., 2006).

37. Authors' calculation from financial data.

38. The other debates are unfortunately of less use. For the first debate there were no instant polls to determine a winner objectively; it took at least one news

cycle for a consensus to emerge that Kerry had won, and this leaves us with too long an event window. The second debate was on a Friday evening, when futures markets were closed, and the vice-presidential debate was considered to be approximately a draw.

39. The slow incorporation of information in prediction markets is illustrated by figure 2-4. The bulk of the exit poll–related movement occurred between 2:50 p.m. and 3:30 p.m. eastern time in the stock market, whereas it lasted until 5:30 p.m. eastern time in the TradeSports reelection market. Likewise, the subsequent rally began about ten to twenty minutes earlier on the Chicago Mercantile Exchange than on TradeSports.

40. Standard deviations of S&P changes during the 2:50 p.m.–3:30 p.m. and 8:30 p.m.–1:00 a.m. windows are twenty-six and twelve basis points, respectively. These imply standard errors of roughly 1.0 and 0.2 percentage points, respectively.

41. Of course, a sex scandal involving a senior Democrat might affect the general public's views of all Democrats, which would potentially invalidate this instrument.

42. Note that as with most applications of IV methods, we identify a Local Average Treatment Effect (LATE). Naturally, whether this is the causal parameter of interest depends on the context. For example, if Edwards is of higher average quality in states of the world in which he can take advantage of a small scandal than in states of the world where he can take advantage of a large scandal, then a LATE estimator based on a small scandal may overstate the performance one could expect from exogenously choosing him as the nominee.

43. Naturally, this example shows only one of many such market designs that can be used to recover the causal parameter of interest.

44. Wolfers and Zitzewitz, "Prediction Markets."

45. Andrei Shleifer and Robert Vishny, "The Limits of Arbitrage," *Journal of Finance* 52, no. 1 (1997): 35–55.

3

Designing Information Markets for Policy Analysis

John O. Ledyard

Policy analysis, be it public or private, is all about acquiring and organizing bits and pieces of dispersed information in a way that will more clearly inform a decision that has to be made.[1] Information aggregation is the process of bringing all the relevant information to bear on the decision. In this chapter I look at an old approach to aggregating information markets and ask whether they might lead to improved policy analysis. I find that there are reasons to believe that information markets based on standard designs will not perform well in environments relevant to policy analysis. Two key reasons are the need for many contracts and the incentives to deviate from the behaviors necessary to achieve accurate aggregation of information. This means that new market designs are necessary if information markets are to be applicable to policy situations. One promising new design, a market-scoring rule with conditional contracts, is described. It performs significantly better than standard markets in experimental environments that mirror difficult information-aggregation situations one might expect to see in practical applications.

Information Markets for Prediction

To get started, let us look at a simple example of a corporate policy decision. A company is significantly upgrading a piece of software that has two major components: A and B. The decision to be made is when to launch the marketing effort that will drive the sales of the new software.

Getting the time of the launch right is worth a lot to the company. There are people in the company who have a good sense for the development of A, and who can make an informed prediction on the basis of their information. They know a little about B. There are also people who are symmetrically placed with respect to B. The predictions of the two groups may well be different, based on what they know. Who should be listened to?

The obvious answer is both. In fact, it is most desirable that the information of the two groups be merged or aggregated and predictions made on the basis of the total information. If all the individuals completely share their information, then, ultimately, their predictions will agree and be the same as those that would have been made by someone who had all the facts from the beginning.[2]

The standard methods used to collect and aggregate information, including committees, group retreats, bureaucracies, outside consultants, opinion polls, and surveys, are well known. Many have been around a very long time. More modern approaches include computer search engines. All have their advocates, and all have drawbacks. A newer approach uses the power of carefully focused markets. These have come to be known as information or prediction markets.

What is an information market? One of the earliest examples of a market created specifically to aggregate information was the Iowa Electronic Markets (IEM). The familiar question the market was designed to answer was, who will win an election? In 1988, some faculty at the University of Iowa Business School securitized the presidential-election prediction and provided a trading system on the Internet. For $1.00, IEM stood ready to sell to you or buy from you a set of three securities that covered all possible outcomes of the election; Bush, Dukakis, Other. Each security paid $1.00 if and only if that person won. Securities were traded.

How this looks from the point of view of one trader is illustrated in table 3-1. You, as a trader, have bought a dollar's worth of securities from the IEM that gives you one unit each of Bush, Dukakis, and Other. As indicated in the last column, your expected earnings if you did nothing else are $0.00. One of the three assets will pay you $1.00, and you have paid $1.00. Now you look at the market prices on the IEM and see that they are $0.50, $0.40, and $0.10, respectively, for Bush, Dukakis, and Other. But you believe, *on the basis of the information that you have*, that Bush has a

TABLE 3-1
TRADING IN AN INFORMATION MARKET

	Bush	Dukakis	Other	E(V)
You have	1 unit	1 unit	1 unit	\$1 – \$1 = \$0
Prices	\$0.50	\$0.40	\$0.10	
You think	70%	30%	0	
So trade	1 @ \$0.60	–1 @ \$0.35	–1 @ \$0.05	–\$0.20
You have	2 units	0 units	0 units	\$1.40 – \$1.20 = \$0.20

SOURCE: Author's calculations.

70 percent chance of winning, and that Other has no chance at all. How can you make money? You buy one Bush for \$0.60, sell your Dukakis for \$0.35, and sell your Other for \$0.05.[3] This trade costs you an additional \$0.20, but you are better off. You now have two Bushes, each of which you believe has a 70 percent probability of paying \$1.00. So your expected payment is \$1.40. You expect to make \$0.20 on your \$1.20 investment.

Other traders, *with different information from yours*, will look at these price changes, integrate the information conveyed by them, and adjust their beliefs in response. They will also trade if their beliefs are different from the market prices. Eventually, prices will settle down. On the basis of theoretical, experimental, and empirical evidence, there is reason to believe that, in equilibrium, the market prices for Bush, Dukakis, and Other will be an accurate evaluation of the probability that each will win, based on all of the information of those participating in the market. Since 1988, the prices of the Iowa Election Markets have bettered the standard polls 451 out of 596 times in predicting the election of candidates in a wide range of candidate competitions.[4]

In assessing the potential of information markets, one does not need to rely only on the evidence from the IEM, no matter how persuasive it is. There are by now many more information markets than just IEM.[5] There is also a growing body of scientific evidence to support the contention that information markets can provide significant aggregation. I turn to that evidence now.

The Field Evidence. There are many naturally occurring information markets. Stock markets, futures markets, and parimutuel betting are just some examples. In direct comparisons with other institutions, they seem to perform very well. Racetrack odds beat track experts,[6] orange juice futures improve on weather forecasts,[7] and stock prices beat the panel of experts in the post-Challenger probe.[8]

One can also create information markets. In direct comparisons to other institutions, these designer markets, created explicitly to aggregate information, also seem to perform very well. I have already indicated the successful performance of the IEM. A market designed by Kay-Yut Chen and Charles Plott for Hewlett-Packard beat the internal sales forecast process six out of eight times.[9] Other evidence can be found in Wolfers and Zitzewitz.[10]

This positive evidence is all drawn from field studies. There is a lot going on in these situations that might interfere with accurate inferences, not the least of which is the uncontrolled timing of the arrival of new information and the inability of the researcher to know the true, fully aggregated information. I turn next to the evidence from more scientific approaches.

The Scientific Evidence. Two basic strands of scientific work support the hypothesis that information aggregation is possible. One relies on the intuition I gave in our first example that if information-holders interact iteratively, they will eventually agree, and that agreement will involve complete aggregation of their information. The second comes from the theory of rational expectations equilibrium—an equilibrium theory of information aggregation through markets rather than through personal interactions. I look at each in turn.

Iterative Aggregation. In his seminal paper, Aumann considered the situation in which two people have a common prior belief, and then each privately learns something about the state of the world.[11] He proved that if their posterior beliefs become common knowledge, then they must have the same posterior, or final, beliefs.[12] Loosely stated, when one of them sees the other's beliefs, he will be able to infer something about the other person's information and add this to his own information. So will the other. This revision process continues until they have the same beliefs, and these will be the full-information beliefs. Geanakopolos and Polemarchakis were able to specify a precise dynamic process that implemented Aumann's insight for two people who follow the rules of Bayesian updating.[13] The process converges to full-information beliefs in a finite number of steps. McKelvey and Page generalized the process to an arbitrary number of people.[14] They were also able to achieve full aggregation of information using only a public aggregate statistic to convey information from one to another. The conclusion to draw from this work is that if individuals are willing to share their information honestly, and if they are able to process information as a Bayesian should, then iterative processes can lead to full-information aggregation.

There has been at least one set of experiments to test whether iterative aggregation will work in practice. McKelvey and Page created an experiment in which subjects gave sequential reports in a series of rounds.[15] Between rounds there was a public report. They used a scoring rule[16] to try to provide some incentives for the correct revelation of information. They came to two conclusions: First, observed individual behavior corresponded roughly to the predicted Bayesian updating; and, second, some information aggregation occurred.[17]

Equilibrium Aggregation. The second strand of work that supports the hypothesis that information aggregation is possible rests on the equilibrium analysis of markets and other institutions. At the core of the analysis is rational expectations theory.[18] Individuals' demands reflect their beliefs about the world, as in the example in table 3-1. Prices respond to those demands, and so are public signals that convey information about the world. Traders incorporate that public information into their private expectations. With these new expectations come new demand functions and, therefore, new prices. In equilibrium, all is revealed, and expectations are fully informed.

Putting this theory to work, one can create securities that pay $1.00 in a particular state. These are called a complete set of Arrow-Debreu securities[19] if there is one for every possible state.[20] If traders are risk-neutral and price-taking, and if markets fully equilibrate, then in equilibrium the prices of each security will equal the common-knowledge posterior probability of that state. Market equilibrium will aggregate all of the information of the traders.

Experimental work has evaluated whether the equilibrium theory accurately describes a real situation. Forsythe, Palfrey, and Plott created a laboratory securities market and demonstrated convergence to a rational expectations equilibrium.[21] McKelvey and Ordeshook were able to show that information aggregation occurred in a laboratory election where individuals had private information about the candidates and polls provided the public signal.[22] This aggregation was consistent with rational expectations theory. In an important paper in this area, Plott and Sunder created laboratory securities markets where multiple securities were traded in an uncertain world.[23] Individuals had private information about the probability of some states. One of their key findings was that if individuals have the same preferences, and if there is a complete set of Arrow-Debreu securities, then there is rapid pooling of information, consistent with rational expectations equilibrium theory.

Some Storm Clouds. To this point, things look pretty good for the claim that markets can be created to aggregate information. Both iterative and equilibrium theories are positive. The experimental evidence is positive. And the field evidence is positive. But there are also some cautionary notes in the literature.

Grossman and Stiglitz point out an apparent paradox that must be confronted at some point: Why pay to gather information if it is just going to be revealed to others for free?[24] The idea can be illustrated simply as follows: Suppose a trader knows the state for sure. He is willing to pay up to $1.00 for an Arrow-Debreu security on that state and sell all other securities at any positive price. But if the others know that someone might know something,[25] then as soon as this trader bids up the price of the one security, the information will be revealed, and no one will sell that security for less than $1.00. And no one will buy the other at any price. Prices have converged to the full-information probabilities with $1.00 on the true state. But—and here is the potential problem—the trader with the information cannot make any money by trading, so why bother? And if the trader does not bother, the equilibrium is never revealed.[26]

This kind of intuition is also captured in the "no trade" theorem of Milgrom and Stokey.[27] They consider the same situation Aumann did. Two traders begin with a common prior belief, and then each learns something privately. It can be shown that they will never trade solely on the basis of differing information.

The intuition is fairly easy to understand. Suppose I have two coins: One is weighted so that heads comes up 80 percent of the time, and the other is weighted so that tails comes up 80 percent of the time. I randomly pick one of these, and, for each of two people, flip the coin twice. Neither sees the results of the other's flips. I then create an information market by allowing trade in an asset that pays $1.00 if the coin is the one weighted toward heads. Suppose person 1 sees a head and a tail, denoted (1H, 1T). His posterior belief is then that the probability the coin is weighted heads is 50 percent. Suppose person 2 offers to sell two units of the asset for $0.30 each. Person 1 can immediately infer that person 2 saw (0H, 2T)[28] and therefore knows that the total information is (1H, 3T) giving a full-information posterior that A is weighted heads of 6 percent. So, person 1 will reject the offer (and, indeed, any offer above $0.06). From this rejection, person 2 knows that person 1 did not see (2H, 1T), and person 2 knows that the full-information posterior probability the coin is weighted heads is less than or equal to 6 percent.[29] At this point, there is no basis for a trade to take place. This strongly suggests that if traders have a common prior belief and are risk-neutral, information markets will not work as advertised.

In another paper casting doubts on rational expectations equilibrium theory, Jordan showed that there are situations in which there are "under-revealing" rational expectations equilibria, and there are situations in which the rational expectations equilibrium will not even exist.[30] The first situation can cause information aggregation to be stopped before it is complete. The second situation means that these markets will not equilibrate as expected. Both Jordan and Milgrom and Stokey indirectly raised important questions about the dynamics of these markets—the process of price-discovery.

Finally, although Plott and Sunder had success in getting information aggregation under the right conditions, they also demonstrated that if the preferences of individuals differ and there is only a single asset without contingent claims, then relatively little aggregation of information happens.[31]

The iterative approach has been less extensively discussed than rational expectations equilibrium theory. McKelvey and Page point out that the individual behavior they observed in the lab is not generally fully rational.[32] Bayesian updating by the subjects is incomplete—and complete updating is required to get full-information aggregation.

Summary of the Scientific Evidence on Prediction. At this point, it seems fair to summarize the scientific evidence as cautiously optimistic. We have seen numerous papers suggesting that information aggregation is possible, either iteratively or in equilibrium. But some storm clouds threaten the parade. The iterative theory assumes individuals will honestly reveal their beliefs when asked, though this may not be compatible with the actual incentives faced by participants. If it is not, then there is no reason to expect full or accurate aggregation. The equilibrium theory requires a complete set of securities, price-taking behavior, and adequate price-discovery. In thin markets, price-taking may not be compatible with the traders' incentives, and price-discovery may be incomplete. That is, there can be incomplete or inaccurate aggregation. Both theories rely on each trader's ability and interest in understanding the common-knowledge structure, inverting price and other signals into information about other traders' information, and using Bayesian updating when they revise their beliefs. If traders do not behave this way, then inaccurate and incomplete aggregation will occur.[33] When one tries to transform information markets into policy-analysis markets, incentives, thinness, and incomplete updating will become major issues.

Information Markets for Decisions

Up to now, I have been looking at information markets strictly as a means of improving information retrieval and aggregation. But in policy analysis, one is trying to make a decision, and prediction is only a part of this process. In committees and other processes for information aggregation, many variations in a policy are explored and evaluated before a final recommendation is made. Small variations in key sections can create significant variations in predicted benefits and costs. For markets to duplicate these far-ranging considerations, they must require the trading of many securities simultaneously. Of course, this introduces a number of new potential problems to worry about. Here I consider three.

Information Markets for Decisions Require Many Securities. Consider an example taken, and modified, from Hahn and Tetlock.[34] A policymaker wants to improve the standardized scores of a school district. He is considering a policy that would delegate the right to run the schools. To estimate the benefits of such a policy, he decides to set up two markets. After the markets close, a decision will be made whether to implement the policy.

- In market 1, a contract is traded that pays $\$x$ if the average score is x, conditional on the policy not being implemented. If the policy is implemented, you get your money back.[35]
- In market 2, a contract is traded that pays $\$y$ if the average score is y, conditional on the policy being implemented. If the policy is not implemented, you get your money back.

The policy is described before the markets open.

Suppose June 30 arrives, and the prices of the contracts in market 1 and 2 both equal \$100. Such prices clearly suggest that the policy will have no effect, so if it costs anything, it should not be implemented. The policy had a number of key clauses that described what the firm could and could not do in running the schools. Any one of these could have caused the market valuation to be so low. The policymaker may wonder what went wrong, and question how to revise the policy to improve it. But there is no way to know. If markets are to replace other aggregation procedures, they will need to be more informative than this.[36]

But suppose that the policymaker has two versions he can live with for each of, say, three clauses. Let the clauses be identified by A, B, C, and let the versions of each be either 0 or 1. If the policymaker sets up the markets so that one can buy or sell the contracts in market 1 conditional on, say, $A = 1$ or $A = 0$, and $B = 1$, then the prices of these conditional contracts will signal what the increase in scores will be, conditional on the particular version of the policy. Of course, if there are N clauses with K versions, then there will need to be $4x(N^K)$ securities traded, only two of which will actually pay off in the end. For the example here, that means thirty-two securities.[37]

The main point is that the number of securities to be traded increases exponentially in the fineness of the detail desired. Better analysis requires a significant number of simultaneous markets. The more markets, the more likely it is that neither price-taking nor honest revelation of information will be incentive-compatible if the markets are organized in the usual way. This means that the market design is going to be crucial. New processes will be needed that can encourage the aggregation of information, even though there are many securities and few traders.

Policymaker Temptation. Problems in the use of information markets as decision tools may arise because of the situations in which they are embedded. Decisions made on the basis of the markets may have consequences for both the policymaker and the traders. If the consequences are large, then each party's interest in the decision can easily outweigh his interest in the markets themselves.

Let us look at an example of the temptations faced by the policymaker. Acme Software Inc. plans to ship its product, Zeus, next July. It is built from components *A*, *B*, and *C*; each can be new or old. Acme management is crucially interested in getting as much information possible on the shipment date so they can correctly time the massive marketing campaign and deployment of its sales force. Shipping in October could cost them $70 million in forgone sales. In January, Acme opens a market to predict the Zeus shipment date, allowing trade in the following securities: *{before Aug}*, *{Aug}*, *{Sept}*, *{Oct}*, *{Nov}*, and *{later than Nov}*. In March, the October prediction is 75 percent because the price is $0.75. Management orders a review, identifies component *A* as the problem, stops production of A_{new}, and retains A_{old}. Prices soon move to $0.03 for October and $0.45 for both August and September. Zeus ships in August.

So what is the problem here? Under this scenario, the traders who signaled October (assuming A_{new}) by buying at prices up to $0.75 lose.[38] If they had correctly anticipated the actions of management, they would not have revealed their information. But if they had revealed no information, and the October price had stayed low, management would have lost money. Without any changes in the market setup, the traders will include in their probability estimates what they think management might do. This will significantly dilute the quality of the information being revealed by the market.

There are at least two ways to redesign the markets so that the type of problem faced above by Acme Software will not happen. One is for the policymaker to commit to not doing anything to change the outcomes on which everyone is trading. But living up to that commitment could be very costly. In our example, it would have cost Acme up to $70 million to do so. The second, cheaper way is to let traders hedge against the risk of adverse decisions. In our example, that is done by creating options such as *{Zeus in October if* A_{new}*}* and *{Zeus in August if* A_{old}*}*. If the condition does not occur, then the trader is off the hook. With these options, traders who know that the October delivery is likely because of the problem with A can indicate their beliefs by selling *{Zeus in October if* A_{new}*}* and buying *{Zeus in August if* A_{old}*}*. There is no need for them to worry about the effect of management's response on their market earnings.[39]

There is, of course, an added benefit and an added cost. The added benefit is that management will not need to enter into a costly review to locate a problem. It will be easy to identify from the prices. As I argued earlier, having more markets potentially provides better information. But the added cost arises in the same way it did then. One now needs to have six dates, two features, and two states for each feature, giving us twenty-four securities. If there were four features, one would need $6x(4^2)$, or ninety-six, securities. The cost of hedging is an exponential increase in the number of securities to be traded. This increase leads to a thinning of the market, which can lead to a loss in accurate price-discovery. The trade-off faced by the market designer is between bad information revelation for fear of future decisions and bad information revelation because of thin markets. New market processes that create better price-discovery in thin situations would alleviate the latter.

Trader Temptation—Information Monopoly. Even if traders do not care about and cannot affect the outcomes that determine the payoffs of the securities, they may be tempted to manipulate the market itself in order to increase their profits. If a single trader knows something no one else knows (inside information), he has a monopoly in that information and can gain, at least in standard market designs, by manipulating the price. Just as a product monopolist can create "artificial scarcity" and thus keep the price of his sales up, so can the information monopolist. The argument is simple: If the final prices reflect aggregate information, then they are a well-defined function of the various pieces of information each has.

Suppose I create a very simple information market in which I want to know the probability it will snow in New York City on January 1, 2006. In a rational expectations equilibrium, if I am risk neutral, my willingness to pay is $q^i(s^i, p^*(s))$, where q^i is my belief it will snow, s^i is the private information I have, and $p^*(s)$ is the equilibrium market price given s, the signals of everyone. In a rational expectations equilibrium, at the final prices under price-taking competitive behavior with risk-neutral preferences, it must be true that $q^i(s^i, p(s)) = p(s)$ for all of us; otherwise I will still want to trade. Let the price that satisfies all n equations be $p^* = g(s^1, s^2, \ldots, s^n)$. If the markets accurately aggregate the information as predicted by the theory, then $g(s)$ should be the posterior based on the full information in the vector of private signals s. So, if markets are performing their predicted function of information aggregation, they must be sensitive to each individual's information. But it is just this sensitivity that gives the monopolist his leverage.[40]

How might a monopolist pull off his manipulation? If everyone knows he is a monopolist, then by closely tracking his bids and offers, they can infer his position and eliminate his advantage. But he can prevent this by acting competitively (in a way that is indistinguishable to an outside observer from the price-taking behavior normally assumed) while mimicking the behavior of a trader like himself who has different information. In doing so, he can guide the market to a different equilibrium, the one that assumes different information is correct. In many cases, this can be done in a way that leaves the monopolist better off. To see how this works, consider a very simple example. Suppose each agent receives a signal that is *H*, *M*, or *L*. If it is *H*, the agent knows for sure that it will snow on January 1 in New York City; if it is *M*, then it is likely; and if *L*, then it will not.[41] The more *M*s, the higher the price will be in equilibrium. Suppose there are five people in this market, and the information is *2 M*, *2 L*, and *1 H*. As predicted by rational expectations equilibrium theory, when the holder of *H* bids the price of the security up, all others will infer *H*, and the price will instantaneously jump to 1. The holder of *H* will complete few, if any, trades at a price lower than 1, and, therefore, in equilibrium, prices will reflect the true probabilities, but no one will have made any money. But if the holder of *H* pretends to be *M*, then they will be able to buy assets at prices reflecting the difference between $p(2\,M, 3\,L)$ and $p(3\,M, 2\,L)$. The monopolist knows for sure that the security will pay off at $1.00, and so the monopolist makes more money by using this strategy than by behaving competitively. And, the equilibrium price will not reflect the full-information posterior for which $p = 1$.

I have purposely exaggerated this example to make the point that if information is not widely held, competitive behavior may not be incentive-compatible, and information may be hoarded, causing prices not to reflect the full market information. If there are one hundred people instead of five, the gains from this type of manipulation will obviously be lower and might, in fact, be less than those from acting like *H*. Also, if two people hold the information *H* in our example above, then neither will be a monopolist, and competition might drive the price to 1.[42] If information is more dispersed, then the example will not be as sharp. But if the markets are thin, the number of traders is small, and some individuals' information is important, then standard markets will provide temptations to misrepresent that information and may lead to incomplete aggregation of information.

There is a way to design the markets so that the temptation to manipulate price is reduced or eliminated. The design does not rely on rational expectations theory and its companion assumption of competitive behavior. Instead, it builds on a method known as proper scoring rules. According to this method, originally suggested by such statisticians as Brier[43] and Savage[44] who were trying to elicit probability beliefs from weather forecasters and others, scoring rules accept the incentives of the individuals and create a mechanism to deal with them.

It is very easy to see how scoring rules work. An individual who is asked to report a probability r will be rewarded with $\$s_i(r)$ if the actual outcome is i. Although scoring rules come in many forms, a classic example from Good uses logarithms. For two possible outcomes, the Good rule pays $ln(r_1/.5)$ if outcome 1 occurs and $ln((1 - r_1)/.5)$ if outcome 2 occurs. A risk-neutral, expected-value maximizing agent faced with this rule and believing the true probability of state 1 is q will want to report r to maximize $q\ [ln(r/.5)] + (1 - q)\ [ln((1 - r)/.5)]$.[45] It is easy to see that $r = q$ solves this problem uniquely.[46] So, as long as one is willing to pay for it, one can elicit correct information from an information monopolist.

Can scoring rules be made to work for a group of people? The answer is yes. Hanson has provided a clever way to do this by introducing a shared scoring rule.[47] A market-maker (easily automated) stands ready to trade with any of the N traders. A trader proposes a price p, and the market-maker offers to change his assets so that he gets $s_k(p) - s_k(p_{t-1})$ of the asset that pays \$1.00 if and only if k occurs, where $s(p)$ is one of the scoring rules, and p_{t-1} is the last price at which the market-maker traded. As Hanson puts it, "Anyone can use the scoring rule if they pay off the last user." If agents follow their dominant strategy to tell the truth—to report their current posterior as their price proposal—at the time they trade, then iterative aggregation theory applies, and full aggregation of information will occur.

By now I have moved a long way from standard market designs with securities that only predict and from bulletin board trading systems. But that is the point. If I want to use markets to aggregate information for decisions, then there will be many frictions and temptations if I stick to traditional approaches. Good market designs will have to be guided by the principles of incentive-compatible mechanism design. Two suggestions from our earlier analysis to obtain the desired conditional information and to ensure against adverse behavior are (a) the use of extensive conditional contracts to inform decisions better and to protect against policymaker incentives to use the information prematurely, and (b) the use of market scoring rules to protect against the information-monopolist incentives to manipulate prices.

Conditional contracts mean a large number of contracts, thinning out the process. Scoring rules mean complex formulae, causing potential behavioral problems. Equilibrium and iterative aggregation theory are unlikely to be good predictors of how well information aggregation will actually occur. How will one really know what works?

Knowing What Works

I have found the use of experimental test beds to be of considerable help in identifying how mechanism designs may work when confronted with reality. The idea is to create an economics wind tunnel in which one can try out various designs in a controlled environment and measure their performance. The closer the environment is to capturing the situation in which the mechanisms are to be used, the better. To test information markets, we[48] created two very difficult environments. In earlier experimental analyses such as those in Plott and Sunder[49] and McKelvey and Page,[50] the primary purpose was to show that, in fairly simple environments, market aggregation occurs. Our goal was to stress-test the claims seriously.[51] We succeeded.

The Experimental Test Beds. We created two environments. The first had three traders and three correlated events. An event is that for which one wants to estimate a probability. An example would be, "Test scores in district A increase over last year's scores" or "Syrian GDP declines in 2005." In our experiments, each event has an outcome that can either be 1 or 0. A set of simple markets can be set up in this situation—one for each event. But in our experiments, the events are partially correlated so that a complete set of markets would require $2^3 = 8$ markets. The second environment had six traders and eight events, requiring 256 securities for a complete set. These environments really are very thin. One measure by which to see this is the number of traders per state of the world. In simple asset experiments with standard markets, such as those in Bossaerts and Plott,[52] there are three states and forty or more traders, or 13.33 traders/state. When markets are thinner, as in an earlier study by Bossaerts and Plott,[53] there may be twelve traders and three states, meaning there are four traders per state; standard markets do not equilibrate well, although call markets do.[54] In comparison, the three-event environment has 0.375 traders per state, and the eight-event environment has 0.0325 states per trader. I believe this is a significant challenge to any mechanism, much less standard designs.

In each environment we induced a common-knowledge prior.[55] We described a set of possible urns of balls, each ball containing an outcome such as ($A = 1$, $B = 0$, $C = 1$). In the three-event environment there were six possible urns. In the eight-event environment there were 40,320 possible urns. We then selected one of these urns at random, with equal probability. To provide private information, we drew ten balls at random from the urn we had chosen. In the three-event environment, this meant there were ten outcomes, such as (1, 0, 1), (0, 1, 1), (1, 1, 1), and so forth, representing the outcomes for (A, B, C). We then showed part of these data to each trader. In particular, we showed the results for A and B to one trader, the results for B and C to another trader, and the results for A and C to the third trader. The feature of reality we were trying to capture was that of an "area expert." Someone may know and observe outcomes only in, say, Iraq and Iran. Another may know and observe results in Iran and Syria, and so forth. These experts' areas may overlap but are seldom identical. Everyone knew the descriptions and the selection process. From these, all traders could compute a prior and an individual posterior over the possible states of the world. In addition, the experimentalist, knowing all the draws, had a sample of ten and could compute the "full information posterior," which completely aggregates all the private information. One does not have this information if one is using field data, which is a key reason experiments can be significantly more informative.

After trading or whatever mechanism was employed, we would draw one hundred new balls and pay the subjects according to that draw. That is, if they hold one unit of the security (1,1,1) then they are paid $1.00 multiplied by the percentage of the draws that yield $A = 1$, $B = 1$, and $C = 1$.

Measuring Performance. In the environments we create, we can run a series of trials using different mechanisms, such as opinion polls, standard markets, or new designs we might want to test. At the end of the trials we will know the probability density over states that the process produced. Because we control everything, we will also know the full-information aggregation probability density. We can measure the difference between the two. In the analysis below, we did this using the Kulback-Leibler measure of the difference between a process prediction, p, and the full-information prediction, q.[56] The measure is $\Sigma_k q_k ln(p_k/q_k)$, which equals zero when $p = q$.

To illustrate both how this measure works and to indicate the scope for information aggregation in our environments, we provide two figures (see figures 3-1 and 3-2), one for each basic environment. In each figure, the horizontal axis indicates the distance to the full-information posterior, where further to the left is closer. For each information draw in an environment, we compute the distance from the full-information posterior of the individual priors and the individual posteriors.[57] We also include the distance of the uniform density (the completely uninformative density) from the fully informed posterior as a lower bound on what one might expect to see in any data. We then plot the cumulative distribution function of those distances.

The height of the curve at a point on the x-axis in the figures represents the percentage of the environments that were within that distance of the full-information posterior. A curve that lies to the left of another is, in some sense, more informative. In figures 3-1 and 3-2, we provide the basic data respectively for the three-trader–three-event environment and the six-trader–eight-event environment. In each case, the individual posteriors are more informative than the individual priors, and those, in turn, are more

FIGURE 3-1
THEORY BENCHMARKS FOR THE THREE-EVENT ENVIRONMENTS

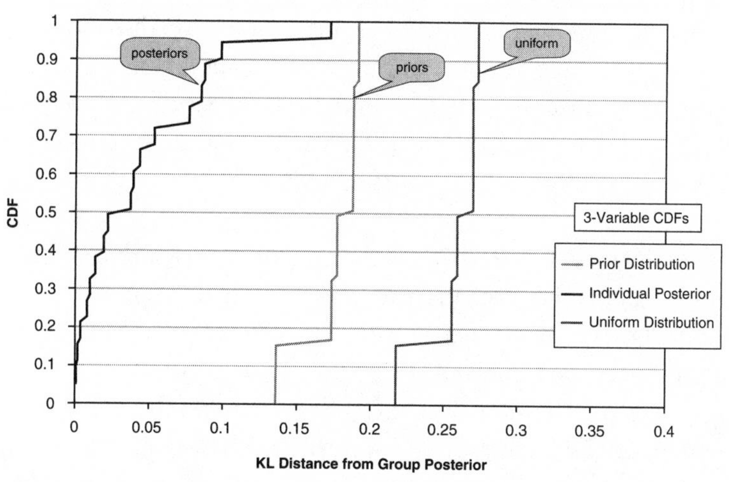

SOURCE: Author's calculations.

FIGURE 3-2
THEORY BENCHMARKS FOR THE EIGHT-EVENT ENVIRONMENTS

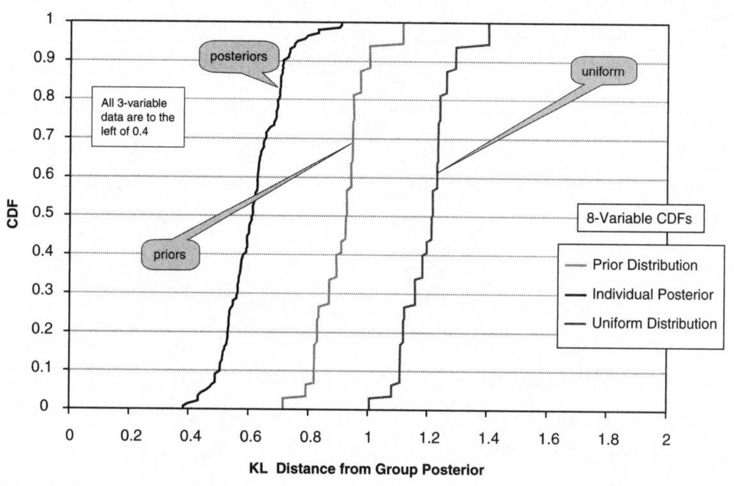

SOURCE: Author's calculations.

informative than the uniform beliefs. If the traders are competent Bayesians, they will begin with their prior and, after seeing their individual information, will believe their individual posterior. If a process is successful at fully aggregating the information available, the cumulative distribution of its predictions will be a vertical line at zero. A key point to note for later is that the scales are significantly different. All the curves in the eight-event case lie to the right of the curves in the three-event case, indicating that eight events and 256 states is a significantly more difficult world.

Process Performance. We looked at the performance of four different information aggregation processes in each of the two environments. We looked at two standard processes: opinion surveys and bulletin-board markets. For the first of these, we asked individuals to describe their beliefs, and we used a scoring rule to provide some incentives for them to do this accurately. They were not involved with anyone else and received no feedback from anyone. For the second, we used Marketscape, a web-based, multiple-market system developed by Charlie Plott (www.eeps.caltech.edu). There was one market for each event. We also looked at two less-standard mechanisms suggested by our earlier analysis: an iterative call market with conditional contracts and a shared scoring rule with conditional contracts. For each process we ran sixty trials, where each trial involved a new draw of information and a complete run-through of the process. For the three-event environment, we ran twenty-four trials (with four groups of three subjects each participating in six trials). In each trial, three individuals computed seven independent prices in twelve minutes. For the eight-event environment, we ran thirty-six trials (with six groups of six subjects participating in six trials each). In the eight-event environments, at least twelve of the trials involved subjects who had already participated in six of the three-event trials and six of the eight-event trials. In each trial, six individuals computed 255 independent prices in twelve minutes.

The data suggest that subjects were having problems understanding these difficult environments. In figures 3-3 and 3-4, I graph the cumulative distributions summarizing the performance of the individual scoring rule in the three-event and eight-event environments. The cumulative distribution provides the probability that a randomly selected individual will provide a probability estimate within that distance from the full-information density. As one can see, in the three-state world, two-thirds of the individuals

FIGURE 3-3
KL DISTANCES FOR THE EXPERIMENTS USING INDIVIDUAL SCORING RULES IN THREE-EVENT ENVIRONMENTS

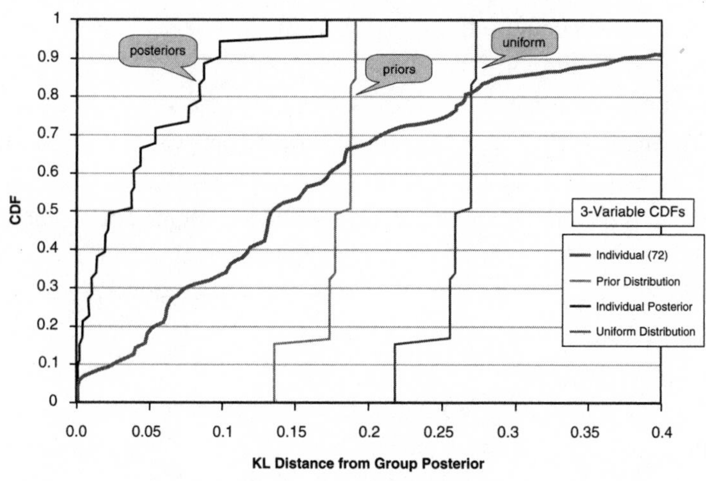

SOURCE: Author's calculations.

FIGURE 3-4
KL DISTANCES FOR THE EXPERIMENTS USING INDIVIDUAL SCORING RULES IN EIGHT-EVENT ENVIRONMENTS

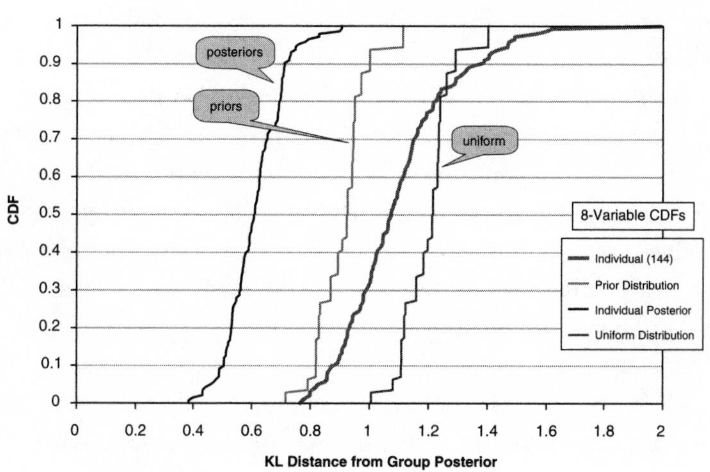

SOURCE: Author's calculations.

managed to beat the theoretical prior, but fewer than 5 percent actually provided as much information as they could have had in their individual posterior.[58] In the eight-state world, performance was worse. The subjects were better informed than the uniform prior, but they were not as well-informed as the theoretical priors, again providing an indication that this was is a very difficult world for them to deal with.

One might wonder at this point whether the subjects really understood the environment and, if not, whether the data from various mechanisms should be taken seriously. I think the answers are no and yes. That is, the subjects had difficulty understanding the environment, and some were obviously better at it than others. But each had information about the world that could be aggregated. The real question could still be asked and answered: Can any process sharpen the signal-to-noise ratio in a complex situation? I turn to that now.

In our first attempt to create information aggregation, we used standard markets. We created two securities for each event,[59] provided subjects with an initial endowment of each, and let them trade through a bid-ask system with an open book. Surprisingly, these standard markets did not help. In fact, the final predictions were even worse than those provided by individuals acting on their own. The data are graphed in figures 3-5 and 3-6. With the exception of the bottom 15 percent of the trials, the cumulative distribution for the market experiments lies to the right of that for the individual data. In these very thin environments, very little trading takes place, price-discovery does not occur, and equilibria are hard to find. The markets seem to garble the aggregate information rather than sharpen it. In the whirlwind we created in the lab, one can do better than markets by randomly selecting someone and asking him what he thinks. The implication is that unless one is convinced that there will be thick markets, one cannot achieve good information aggregation simply by creating a collection of securities and then declaring, "Let there be markets." It just will not work. New designs are necessary.

A natural conjecture based on the work of Bossaerts, Fine, and Ledyard[60] is that the process should work better in thin situations if one includes conditional contracts and uses a call market.[61] With conditional contracts, a trader can buy or sell securities such as (A = 1 if B = 0), which pays $1.00 if both ($A$ = 1 and B = 0), pays $0.00 if ($A$ = 0 and B = 0), and returns one's

FIGURE 3-5
KL DISTANCES FOR THE EXPERIMENTS USING STANDARD DOUBLE AUCTIONS IN THREE-EVENT ENVIRONMENTS

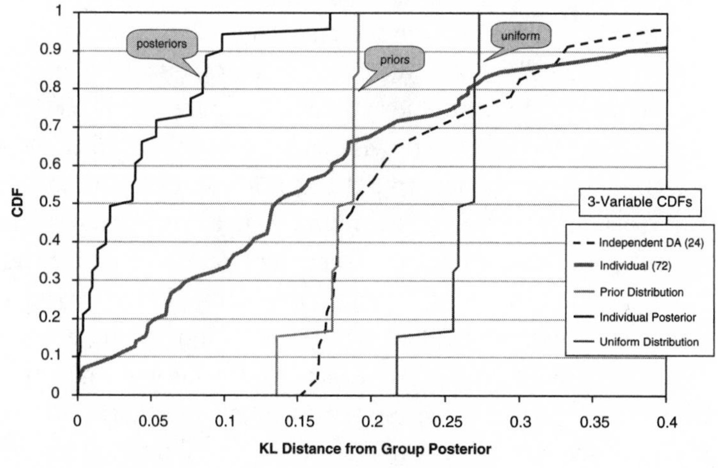

SOURCE: Author's calculations.

FIGURE 3-6
KL DISTANCES FOR THE EXPERIMENTS USING STANDARD DOUBLE AUCTIONS IN EIGHT-EVENT ENVIRONMENTS

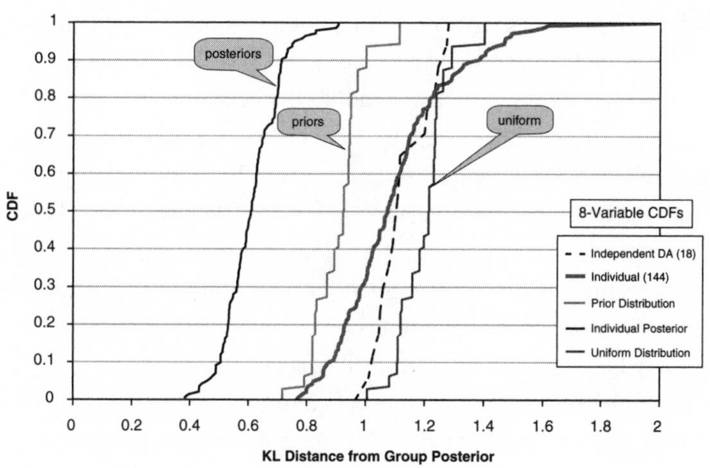

SOURCE: Author's calculations.

money if (B = 1). In this way, traders can display and trade on partial information with which they may feel more comfortable. Furthermore, the process should also work better if we use a call market to "thicken up" the trading by clearing a larger number of contracts at one time.

Following this intuition, we created and ran a call market with conditional contracts. The call market was an iterative process where, in a series of rounds, subjects submitted bids on the complete set of contingent contracts, and then an algorithm provisionally cleared the market and set a price for each state. Then a new round began for up to five rounds. Bids that were provisionally cleared in one round were automatically resubmitted to the next. The data from our experiments are provided in figures 3-7 and 3-8. In the three-event environments, this design provided an improvement over both individual observations and standard markets. The predictions of the call market were closer to the full-information prior. But this was only a qualified success at best. Despite a sharpening of the information, the subjects still did not get to the distribution of theoretical individual posteriors. Furthermore, in the eight-event environment, there was actually no improvement over standard mechanisms. There was no difference in the top 50 percent of the distributions for any of the three processes: individual observations, standard markets, or call markets with conditional contracts. Further design was clearly necessary.

From earlier discussions, one might conjecture that one of the inhibiting factors to the full aggregation of information could be the fact that subjects are not "small" in these environments. In thin markets, informational monopoly power exists and can lead to incomplete bidding. It is not incentive-compatible for traders to behave as required for markets to aggregate information fully. To mitigate such frictions, we turned to a shared scoring rule with conditional contracts. The data from those trials are summarized in figures 3-9 and 3-10. Here there was some success, with a significant improvement in the eight-event world and some improvement in the three-event trials. The shared scoring rule did better than the traditional approaches to market design. But it is also true that the subjects still did not get to the distribution of theoretical individual posteriors. We have found a process that does sharpen the signal-to-noise ratio through some type of aggregation process. We have not found a process that fully aggregates all information.

FIGURE 3-7

KL DISTANCES FOR THE EXPERIMENTS USING A CALL MARKET WITH CONTINGENT CONTRACTS IN THREE-EVENT ENVIRONMENTS

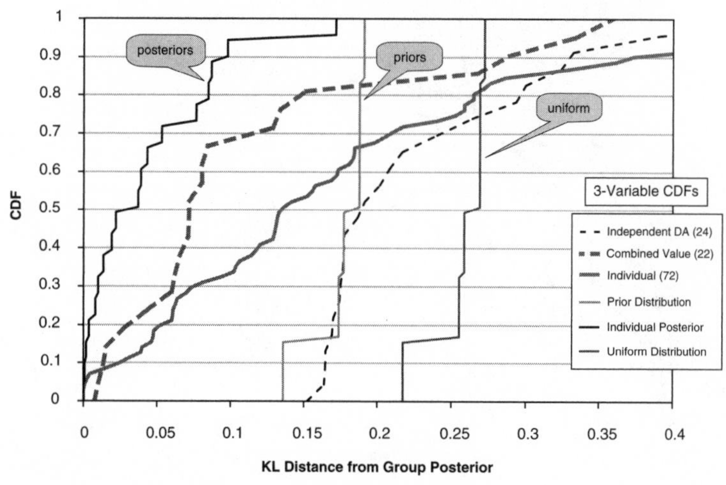

SOURCE: Author's calculations.

FIGURE 3-8

KL DISTANCES FOR THE EXPERIMENTS USING A CALL MARKET WITH CONTINGENT CONTRACTS IN EIGHT-EVENT ENVIRONMENTS

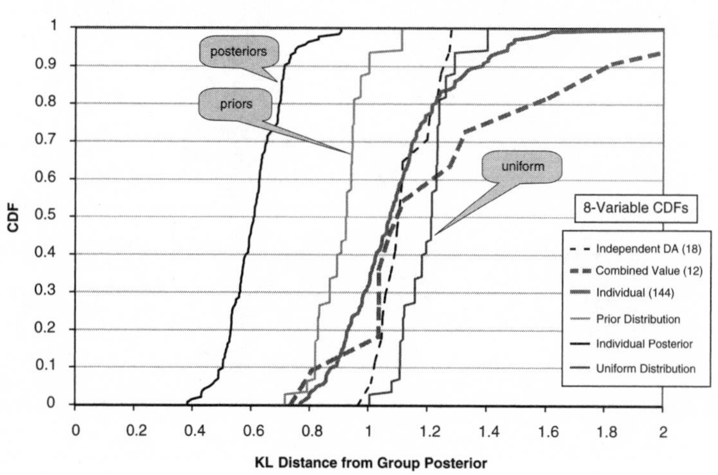

SOURCE: Author's calculations.

FIGURE 3-9

KL DISTANCES FOR THE EXPERIMENTS USING SHARED SCORING RULES WITH CONTINGENT CONTRACTS IN THREE-EVENT ENVIRONMENTS

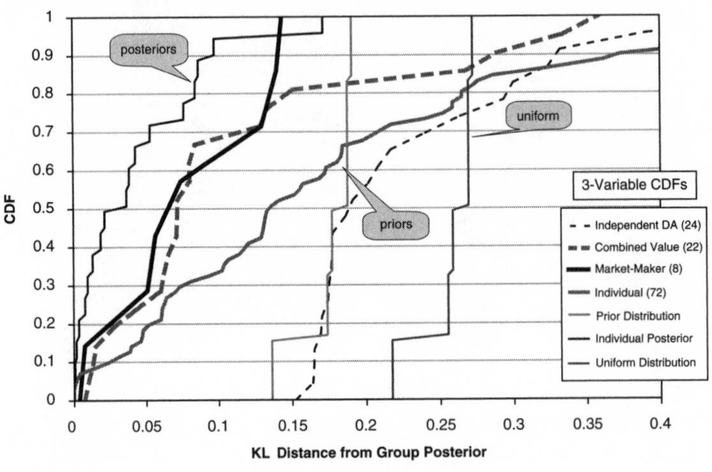

SOURCE: Author's calculations.

FIGURE 3-10

KL DISTANCES FOR THE EXPERIMENTS USING SHARED SCORING RULES WITH CONTINGENT CONTRACTS IN EIGHT-EVENT ENVIRONMENTS

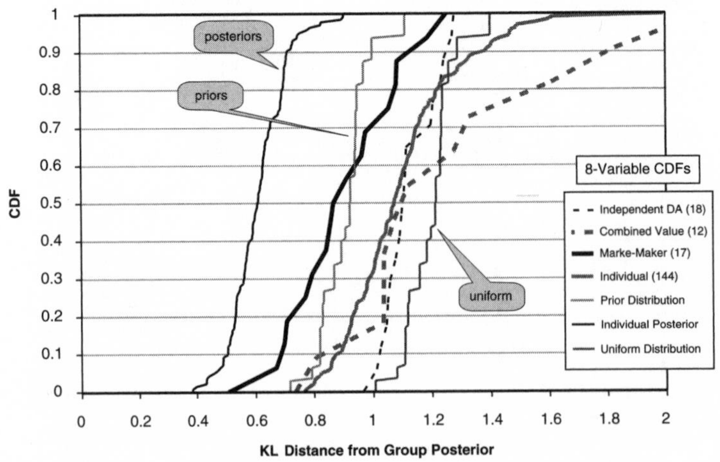

SOURCE: Author's calculations.

Final Thoughts

Information markets for predictions are possible and desirable. A growing body of scientific evidence supports the ability of carefully focused markets to aggregate privately held, widely dispersed information into probability estimates that approximate the full-information posterior. Moreover, a growing body of applications supports the hypothesis that markets improve on other more traditional methods, such as polls, committees, and other forms of expert opinion. Markets seem to work best in thick situations where there are many traders with small bits of information; where traders behave competitively as price-takers, are risk-neutral, and are good at Bayesian updating; and where traders do not have a direct stake in the outcomes. The increasing use of these markets will improve our ability to recognize and deal with uncertainty.

The evidence for the use of information markets to support policy decisions is not as straightforward. Many policy applications will be in thin situations. Better policy analysis requires more contracts, which exponentially explode in the number of alternatives considered. There are often a small number of traders, whom I have called informational monopolists, with exclusive and important pieces of information. And there are temptations for both the policy analyst operating the market and the traders in the market to take actions that will cause information not to be revealed. Traditional market designs do not work well under these conditions, and there is no reason to expect them to create a full aggregation of information.

New market designs will be needed. Designs must be able to operate effectively in thin situations. They must be sensitive to issues of incentive compatibility, computational complexity, and immediacy. We looked at two possible alternatives to traditional approaches: call markets and shared scoring rules. We found that the shared scoring rule design definitely sharpens the signal-to-noise ratio in thin and ultrathin markets over that achieved by traditional markets. But we did not find a process that did even as well as the theoretical individual posteriors. It is not clear one exists, but it is highly likely there are other designs that can do better.[62]

Notes

1. Policy analysis can, of course, also be about persuasion and obfuscation and not about clearing up the issues. But most groups, even those that intend ultimately to cloud issues, privately want to know as much as they can about the true situation before doing so.

2. All beliefs will be the same and will be equal to the full-information posterior probability distribution function.

3. Actually, as long as the price of Bush is less that $0.70, the price of Dukakis is more than $0.30, and the price of Other is more than $0, you will be better off after the trade. I am, of course, assuming throughout this example that you are risk-neutral.

4. Joyce E. Berg, Robert Forsythe, and Tom A. Rietz, "The Iowa Electronic Market," in *Blackwell Encyclopedic Dictionary of Finance*, ed. Dean Paxson and Douglas Wood (Oxford: Blackwell Press, 1997), 111–13.

5. Examples can be found at the websites of Common Knowledge Markets, HedgeStreet, Goldman Sachs and Deutsche Bank, NewsFutures, and TradeSports.

6. Stephen Figlewski, "Subjective Information and Market Efficiency in a Betting Model," *Journal of Political Economy* 87 (1979): 75–88.

7. Richard Roll, "Orange Juice and Weather," *American Economic Review* 74, no. 5 (1984): 861–80.

8. Michael Maloney and J. Harold Mulherin, "The Complexity of Price Discovery in an Efficient Market: The Stock Market Reaction to the Challenger Crash," *Journal of Corporate Finance* 9, no. 4 (September 2003): 453–79.

9. Kay-Yut Chen and Charles Plott, "Information Aggregation Mechanisms: Concept, Design and Implementation for a Sales Forecasting Problem" (Working Paper 1131, Caltech Social Science, Pasadena, Calif., 2002).

10. Justin Wolfers and Eric Zitzewitz, "Prediction Markets," *Journal of Economic Perspectives* 18, no. 2 (Spring 2004): 107–26.

11. Robert Aumann, "Agreeing to Disagree," *Annals of Statistics* 4 (1976): 1236–39.

12. "Common knowledge" means that each knows the other's beliefs, each knows the other knows that each knows the other's beliefs, and so on. This will be true if, for example, they each announce their beliefs when they are physically in the presence of each other.

13. John Geanakopolis and Heracles Polemarchakis, "We Can't Disagree Forever," *Journal of Economic Theory* 28 (1982): 192–200.

14. Richard McKelvey and Talbot Page, "Common Knowledge, Consensus and Aggregate Information," *Econometrica* 54, no. 1 (1986): 109–27.

15. Ibid.

16. Scoring rules are of real interest in this paper and will be covered in detail later. They are one way to provide monetary incentives to someone to reveal his probability beliefs accurately.

17. Each of these conclusions was somewhat qualified, as we will see later.

18. See, for example, Jerry Green, "Temporary General Equilibrium in a Sequential Trading Model with Spot and Future Transactions," *Econometrica* 41 (1973): 1103–23; Sanford Grossman, "The Existence of Futures Markets, Noisy Rational Expectations, and Informational Externalities," *Review of Economic Studies* 44 (1977): 431–49; Robert Lucas, "Expectations and the Neutrality of Money," *Journal of Economic Theory* 4 (1972): 103–24; Beth Allen, "General Equilibrium with Rational Expectations," in *Contributions to Mathematical Economics in Honor of Gerard Debreu*, ed. Werner Hildenbrand and Andreu Mas-Colell (Amsterdam: North-Holland, 1986), 1–23.

19. See, for example, Kenneth Arrow, "The Role of Securities in the Optimal Allocation of Risk Bearing," *Review of Economic Studies* 31 (1964): 91–96; Gerard Debreu, *Theory of Value* (New York: John Wiley and Sons, 1959).

20. In the IEM example above, there are three mutually exclusive states: Bush wins, Dukakis wins, and Other wins. It is a complete set of securities.

21. Robert Forsythe, Thomas Palfrey, and Charles Plott, "Asset Valuation in an Experimental Market," *Econometrica* 50 (1982): 537–68.

22. Richard D. McKelvey and Peter C. Ordeshook, "Sequential Elections with Limited Information," *American Journal of Political Science* 29 (1985): 480–512.

23. Charles R. Plott and Shyam Sunder, "Rational Expectations and the Aggregation of Diverse Information in Laboratory Security Markets," *Econometrica* 56, no. 5 (1998): 1085–1118.

24. Sanford J. Grossman and Joseph Stiglitz, "Information and Competitive Price Systems," *American Economic Review* 66, no. 2 (1976): 246–53.

25. If they do not know this, then there is no way for them to make inferences from the prices.

26. Robin Hanson and Ryan Oprea, however, provide a financial trading model in which traders actually acquire more information when a potential manipulator is present. Hanson and Oprea, "Manipulators Increase Information Market Accuracy" (working paper, Department of Economics, George Mason University, Fairfax, Va., 2004).

27. Paul Milgrom and Nancy Stokey, "Information, Trade, and Common Knowledge," *Journal of Economic Theory* 26 (1982): 17–27.

28. If he saw (H, H) or (H, T), person 1 would not be willing to part with his assets for any price less than $0.50.

29. It would be less than if person 1 had seen (0H, 2T).

30. James S. Jordan, "The Generic Existence of Rational Expectations Equilibrium in the Higher Dimensional Case," *Journal of Economic Theory* 26 (1982): 224–43.

31. Plott and Sunder, "Rational Expectations."

32. Richard McKelvey and Talbot Page, "Common Knowledge."

33. Incomplete updating is a problem for all information-aggregation procedures, including polls and committees.

34. Robert W. Hahn and Paul C. Tetlock, "Using Information Markets to Improve Public Decision Making," *Harvard Journal of Law and Public Policy* 29, No. 1 (Fall 2005): 213–89.

35. IEM has a particularly clever way to implement this market, as they did for the Google initial public offering. Two securities are issued: one that pays $0 if the policy is not implemented and $\$(ax)$ if the policy is implemented and the average score is x (where $a(max\ x) = \$1$ and $max\ x$ is the highest score possible). The other pays $1 if the policy is not implemented and pays $\$(1 - ax)$ if the policy is implemented. Note that no matter what happens, the portfolio value of 1 of each security is $1. The market-maker can offer to buy or sell this portfolio at the price of $1 risk-free.

36. It is also true that if the price of security 2 were $0.10 higher than the price of security 1 so that a predicted increase of $0.1a$ were being made, the policymaker would never know whether more could have been done for less.

37. As an indication of how quickly this can get out of hand in real applications, consider the Policy Analysis Market proposed by Net Exchange for the Defense Advanced Research Projects Agency. It would have involved five quarterly indices for each of eight countries (plus five other indices) for four quarters. Each market was whether the index went up or down. There were initially to be one thousand traders, growing eventually to ten thousand. A complete set of contracts would have required $2^{180} = 1.54E + 50$ contracts.

38. Even if management does not reopen the markets after its inquiry, these folks lose because the August securities end up out of the money. Alternatively, if management gives everybody their money back, the traders will be not very interested the next time information markets are tried. In all cases, there is a serious problem.

39. This does not eliminate another trader problem that can arise from management reaction to the information in the market—loss of one's job. If the individual who signals that A_{new} is in trouble works exclusively on A_{new}, then the individual's gains from transactions in the information market may well be outweighed by his losses from the cancellation. The individual will suppress any information that is bad for him—especially if he is the unique holder of the information.

40. It is a well-known theorem in mechanism design (see Leo Hurwicz, "On Informationally Decentralized Systems" in *Decision and Organization: A Volume in Honor of Jacob Marschak*, ed. Roy Radner and C. Bart McGuire [Amsterdam: North-Holland, 1972], 297–336); as long as there are a finite number of traders, each trader—whether an informational monopolist or not—has some market power and can, through misrepresentation of preferences, cause the outcome to move in a direction he would prefer. Of course, the incentive to do this usually decreases as the number of traders increases.

41. Do not ask me how they will know this; this is just an example. We could change the example prediction to "a whaler will land in Boston on 12/25/1850" and allow this person to have a very powerful telescope.

42. This is a form of Bertrand competition. Charlie Plott reports this type of phenomenon in many of his experiments where the two insiders compete with each other in the order queue until they drive the price to 1 and no one gains anything. They act as if they are competitive even if they are not. He argues that this is an important mechanism in getting private information out into the marketplace.

43. Glenn W. Brier, "Verification of Forecasts Expressed in Terms of Probability," *Monthly Weather Review* 75 (1950): 1–3.

44. Leonard J. Savage, "Elicitation of Personal Probabilities and Expectations," *Journal of the American Statistical Association* 46 (1971): 783–801.

45. I. J. Good, "Rational Decisions," *Journal of the Royal Statistical Society* 14 (1952): 107–14.

46. Risk-averters will report a probability density that is flatter than the truth.

47. Robin Hanson, "Combinatorial Information Market Design," *Information Systems Frontiers* 5, no. 1 (2003): 105–19.

48. I am now reporting on material that is in Robin Hanson, Takashi Ishikida, and John Ledyard, "An Experimental Test of Combinatorial Information Markets" (manuscript, Caltech, Pasadena, Calif., 2005). Hanson was the prime designer of the experimental environments. Ishikida was the prime implementer.

49. Plott and Sunder, "Rational Expectations," 1085–1118.

50. Richard McKelvey and Talbot Page, "Public and Private Information: An Experimental Study of Information Pooling," *Econometrica* 58, no. 6 (1990): 1321–39.

51. We were analyzing designs for the Policy Analysis Market. That environment is really thin, and we did not expect standard market designs to do well.

52. Peter Bossaerts and Charles Plott, "Basic Principles of Asset Pricing Theory: Evidence from Large-Scale Experimental Financial Markets," *Review of Finance* 8 (2004): 1–35.

53. Peter Bossaerts and Charles Plott, "The CAPM in Thin Experimental Financial Markets," *Journal of Economics Dynamics and Control* 26 (2002): 1093–1112.

54. Peter Bossaerts, Leslie Fine, and John Ledyard, "Inducing Liquidity in Thin Financial Markets through Combined-Value Trading Mechanisms," *European Economic Review* 46 (2002): 1671–95.

55. It would be perhaps more appropriate to say, "We tried to induce a common prior." We handed out instructions, available on request, with much detail. We repeated the markets within each session, and we brought back subjects for further sessions. But one never knows for sure what the subjects have in their heads.

56. There are many possible measures one might use. This measure is reasonably standard in the literature, so we use it here. It does have a problem if probabilities are close to zero, but we ignore that here.

57. In the three-event environment experiments, there were six different priors and full-information posteriors. And, because there were three subjects in each, there were eighteen different individual posteriors. In the eight-event environment,

there were also six priors and full-information posteriors. Because there were six subjects in each, there were thirty-six different individual posteriors.

58. The subject pool was Caltech undergrads. I do not know what would happen with a different pool.

59. One paid $1.00 if and only if the event = 1. The other paid $1.00 if and only if the event = 0.

60. Bossaerts, Fine, and Ledyard, "Inducing Liquidity," 1671–95.

61. In a call market, as opposed to, say, Marketscape, where bids, offers, and acceptances occur asynchronously, all bids and offers are collected over some prespecified period of time. At the end of that period, the bids and offers are matched in a way that maximizes the total gains from trade. This allows time to accumulate trades so that, at the call, the market is thicker.

62. A lot of research is going on in this area, significantly aided by experimental methods. See Charles Plott, Jorgen Wit, and Winston Yang, "Pari-mutuel Betting Markets as Information Aggregation Devices: Experimental Results," *Economic Theory* 22 (2003): 311–51; Kay-Yut Chen, Leslie Fine, and Bernardo Huberman, "Eliminating Public Knowledge Biases in Information Aggregation Mechanisms," *Management Science* 7 (2004): 983–94; and David Pennock, "A Dynamic Pari-mutuel Market for Hedging, Wagering, and Information Aggregation" (ACM Conference on Electronic Commerce, New York, N.Y., May 2004).

4

Deliberation and Information Markets

Cass R. Sunstein

Many institutions, both public and private, make their decisions through deliberation. But why, exactly, is deliberation important or even desirable? A central answer must be that deliberation will result in wiser judgments and better outcomes. But does deliberation actually have this effect? The answer is by no means clear. Group members may impose pressures on one another, leading to a consensus on falsehood rather than truth. The idea of "groupthink," coined and elaborated by Irving Janis, suggests the possibility that groups will tend toward uniformity and censorship, thus failing to combine information and enlarge the range of arguments.[1] Without structural protections, both private and public groups are likely to err, not in spite of deliberation, but because of it. The use of statistical means, or of information markets, will often lead to more accurate decisions.

As an example of a failure of deliberation, consider the account in the 2004 report of the Senate Select Committee on Intelligence, which explicitly accused the Central Intelligence Agency of groupthink. According to the committee, the CIA's predisposition to find a serious threat from Iraq led to its failure to explore alternative possibilities or to obtain and use the information that it actually held.[2] In the committee's view, the CIA "demonstrated several aspects of group think: examining few alternatives, selective gathering of information, pressure to conform within the group or withhold criticism, and collective rationalization."[3] Thus, the agency showed a "tendency to reject information that contradicted the presumption" that Iraq had weapons of mass destruction. Because of that presumption, the agency failed to use its own formalized methods "to challenge assumptions and 'group think,' such as 'red teams,' 'devil's advocacy,' and other types of alternative or competitive analysis."[4] Above all, the committee's conclusions emphasized the CIA's failure to elicit and aggregate information.

This claim is a remarkable and even uncanny echo of one that followed the 2003 investigation of problems at NASA, stressing that administration's similar failure to elicit competing views, including those based on information held by administration employees.[5] The Columbia Accident Investigation Board explicitly attributed the destruction of the space shuttle Columbia to an unfortunate culture at NASA—a culture that did too little to elicit information. In the board's words, NASA lacked "checks and balances." It pressured people to follow a "party line." It made it "difficult for minority and dissenting opinions to percolate up through the agency's hierarchy"—even though, the board contended, effective safety programs required the encouragement of minority opinions and the reporting of bad news.[6]

My aim here is to compare deliberation with information markets and to show the advantages of the latter over the former. To explain why deliberation fails, I explore the consequences of two sets of influences on members of deliberating groups.[7] The first consists of informational influences, by which group members fail to disclose what they know out of deference to the information publicly announced by others. The second involves social pressures, which lead people to silence themselves in order not to face reputational sanctions, such as the disapproval of relevant others. As a result of these problems, groups often amplify rather than correct individual errors; emphasize shared information at the expense of unshared information; fall victim to cascade effects; and tend to end up in more extreme positions in line with the predeliberation tendencies of their members. Even federal judges are vulnerable to the relevant pressures, as both Republican and Democratic appointees show especially ideological voting when they are sitting with other judges appointed by presidents of the same political party.[8]

Because of these pressures, deliberative processes often fail to achieve their minimal goal of aggregating the information actually held by the deliberators. Indeed, such processes often fail to aggregate information even as they decrease variance, and increase confidence, among their members. A confident, cohesive, error-prone group is nothing to celebrate. On the contrary, it might be extremely dangerous, both to itself and to others.[9]

As we shall see, information markets often outperform deliberating groups, simply because they are so effective at pooling information. Indeed, information markets realign private incentives in a way that makes them exceptionally well-designed to reduce the problems that infect deliberating groups. Such markets are worth investigating, in part because they provide an illuminating route by which to explore some characteristic defects in deliberative processes—and by which to identify reforms that should make them work better. If deliberative processes are to be improved, it might well be by building on the insights provided by the large successes of information markets. In addition, such markets are worth investigating in their own right, if only because they promise to provide a supplement to deliberation that should improve social decisions.

Deliberating Groups

To make the analysis tractable, let us focus on how deliberating groups might be able to solve factual questions or cognitive puzzles that have correct solutions. Results in these domains provide a good test of when and whether deliberating groups perform well.

If deliberating groups do well, we can imagine three principal reasons:

- *Groups are equivalent to their best members.* One or more group members will often know the right answer, and other members might well become convinced of this fact. For this reason, groups might perform toward or at the level of their best members. If some or many members suffer from ignorance or a form of bias that leads to error, others might correct them. Suppose, for example, that a group of military officials is attempting to assess the strengths and weaknesses of a potential enemy in some part of the world. If one of them is a specialist, all of them can learn what the specialist knows. Many deliberating groups contain at least one expert on the question at hand; if group members listen to the expert, they will do at least as well as he does. For these reasons, deliberation might correct individual errors rather than propagate them, in a way that allows convergence on the judgment of the most accurate group member.

- *The whole is the sum of the parts: aggregating information.* Deliberation could aggregate existing information in a way that leads the group as a whole to know more than any individual member does. Suppose that the group contains no experts on the question at issue, but that relevant information is dispersed among members so that the group is potentially one larger expert, even if its members are not. Or suppose that the group contains a number of experts, but that each member is puzzled about how to solve a particular problem. Deliberation might elicit the relevant information and allow the group to make a sensible judgment. Almost everyone has had the experience of being a part of a group that ended up with a solution that went beyond what any individual member could have produced on his own. In this process, the whole is equal to the sum of the parts—and the sum of the parts is what is sought.
- *The whole goes beyond the sum of the parts: synergy.* The give and take of group discussion might sift information and perspectives in a way that leads the group to a good solution to a problem, one in which the whole is actually more than the sum of its parts. In such cases, deliberation is, at the very least, an ambitious form of information aggregation, one in which the exchange of views leads to a creative answer or solution.

To what extent do these mechanisms work in practice? Two points are entirely clear. First, deliberation usually reduces variance.[10] After talking together, group members tend to come into accord with one another.[11] Statistical groups thus show far more diversity of opinion than deliberating groups. Second, group members tend to become far more confident of their judgments after they speak with one another.[12] A significant effect of group interactions is a greater sense that one's postdeliberation conclusion is correct—whether it actually is or not. Corroboration by others increases confidence in one's judgments.[13] It follows that members of deliberating groups will usually converge on a position in which members have a great deal of confidence. This is not disturbing if that position is also likely to be correct—but if it is not, then many group members will end up sharing a view in which they firmly believe, but which turns out to be wrong (a most unfortunate and sometimes quite dangerous situation).

Unfortunately, there is no systematic evidence that deliberating groups will usually succeed in aggregating the information held by their members. This finding presents an extremely serious problem for those who favor deliberation as a method for improving judgments.

With respect to questions with definite answers, deliberating groups tend to do about as well as or slightly better than their average members, but not as well as their best members.[14] Hence, it is false to say that group members usually end up deferring to their internal specialists. Truth does not win out; according to Robert J. MacCoun, the most that can be said is that under some conditions, the group will converge on the truth if the truth begins with "at least some initial support" within the group when the task has "a demonstrably correct answer."[15] Note here that when a group outperforms most of its individual members, it is generally because the issue is one for which a particular answer can be shown, to the satisfaction of all or most, to be right; and that even in that condition, the group might not do well if the demonstrably correct solution lacks significant support at the outset.

In general, simple majority schemes do fairly well at predicting group judgments for many decision tasks. It follows that if the majority is wrong, the group will be wrong as well.[16] With experts, the same general conclusion holds. J. Scott Armstrong writes that a "structured approach for combining independent forecasts is invariably more accurate" than "traditional group meetings," which do "not use information efficiently."[17]

Let us discuss the key sources of deliberative failure, understood as a failure to make good decisions on the basis of the information group members actually have.

Sources of Deliberative Failure

A primary advantage of statistical groups is that members say what they think. But with deliberating groups, this might not happen. Exposure to the views of others might lead people to silence themselves, for two different reasons. The first involves the informational signals provided by the acts and views of other people. If most group members believe that X is true, there is reason to believe that X is in fact true, and that reason might outweigh the purely private reason a particular group member has to believe that X is false. If other group members share a particular belief, isolated or minority members might not speak out, deferring to the informational signal given by the statements of others. Not surprisingly, the strength of the signal will depend on the number and nature of the people who are giving it. People are particularly averse to being sole dissenters. If all but one person in a deliberating group has said that X is true, then the remaining member is likely to agree X is true, even to the point of ignoring the evidence of his own senses. And if the group contains one or more people who are well-known to be authorities, then other group members are likely to defer to them.

The second reason group members might silence themselves involves social influences. If people fear that their statements will be disliked or ridiculed, they might not speak out, even on questions of fact. Their silence might stem not from a belief that they are wrong, as in the case of informational pressure, but instead from the risk of social sanctions of various sorts. In the most extreme cases, those sanctions will take the form of criminal punishment or complete exclusion from the group. In less severe cases, those who defy the dominant position within the group will incur a form of disapproval that will lead them to be less trusted, liked, and respected in the future. Here, too, people are inevitably affected by the number and nature of those with the majority position. A large majority will impose more social pressure than a small one. If certain group members are leaders or authorities willing and able to impose social sanctions of various sorts, others will be unlikely to defy them publicly.

Participation in deliberative processes, and the effects of informational and social influences, can be put into a more general framework. Suppose that group members are deliberating about some factual question; suppose, too, that each member has some information that bears on the answer to that question. Will members disclose what they know?

For each person, the answer may well depend on the individual benefits and the individual costs of disclosure. In many situations, and entirely apart from informational and social influences, the individual benefits of disclosure will be far less than the social benefits. If I say what I know about a legal issue being examined by a team of lawyers, I will probably receive only a fraction of the benefit that comes from an improved decision by the group.

And if each group member thinks this way, the group will receive only a fraction of the available information. In this sense, participants in deliberation typically face a collective-action problem, in which each person, following his rational self-interest, will tell the group less than it needs to know. At least, this is so if each member receives only a small portion of the benefits that come to the group from a good outcome—a plausible view about the situation facing many institutions, including, for example, corporate boards and administrative agencies

If the statements of others suggest that privately held information is wrong or unhelpful, then the private benefit of disclosure is reduced much more. In that event, the group member has reason to believe that disclosure will not improve the group's decision at all. Things are even worse if those who speak against the apparent consensus suffer reputational injury (or more). In that event, the private calculus is straightforward: Silence is golden.

Both informational pressure and social influences help explain the finding that in a deliberating group, those in a minority position often silence themselves or otherwise have disproportionately little weight. There is a more particular finding: Members of low-status groups—less-educated people, African Americans, sometimes women—speak less and carry less influence within deliberating groups than their higher-status peers.[18] Both informational influence and social pressures, likely to be especially strong for low-status members, contribute to this result. The unfortunate consequence can be a loss of information to the group as a whole, in a way that ensures that deliberating groups do far less well than they would if only they could aggregate the information held by group members.

More generally, a comprehensive study has demonstrated that majority pressures can be powerful even for factual questions to which some people know the right answers.[19] The study involved twelve hundred people, forming groups of six, five, and four members. Individuals were asked true-false questions involving art, poetry, public opinion, geography, economics, and politics. They were then asked to assemble into groups, which discussed the questions and produced answers. The majority played a substantial role in determining each group's answers. The truth played a role, too, but a lesser one. If a majority of individuals in the group gave the right answer, the group's decision moved toward the majority in 79 percent of the cases. If a majority of individuals in the group gave the wrong answer, the group's decision nonetheless moved toward the majority in 56 percent of the cases. Hence, the truth did have an influence—79 percent is higher than 56 percent—but the majority's judgment was the dominant one. And because the majority was influential even when wrong, the average group decision was right only slightly more often than the average individual decision (66 percent versus 62 percent). What is most important is that groups did not perform as well as they would have if they had properly aggregated the information that group members had.

Consider four sets of deliberative failures.

Deliberative Failure 1: Amplification of Cognitive Errors

It is well known that individuals do not always process information well. They use heuristics that lead them to predictable errors; they are also subject to identifiable biases, which also produce errors.[20] A growing literature explores the role of these heuristics and biases and their relationship to law and policy.[21] For example, most people follow the representativeness heuristic, in accordance with which judgments of probability are influenced by assessments of resemblance (the extent to which A "looks like" B).[22] The representativeness heuristic helps explain what Paul Rozin and Carol Nemeroff have called "sympathetic magical thinking," including the beliefs that some objects have contagious properties, and that causes resemble their effects.[23] The representativeness heuristic often works well, but it can also lead to severe blunders. People often err because they use the availability heuristic to answer difficult questions about probability. When people use the availability heuristic, they answer a question of probability by asking whether examples come readily to mind.[24] Consider, for example, the question whether we should fear a hurricane, a nuclear power accident, or a terrorist attack. If it is easy to think of a case in which one of these hazards created serious harm, the assessment of probability will be greatly affected. Of course, use of the availability heuristic is not irrational, but it, too, can produce both excessive and insufficient fear.

For purposes of assessing deliberation, a central question is whether groups avoid the errors of the individuals who comprise them. There is no clear evidence that they do, and often they do not—a vivid illustration of the principle, "garbage in, garbage out," in a way that mocks the aspiration to collective correction of individual blunders. In fact, individual errors are not merely replicated but actually amplified in group decisions—a process of "some garbage in, much garbage out."

Consider some key findings. If individual jurors are biased because of pretrial publicity that misleadingly implicates the defendant, or even because of the defendant's unappealing physical appearance, juries are likely to amplify rather than correct those biases.[25] Groups have been found to amplify, rather than to attenuate, reliance on the representativeness heuristic;[26] to reflect even larger framing effects than individuals;[27] to show more overconfidence than group members;[28] to be more affected by the biasing effect of spurious arguments from lawyers;[29] to be more susceptible to the "sunk cost fallacy";[30] and to be more subject to choice-rank preference reversals.[31] In an especially revealing finding, groups have been found to make more, rather than fewer, conjunction errors than individuals when individual error rates are high—though fewer when individual error rates are low.[32] In addition, groups demonstrate essentially the same level of reliance on the availability heuristic, even when use of that heuristic leads to clear errors.[33]

Deliberative Failure 2: Hidden Profiles and Common Knowledge

Suppose group members have a great deal of information—enough to produce the unambiguously right outcome if that information is properly aggregated. Even if this is so, an obvious problem is that groups will not perform well if they emphasize shared information and slight information that is held by one or a few members. Unfortunately, countless studies demonstrate that this regrettable result is highly likely.[34] "Hidden profiles" is the term for accurate understandings that groups could but do not obtain. Hidden profiles are, in turn, a product of the *common-knowledge effect,* through which information held by all group members has more influence on group judgments than information held by only a few members.[35] The most obvious explanation of the effect is the simple fact that as a statistical matter, common knowledge is more likely to be communicated to the group; but social influences play a role as well.

Hidden Profiles. Consider a study of serious errors within working groups, both face-to-face and online.[36] The purpose of the study was to see how groups might collaborate to make personnel decisions. Resumes for three candidates applying for a marketing manager position were placed before group members. The attributes of the candidates were rigged by the experimenters so that one applicant was clearly the best for the job described. Packets of information were given to subjects, each containing a subset of information from the resumes, so that each group member had only part of the relevant information. The groups consisted of three people, some operating face-to-face, some operating online. Almost none of the deliberating groups made what was conspicuously the right choice. The reason is simple: They failed to share information in a way that would permit the group to make that choice. Members tended to share positive information about the winning candidate and negative information about the losers. They suppressed negative information about the winner and positive information about the losers. Hence, their statements served to "reinforce the march toward group consensus rather than add complications and fuel debate."[37]

Or consider a simulation of political elections, in which information was parceled out to individual members about three candidates for political office, and in which properly pooled information could have led to what was clearly the best choice, candidate A.[38] In the first condition, each member of the four-person groups was given most of the relevant information (66 percent of the information about each candidate). In that condition, 67 percent of group members favored candidate A before discussion and 85 percent after discussion.[39] This is a clear example of appropriate aggregation of information. Groups significantly outperformed individuals, apparently because of the exchange of information and reasons. Here, then, is a clear illustration of the possibility that groups can aggregate what members know in a way that produces sensible outcomes.

In the second condition, by contrast, the information that favored candidate A was parceled out to various members of the group so that only 33 percent of information about each candidate was shared. As the condition was designed, the shared information favored two unambiguously inferior candidates, B and C; but if the unshared information emerged through discussion, and were taken seriously, candidate A would be chosen. In that condition, fewer than 25 percent of group members favored candidate A before discussion, a natural product of the initial distribution of information. But (and this is the key result) that number actually *fell* after discussion, simply because the shared information had a disproportionate influence on group members.[40] In other words, groups did worse, not better, than individuals when the key information was distributed selectively. In those conditions, the commonly held information was far more influential than the distributed information, to the detriment of the group's ultimate decision.

From this and many similar studies, the general conclusion is that, as Stasser and Titus put it, when "the balance of unshared information opposes the initial most popular position . . . the unshared information will tend to be omitted from discussion and, therefore, will have little effect on members' preferences during group discussion."[41] That conclusion has a clear connection with the judgments, mentioned above, about large-scale information failures at the CIA and similar failures at NASA. It follows that "group decisions and postgroup preferences reflect the initial preferences of group members even when the exchange of unshared information should have resulted in substantial shifts in opinion."[42] Nor does discussion increase the recall of unshared information. On the contrary, its major effect is to increase recall of the attributes of the initially most popular candidate.[43] The most disturbing conclusion is that when key information is unshared, groups are "more likely to endorse an inferior option after discussion than [are] their individual members before discussion."[44]

The Common-Knowledge Effect. These results are best understood as a consequence of the common-knowledge effect, by which information held by all group members has far more influence on group judgments than information held by one member or a few.[45] More precisely, the "influence of a particular item of information is directly and positively related to the number of group members who have knowledge of that item before the group discussion and judgment."[46] Under conditions of unshared information, group judgments have been found by Gigone and Hastie to be "not any more accurate than the average of the individual judgments, even though"—and this is the central point—the groups were "in possession of more information than were any of the individuals."[47]

In this study, deliberating groups would have lost nothing in terms of accuracy if they had simply averaged the judgments of the people involved—a clear finding that deliberation might not improve on the judgments of a statistical group.[48] The more shared information is (the more that it stands as "common knowledge"), the more impact it will have on group members before discussion begins—and the more impact it will have as discussion proceeds, precisely because commonly held information is more likely to be discussed.

As might be expected, the group's focus on shared information increases with the size of the group.[49] In a study by Stasser and colleagues designed to test judgments about candidates for office, involving both three-person and six-person groups, all discussions focused far more on shared than on unshared information—but the effect was significantly greater for six-person groups. Most remarkably, the researchers write, "It was almost as likely for a shared item to be mentioned twice as it was for an unshared item to be mentioned at all."[50] And, despite the failures of their deliberations, group members were significantly more confident in their judgments after discussion.[51]

Deliberative Failure 3: Cascades

A cascade is a process by which people influence one another, so much so that participants ignore their private knowledge and rely instead on the publicly stated judgments of others. There are two kinds of cascades: informational and reputational. In informational cascades, people silence themselves out of deference to the information conveyed by others. In reputational cascades, they silence themselves so as to avoid the opprobrium of others.

Informational Cascades. Hidden profiles are closely related to informational cascades, which greatly impair group judgments. Cascades need not involve deliberation, but deliberative processes often involve cascades. As in the case of hidden profiles, the central point is that those involved in a cascade do not reveal what they know. As a result, the group does not obtain important information.

To see how informational cascades work, imagine a deliberating jury that is deciding whether a defendant should be subject to a punitive damage award and, if so, in what amount.[52] Let us also assume that the jurors are announcing their views in sequence, in a temporal queue, and that each juror knows his place in that queue. From his own recollection of the evidence and the jury instructions, and from some personal experience, each juror has some private information about what should be done. But each also attends, reasonably enough, to the judgments of others. Mr. Andrews is the first to speak. He suggests that the defendant be subject to a high punitive award—say, $5 million. Ms. Barnes now knows Andrews's judgment; it is clear that she, too, should certainly urge a high punitive award if she agrees independently with Andrews. But if her independent judgment is that no award should be imposed, she would—if she trusts Andrews no more and no less than she trusts herself—be indifferent about what to do and might simply flip a coin.

Now turn to a third juror, Mr. Carlton. Suppose that both Andrews and Barnes have favored a multimillion-dollar punitive award but that Carlton's own information, though inconclusive, suggests that no award should be imposed. In that event, Carlton might well ignore what he knows and follow Andrews and Barnes. It is likely in these circumstances that both Andrews and Barnes had reasons for their conclusion, and unless Carlton thinks that his own information is better than theirs, he should follow their lead. If he does, Carlton is in a cascade. Now suppose that Carlton is acting in response to what Andrews and Barnes did, not on the basis of his own information, and that subsequent jurors know what Andrews, Barnes, and Carlton did. On reasonable assumptions, they will do exactly what Carlton did: favor a high punitive damage award regardless of their private information (which, we are supposing, is relevant but inconclusive). This will happen even if Andrews initially blundered.[53]

If this is what is happening, there is a serious social problem: Jurors who are in the cascade do not disclose the information that they privately hold. In the example just given, jury decisions will not reflect the overall knowledge, or the aggregate knowledge, of those on the jury—even if the information held by individual jurors, if actually revealed and aggregated, would produce a quite different result. The reason is that individual jurors are following the lead of those who came before. Subsequent jurors might fail to rely on, and fail to reveal, private information that actually exceeds the information collectively held by those who started the cascade.

Cascades often occur in the real world within deliberating groups or elsewhere;[54] they are easy to create in the laboratory. The simplest experiment asked subjects to guess whether the experiment was using urn A, which contained two red balls and one white, or urn B, which contained two white balls and one red.[55] Subjects could earn $2.00 for a correct decision, and hence an economic incentive favored correct individual decisions (a point to which I will return). In each period, the contents of the chosen urn were emptied into a container. A randomly selected subject was asked to make one (and only one) private draw of a ball in each round. The subject recorded the color of that draw on an answer sheet and his own decision about which urn was involved. The subject did not announce his draw to the group, but he did announce his own decision to everyone. Then the urn was passed to the next subject for his own private draw, which again was not disclosed, and his own decision about the urn, which again was disclosed. This process continued until all subjects had made draws and decisions. At that time, the experimenter announced the actual urn used. If the subject had picked the urn only on the basis of his private information, he would have been right 66.7 percent of the time. The point of the experiment was to see whether people will decide to ignore their own draw in the face of conflicting announcements by predecessors—and to explore whether such decisions will lead to cascades and errors.

In the experiment, cascades often developed and often produced errors. After a number of individual judgments were revealed, people sometimes announced decisions that were inconsistent with their private draws, but that fit with the majority of previous announcements.[56] More than 77 percent of "rounds" resulted in cascades, and 15 percent of private announcements did not reveal a "private signal," that is, the information provided by people's own draws. Consider cases in which one person's draw (say, red) contradicted the announcement of his predecessor (say, urn B). In such cases, the second announcement nonetheless matched the first about 11 percent of the time—far less than a majority, but enough to ensure cascades. And when one person's draw contradicted the announcement of two or more predecessors, the second announcement was likely to follow those who went before. Of note, the majority of decisions were rationally based on the available information[57]—but erroneous cascades nonetheless developed. Table 4-1 shows an example of a cascade that produced an inaccurate outcome (the urn used was B).[58]

TABLE 4-1
AN INFORMATIONAL CASCADE

	1	2	3	4	5	6
Private draw	a	a	a	b	b	b
Decision	A	A	A	A	A	A

SOURCE: Willinger and Ziegelmeyet, "Are More Informed Agents," 291.

What is noteworthy here, of course, is that the total amount of private information—four whites and two reds—justified the correct judgment, which was in favor of urn B. But the existence of two early signals, producing rational but incorrect judgments, led everyone else to fall in line. As Anderson and Holt have written of a related experiment, "Initial misrepresentative signals start a chain of incorrect decisions that is not broken by more representative signals received later."[59] This result maps directly onto real-world decisions by deliberating groups, in which people fail to disclose what they know, to the detriment of the group as a whole.

Reputational Cascades. In a reputational cascade, people think they know what is right, or what is likely to be right, but they nonetheless go along with the crowd in order to maintain the good opinion of others. Suppose Albert suggests that global warming is a serious problem and that Barbara concurs with Albert, not because she actually thinks that Albert is right, but because she does not wish to seem, to Albert, ignorant or indifferent to environmental protection. If Albert and Barbara seem to agree that global warming is a serious problem, Cynthia not only might not contradict them publicly, but also might even appear to share their judgment, not because she believes that judgment to be correct, but because she does not want to face their hostility or lose their good opinion.

It should be easy to see how this process might generate a cascade. Once Albert, Barbara, and Cynthia offer a united front on the issue, their friend David might be most reluctant to contradict them, even if he thinks they are wrong. In the actual world of group decisions, people are, of course, uncertain whether publicly expressed statements are a product of independent information, participation in an informational cascade, or

TABLE 4-2
CONFORMITY AND CASCADES

	1	2	3	4	5	6	7	8	9	10
Private draw	a	b	b	b	a	b	b	b	a	b
Decision	A	A	A	A	A	A	A	A	A	A

SOURCE: Hung and Plott, "Information Cascades."

reputational pressure. Much of the time, listeners and observers undoubtedly overstate the extent to which the actions of others are based on independent information.

The possibility of reputational cascades is demonstrated by an ingenious variation on the urn experiment mentioned above.[60] In this experiment, people were paid $0.25 for a correct decision, but $0.75 for a decision that matched the decision of the majority of the group. There were punishments for incorrect and nonconforming answers as well. If people made an incorrect decision, they lost $0.25; if their decision failed to match the group's decision, they lost $0.75.

In this experiment, cascades appeared almost all of the time. No fewer than 96.7 percent of rounds resulted in cascades, and 35.3 percent of people's announcements did not match their private signal, that is, the signal given by their own draw. And when the draw of a subsequent person contradicted the announcement of the predecessor, 72.2 percent of people matched the first announcement. Consider, as a dramatic illustration, table 4-2, which shows this period of the experiment (the actual urn was B).[61]

This experiment shows that especially unfortunate results should be expected if people are rewarded not only or not mostly for being correct, but also or mostly for doing what other people do. The problem is that people are not revealing the information they actually have.

Deliberative Failure 4: Group Polarization

There are clear links among hidden profiles, social cascades, and the well-established phenomenon of group polarization, by which *members of a deliberating group end up adopting a more extreme version of the position toward which they tended before deliberation began.*[62] Group polarization is the typical pattern with deliberating groups, and it has been found in hundreds of studies involving more than a dozen countries, including the United States, France, Afghanistan, and Germany.[63] For example, those who disapprove of the United States and are suspicious of its intentions will increase their disapproval and suspicion if they exchange points of view. Indeed, there is specific evidence of the latter phenomenon among citizens of France.[64]

Group polarization occurs for matters of fact as well as issues of value, though it is easier to demonstrate the latter. If the question is whether a terrorist attack will occur in the United States in the next year, group polarization will not be easy to test, simply because the answer is either yes or no, and it is not simple to demonstrate greater extremism in binary choices. But suppose that people are asked, on a bounded scale of zero to eight, how likely it is that a terrorist attack will occur in the United States in the next year, with zero indicating "zero probability," eight indicating "absolutely certain," seven indicating "overwhelmingly likely," six "more probable than not," and five "fifty-fifty." In that event, the answers from a deliberating group will tend to reveal group polarization, as people move toward more extreme points on the scale depending on their initial median point. If the predeliberation median is five, the group judgment will usually be six; if the predeliberation median is three, the group judgment will usually be two.[65] Recall here that federal judges are highly susceptible to group polarization, as both Democratic and Republican appointees show far more ideological voting patterns when sitting with other judges appointed by a president of the same political party.[66] Juries polarize as well.[67]

Why does group polarization occur? There are three reasons.[68] The first and most important involves the now-familiar idea of informational influence, but in a distinctive form. People respond to the arguments made by other people—and the "argument pool" in any group with some predisposition in one direction will inevitably be skewed toward that predisposition. As a statistical matter, the arguments favoring the initial position will be more numerous than those pointing in the other direction. Individuals will have heard of some, but not all, of the arguments that emerge from group deliberation. As a result of the relevant arguments, deliberation will lead people toward a more extreme point in line with what group members initially believed.

The second explanation involves social influences. People want to be perceived favorably by other group members. Sometimes people's publicly stated views are, to a greater or lesser extent, a function of how they want to present themselves. Once they hear what others believe, some will adjust their positions at least slightly in the direction of the dominant position in order to hold onto their preserved self-presentation. They shift accordingly.[69]

The third explanation stresses that people with extreme views tend to have more confidence that they are right, and that, as people gain confidence, they become more extreme in their beliefs.[70] In a wide variety of experimental contexts, people's opinions have been shown to become more extreme simply because their views have been corroborated and because they have been more confident after learning of the shared views of others.[71]

Information Markets

Deliberation is one way to aggregate privately held information, but there are many other possibilities. An obvious alternative is to rely on the price signal, which has a similar aggregative function. And if an emphasis is placed on the information-aggregating properties of markets, it would seem plain that, to improve on the answer produced by statistical means and deliberating groups, we might consider an increasingly popular possibility: *Create a market.*[72] Information markets, a recent innovation, have proved remarkably successful at forecasting future events; they seem to do far better, in many domains, than deliberating groups. Such markets are worth sustained attention, in part because they offer important lessons about how to make deliberation go better or worse, and in part because they provide a useful model for many private and public organizations.

Potential and Promise. A central advantage of information markets is that they impose the right incentives for people to disclose the information they hold. Recall that in a deliberating group, members often have little incentive to say what they know. By speaking out, they provide benefits to others while possibly facing high private costs. Information markets realign incentives in a way that is precisely designed to overcome these problems. Because investments in such markets are generally not disclosed to the public, investors need not fear reputational sanctions if, for example, they have predicted that a company's sales will be low or that a certain candidate will be elected president. And because people stand to gain or lose from their investments, they have a strong incentive to use (and in that sense to disclose) whatever private information they hold; they can capture, rather than give to others, the benefits of disclosure. The use of private information will be reflected in the price signal. In these crucial ways, the problems that infect deliberating groups are largely eliminated in information markets.

Optimal deliberation is structured in a way that permits relevant and correct information to emerge—and that reduces the likelihood that useless, biased, or incorrect information will undermine deliberation. For their part, information markets impose strong incentives for traders to ferret out accurate information. Traders do not trade blindly, and they are entirely able to stop trading, for a moment or more, in order to retrieve better information that will give them an advantage. But in many deliberative groups, participants cannot leave; they must continue deliberating, and the necessary information is, at best, dispersed and locked within individual participants. Well-functioning systems of deliberation encourage group members to act dynamically to acquire further information, just as markets do.

Of course, investors, like everyone else, are subject to the informational pressure imposed by the views of others. But a market creates strong incentives for revelation of whatever information people actually hold. For small groups, of course, information markets are likely to be too "thin" to be useful; a certain number of investors is required to get a market off the ground. Hence, feasibility is a serious constraint on the use of information markets. In some contexts, however, private and public organizations might use markets as a complement to or even a substitute for deliberation. Perhaps most important, information markets have been found not to amplify individual errors but to eliminate them; the prices that result from trading prove reliable even if many individual traders err.

How might information markets be used? Consider a few possibilities:

- Uncertain about sales projections for the future, a company might not ask its employees to make predictions or to deliberate with one another. Instead, it might create an information market in which employees are allowed to place anonymous bets about likely outcomes.[73]

- As an aid to its assessment of future events in the world, the White House and the Department of Defense might maintain an information market in which investors predict outcomes of national importance—for example, the likelihood that the government of Iran will be toppled in the next calendar year, that there will be a terrorist attack in Europe within the same period, and that free elections will be held in Iraq by a specified time.
- The cost of an environmental regulation might be disputed, and experts within government might be unsure about how to resolve the dispute. It would be possible to create an information market asking whether, by a specified date, the projected costs will be above $400 million, $500 million, or $600 million.[74]
- Much of the time, the benefits of environmental regulation are at least as controversial as the costs. Experts might disagree about whether a carcinogen is harmful at low levels or even whether a substance is carcinogenic at all. An information market might be created to make predictions about the benefits of courses of action.[75]
- Movie company executives might want to know which of their movies are most likely to be serious Oscar contenders. Since an Oscar nomination gives a large boost to ticket sales, it is extremely valuable to be able to plan in advance. Existing markets might be enlisted to answer the relevant questions.
- Regulators are interested in trends involving air pollution, including increases or decreases in emissions over time and in concentrations of pollutants in the ambient air. An information market might make projections about sulfur dioxide and particulate concentrations in New York City, Chicago, and Los Angeles in the next decade.

- Officials in a political campaign, or in another nation, often want to know the likelihood of a particular candidate's success at a particular moment in time. Instead of relying exclusively on polling data, they might consult information markets.

- It is important both for government and for outside observers to know the size of federal budget deficits. Government projections are greatly disputed, and some of them may well be self-serving. Information markets might provide more reliable estimates.[76]

- Regulators might be concerned about the likely risks of a new disease or of an old disease that seems to be growing in magnitude. To assess the risks, they might create an information market designed to predict the number of deaths that will be attributed to, say, mad cow disease over a specified period.

- Federal and state agencies monitor a range of institutions to ensure that they are solvent.[77] One problem is that such agencies do not know whether insolvencies are likely to be large or small in a particular year; another is that the solvency of particular institutions can be difficult to predict in advance. Information markets could help with both problems. Most dramatically, according to Abramowicz, they "might have led to earlier recognition of the savings and loans crisis in the 1980s."[78]

- The federal government might want to know the number of people who are likely to be infected by HIV in the United States or Africa by the year 2010; the answer to that question might be relevant to American policy judgments. An information market might be used to make predictions about the future progress of the disease.[79] Such markets might more generally be used to make predictions about the likely effects of development projects, such as those involving vaccinations and mortality reductions.[80]

- The government might seek to predict the likelihood, magnitude, and damage produced by natural disasters such as tornadoes and earthquakes. Accurate information could greatly assist in advance planning. Information markets could easily be created to help in that task.

This is an ambitious agenda. But to date, information markets have been spectacularly successful in terms of the aggregate accuracy of the resulting "prices." Indeed, they have been successful in many domains. Why is this? Note that they do not rely on the median or average judgment of a randomly selected group of people. They are genuine markets. Those who participate are self-selected. They must believe that they have relevant information; it is costly for them to "vote," and they ought not be expected to do so unless they have something to gain. In addition, votes are not weighted equally. If people want to invest a few dollars, they are permitted to do so, but they can invest a great deal more if they are confident of their answers. Intensity of belief is captured in prices.

There is a further point. People are permitted to buy and sell shares on a continuing basis. Moreover, a correct answer is rewarded and an incorrect one punished. Hence, investors have a strong incentive to be right. In these circumstances, accurate answers can emerge even if only a small percentage of participants has good information. In this sense, the judgments of information markets are very different from the ordinary ones of deliberating groups. The resulting prices do not amplify or even perpetuate cognitive errors; on the contrary, they correct them, because shrewd traders are able to invest in a way that corrects for even widespread errors.[81]

Of course, information markets involve a measure of deliberation. Individual investors are likely to have deliberated with others before they invest. In some such markets, investors undoubtedly act as "teams," pooling resources after deliberating together about what to do. The point is that decisions ultimately come not from asking group members to come up with a mutually agreeable conclusion, but by reference to the price signal, which will have aggregated a great deal of diverse information. It is for this reason that information markets outperform deliberative processes.

Failed Predictions? Of Manipulation, Bias, and Bubbles. In what circumstances might information markets fail? To answer this question, we should start with ordinary stock markets.[82] A great deal of recent attention has been paid to the possibility that individual traders are subject to manipulation and identifiable biases, in ways that lead them to blunder.[83] There is also a risk of "prediction bubbles," leading people to inaccurate judgments about future events.

Manipulation. A primary concern is that information markets, no less than ordinary ones, can be susceptible to manipulation by powerful speculators.[84] One attempt to manipulate an information market occurred during the 2000 presidential election. A group of speculators attempted to manipulate the IEM by buying large volumes of futures in presidential candidate Patrick Buchanan. The value of Buchanan shares did increase dramatically, but they fell almost immediately when "well-informed traders . . . seized the opportunity to profit off the manipulative traders."[85] Hence, the Iowa market remained stable despite this attempted manipulation. Perhaps other, more plausible efforts at manipulation would succeed, but none has thus far.

Biases. Another concern is that some of the cognitive biases that afflict individuals will manifest themselves in prediction markets. Just as in group deliberation, investors in a market might be subject to predictable heuristics and biases. The results here are unequivocal: they are. For example, psychologists have found that people overestimate the likelihood that their preferred candidate will win an election—a form of optimistic bias.[86] At a certain point in the 1980 campaign, for example, eighty-seven percent of Jimmy Carter's supporters believed that he would win, and 80 percent of Ronald Reagan's supporters believed their candidate would win.[87] Obviously, at least one side had overestimated its candidate's probability of victory at the relevant time.

In the market context, similar biases can be found. Gamblers in New York are especially likely to bet on the New York Yankees;[88] and some IEM traders show the same kind of "home-team" bias. In 1988, for example, Dukakis supporters were more likely to hold futures in the Massachusetts governor's ill-fated presidential bid than were supporters of George H. W. Bush.[89] More striking still, Dukakis supporters were more likely to view the candidates' debates as helpful to the Democratic candidate, and accordingly bought significant additional futures in his campaign after each debate.[90] Bush supporters showed precisely the same pattern. Traders thus exhibited the "assimilation-contrast" effect.[91] People usually assimilate new information in a way that confirms their view of the world, and those who invest in information markets show the same bias. In general, traders show a tendency to buy and sell in a way that fits with their party identification.[92]

Nonetheless, the Iowa Electronic Markets were more accurate than polls in predicting the outcome of the 1988 presidential election. Even three weeks before the election, the market provided an almost-perfect guess about the candidates' shares of the vote.[93] How is such accuracy possible when many traders showed identifiable biases? The answer lies in the behavior of a small group of "marginal traders" who were far less susceptible to these biases—a demonstration of the "marginal trader" hypothesis. According to this hypothesis, a small group of active traders who were far less susceptible to the relevant biases had a disproportionately large effect on aggregate market behavior. In trading election futures, these traders did not show the same biases as their fellow traders, and they earned significant profits at the expense of their quasi-rational colleagues.[94] Thus, the biased behavior of most traders did not affect the market price because the marginal traders were prepared to take advantage of their blunders. If marginal traders are active and able to profit from the bounded rationality of other participants, there might well be no effect on the aggregate market price.

Another bias that might be expected to affect information markets is the "favorite long-shot" bias. In horse racing, heavy favorites tend to give higher returns than other horses in the field, and long shots tend to offer lower-than-expected returns.[95] Hence, near-certainties are undervalued, and low probabilities are overvalued. If the point generalizes, prediction markets might not be accurate with respect to highly improbable events. The market should be expected to overestimate the likelihood that such events will come to fruition; for example, Pat Buchanan futures would be expected to be (and might well have been) overpriced even before the attempted manipulation of the market. By contrast, an information market might underestimate the probability of events that are highly likely to occur.[96] But with respect to existing prediction markets, there is only slight evidence of systematic errors in this vein.[97]

Bubbles and More. "Prediction bubbles" are also easy to imagine, with investors moving in a certain direction with the belief that many other investors are doing the same.[98] A temporary upsurge in investment in the nomination of Hillary Rodham Clinton as the 2004 Democratic nominee might well have been a small bubble, with some investors thinking not that she would, in fact, be the nominee, but that others would invest in that judgment, thus inflating the value of the investment. Crashes are possible as well.

In any case, informational influences can certainly lead individuals to make foolish investments in any market, including prediction markets.[99] As information markets develop, significant individual errors should be expected, and undoubtedly they will produce some errors in the price signal.[100] In the 2004 presidential election, news of exit polls produced a great deal of volatility in election markets, with a dramatic election-day swing in the direction of Senator Kerry at the expense of President Bush. Large-scale errors are possible when apparently relevant news leads numerous investors to buy or sell; indeed, this particular shift may well have been a cascade, with investors responding to one another's judgments, even though they were based on false information. The erroneous figures were able to last only for a few hours, however, after which the numbers returned to their previous state of considerable accuracy.

In particular contexts, the imaginable problems take a different form. Consider the problem of "terrorism futures." It would be extremely valuable to aggregate privately held information about the risk and location of any attack. But do likely investors actually possess helpful information? Thomas Rietz, a director of the Iowa Electronic Markets, argued that terrorism and world events were fundamentally different from other contexts in which markets have successfully predicted future events.[101] When betting on presidential elections, people can use ordinary information sources, along with their networks of friends, family, and coworkers, to form opinions; but for most investors, there are no such sources of information for terrorist activity. Another skeptic worried that the market would allow the wealthy to "hedge" against the possibility of terrorist activity, while ordinary Americans would remain vulnerable to this threat.[102] In this view, "terrorism futures" could operate as an insurance market that would not serve its purpose of providing information. In any event, government use of the resulting information could be self-defeating, at least if the information were made public. Terrorists would know the anticipated time and location of attacks, and they would also know that the government was aware of this—which would make it most unlikely that the prediction would turn out to be accurate. Where the event's occurrence is endogenous to the outcome of the information market, there is reason for skepticism about its likely performance—certainly if relevant actors have much to lose if the market turns out to be correct.[103]

But many policy issues, including those potentially involved in the now-defunct Policy Analysis Market, did not have this feature. Consider, for example, the question whether the Egyptian economy was likely to grow in the next year, or whether Yasser Arafat would lead the Palestinian Authority at the end of 2005. Perhaps many investors would lack a great deal of information on such questions, but it is most unlikely that the market prediction would turn out to be self-defeating. Of course, the Policy Analysis Market itself raises many questions and doubts. The broader point is that in many domains, information markets are extremely promising and likely to outperform both statistical means and the products of group deliberation.

Feasibility, Markets, and Deliberation Again. Information markets face one pervasive problem: feasibility. A jury, for example, could not enlist such markets to decide on questions of guilt or innocence. Among other things, there is no objective way to test whether the jury, or individual jurors, ended up with the right answer. (And if there were, the jury might well be dispensable!) Moreover, it is not easy to see how information markets could be used by judges. Of course, factual questions are often relevant in court, but such markets could not easily be used to verify one or another answer. In addition, information markets might suffer from a legitimacy deficit, at least at the present time, where they remain unfamiliar. Recall that deliberation increases confidence and decreases variance; in many contexts, reliance on information markets might well breed confusion and distrust.[104]

There is a more general problem. When the relevant groups are small, effective markets may be impossible to create, simply because of the absence of sufficient numbers of investors.[105] A certain number is necessary to ensure that information markets have enough information to aggregate. Nonetheless, administrative agencies might well enlist such markets to resolve a number of questions,[106] and ambitious efforts are underway to examine how government might enlist them to answer an array of disputed questions.[107] But, at a minimum, such markets should be used, where feasible, as an adjunct to deliberative processes. Of course, officials would not be bound by those predictions.[108] They might reasonably believe that investors are wrong. But if the outcomes of information markets prove reliable over time, officials should accept them unless they have grounds to believe they are inaccurate.

As Michael Abramowicz has suggested, governments might use information markets to help make projections about insolvency, budget deficits, and the costs and benefits of proposed regulations.[109] In each of these cases, the predictions of information markets might provide a "reality check" for deliberative processes. It would be possible to go much further. Officials might take into account the markets' predictions of the anticipated damage from a natural disaster, the number of annual deaths from an actual or anticipated disease (such as mad cow disease or AIDS), the number of American casualties from a war effort, the existence of demonstrable harms from global warming by, say, 2010,[110] the likelihood of scarcity of natural resources, shrinkage of tropical forests in the world, demonstrable deterrent effects from capital punishment or other severe punishments, increases or decreases in emissions of specified air pollutants, increases or decreases in concentrations of air pollution in the ambient air, and much more. In all these cases, private or public institutions might create markets to provide information on crucial questions, and public institutions might take that information into account in making judgments about policy.

The broadest point is that, even when information markets are not feasible, an understanding of their virtues helps illuminate the virtues and vices of deliberation—and helps show how to obtain more of the former and less of the latter. Such markets overcome the collective-action problem from which deliberating groups suffer; they also give people a strong incentive to say what they know and to back their best-grounded convictions with money.

Conclusion

Groups often hold a great deal of information, and an important task is to elicit and use the information of their members. Deliberation is generally thought to be the best way of carrying out that task, but deliberative bodies are subject to serious problems. Much of the time, informational influences and social pressures lead members not to say what they know. As a consequence, groups tend to propagate and even amplify cognitive errors.

They also emphasize shared information at the expense of unshared information, resulting in hidden profiles. Cascade effects and group polarization are common.

Information markets have significant advantages over deliberative processes, and in many contexts they might supplement or even replace those processes. Such markets tend to correct rather than amplify individual errors, above all because they allow shrewd investors to take advantage of the mistakes made by others. By providing economic rewards for correct individual answers, they encourage investors to disclose the information they have. As a result, they are often more accurate than the judgments of deliberating groups. To the extent feasible, many groups would often do well to enlist information markets in arriving at their judgments, above all because of the accuracy of the price signal.

Notes

1. Irving L. Janis, *Groupthink*, 2d ed. (Boston: Houghton Mifflin, 1982), 7–9.

2. U.S. Congress, Senate, Select Committee on Intelligence, *Report on the U.S. Intelligence Community's Prewar Intelligence Assessments on Iraq: Conclusions* (Washington, D.C.: GPO, 2004), http://intelligence.senate.gov/ (accessed August 31, 2005).

3. Ibid., 4.

4. Ibid., 7.

5. National Aeronautics and Space Administration, *Report of the Columbia Accident Investigation Board* (Washington, D.C.: GPO, 2003), 97–204, http://www.nasa.gov/columbia/home/CAIB_Vol1.html (accessed August 31, 2005).

6. Ibid., 12, 102, 183.

7. I explore these mechanisms from a different direction in Cass R. Sunstein, *Why Societies Need Dissent* (Cambridge, Mass.: Harvard University Press, 2003), but without attention to statistical groups and information markets, and without focusing on amplification of errors, hidden profiles, and the common-knowledge effect, which are major emphases here.

8. Cass R. Sunstein, David Schkade, and Lisa Ellman, "Ideological Voting on Federal Courts of Appeals: A Preliminary Investigation," *Virginia Law Review* 90 (2004): 301.

9. See the comparison of democratic and nondemocratic regimes in Dominic Johnson, *Overconfidence and War: The Havoc and Glory of Positive Illusions* (Cambridge, Mass.: Harvard University Press, 2004), 180–83.

10. Roger Brown, *Social Psychology*, 2d ed. (New York: Free Press, 1986), 206–7.

11. Ibid.

12. Chip Heath and Rich Gonzalez, "Interaction with Others Increases Decision Confidence but Not Decision Quality: Evidence against Information Collection Views of Interactive Decision Making," *Organizational Behavior and Human Decision Processes* 61 (1995): 305.

13. See Robert S. Baron, S. Hoppe, B. Linneweh, and D. Rogers, "Social Corroboration and Opinion Extremity," *Journal of Experimental Social Psychology* 32 (1996): 537–60.

14. Daniel Gigone and Reid Hastie, "Proper Analysis of the Accuracy of Group Judgments," *Psychological Bulletin* 121 (1997), 149, 161; Reid Hastie, "Experimental Evidence of Group Accuracy," in *Information Pooling and Group Decision Making*, ed. Bernard Grofman and Guillermo Owen (Greenwich, Conn.: JAI Press, 1986), 129.

15. Robert J. MacCoun, "Comparing Micro and Macro Rationality," in *Judgments, Decisions, and Public Policy*, ed. Rajeev Gowda and Jeffrey Fox (Cambridge: Cambridge University Press, 2002), 116, 121.

16. Ibid.

17. J. Scott Armstrong, "Combining Forecasts," in *Principles of Forecasting*, ed. J. Scott Armstrong (Boston: Kluwer Academic, 2001), 433.

18. Caryn Christenson and Ann Abbott, "Team Medical Decision Making," in *Decision Making in Health Care*, ed. Gretchen Chapman and Frank Sonnenberg (New York: Cambridge University Press, 2000), 267, 273–76.

19. Robert L. Thorndike, "The Effect of Discussion upon the Correctness of Group Decisions: When the Factor of Majority Influence Is Allowed For," *Journal of Social Psychology* 9 (1938): 343.

20. For an overview, see Thomas Gilovich, Dale Griffin, and Daniel Kahneman, *Heuristics and Biases: The Psychology of Intuitive Judgment* (New York: Cambridge University Press, 2002).

21. See Cass R. Sunstein, ed., *Behavioral Law and Economics* (New York: Cambridge University Press, 2000).

22. Amos Tversky and Daniel Kahneman, "Judgment under Uncertainty: Heuristics and Biases," in *Judgment under Uncertainty: Heuristics and Biases*, ed. Daniel Kahneman, Paul Slovic, and Amos Tversky (Cambridge: Cambridge University Press), 1982, 3.

23. Paul Rozin and Carol Nemeroff, "Sympathetic Magical Thinking: The Contagion and Similarity 'Heuristics,'" in Gilovich, Griffin, and Kahneman, *Heuristics and Biases*, 201.

24. Tversky and Kahneman, "Judgment under Uncertainty," 3.

25. MacCoun, "Comparing Micro and Macro Rationality," 116, 121.

26. Mark F. Stasson, Kaoru Ono, Suzi K. Zimmerman, and James H. Davis, "Group Consensus Approaches on Cognitive Bias Tasks," *Japanese Psychological Research* 30 (1988): 68.

27. See Norbert L. Kerr, Robert J. MacCoun, and Geoffrey P. Kramer, "Bias in Judgment: Comparing Individuals and Groups," *Psychology Review* 103 (1996): 687, 689, 691–93.

28. Janet A. Sniezek and Rebecca A. Henry, "Accuracy and Confidence in Group Judgment," *Organizational Behavior and Human Decision Processes* 43 (1989): 1. This finding very much bears on excessive risk-taking, including in the context of making war. See Dominic Johnson, *Overconfidence and War*, 180–83.

29. Edward L. Schumann and W. C. Thompson, "Effects of Attorneys' Arguments on Jurors' Use of Statistical Evidence" (unpublished manuscript, 1989).

30. Glen Whyte, "Escalating Commitment in Individual and Group Decision Making," *Organizational Behavior and Human Decision Processes* 54 (1993): 430.

31. James W. Gentry and John C. Mowen, "Investigation of the Preference Reversal Phenomenon in a New Product Introduction Task," *Journal of Applied Psychology* 65 (1980): 715; Julie R. Irwin and James H. Davis, "Choice/Matching Preference Reversals in Groups," *Organizational Behavior and Human Decision Processes* 64 (1995): 325.

32. Whyte, "Escalating Commitment," 430.

33. Stasson et al., "Group Consensus Approaches," 68.

34. Garold Stasser and William Titus, "Hidden Profiles: A Brief History," *Psychological Inquiry* 14 (2003): 304.

35. Daniel Gigone and Reid Hastie, "The Common Knowledge Effect: Information Sharing and Group Judgments," *Journal of Personality and Social Psychology* 65 (1993): 959.

36. See Ross Hightower and Lutfus Sayeed, "The Impact of Computer-Mediated Communication Systems on Biased Group Discussion," *Computers in Human Behavior* 11 (1995): 33.

37. Patricia Wallace, *The Psychology of the Internet* (Cambridge: Cambridge University Press, 1999), 82.

38. See Garold Stasser and William Titus, "Pooling of Unshared Information in Group Decision Making: Biased Information Sampling during Discussion," *Journal of Personality and Social Psychology* 48 (1985): 1467.

39. Ibid., 1473; see also Stasser and Titus, "Hidden Profiles," 304.

40. Stasser and Titus, "Pooling of Unshared Information," 1473.

41. Ibid., 1476.

42. Ibid.

43. Ibid.

44. Stasser and Titus, "Hidden Profiles," 305.

45. See Daniel Gigone and Reid Hastie, "The Common Knowledge Effect: Information Sharing and Group Judgments," *Journal of Personality and Social Psychology* 65 (1993): 959.

46. Ibid., 960.

47. Ibid., 973.

48. Ibid.

49. See Garold Stasser, Laurie A. Taylor, and Coleen Hanna, "Information Sampling in Structured and Unstructured Discussions of Three and Six-Person Groups," *Journal of Personality and Social Psychology* 57 (1989): 67.

50. Ibid., 78.

51. Ibid., 72.

52. I draw here on David Hirschleifer, "The Blind Leading the Blind," in *The New Economics of Human Behavior*, ed. Marianno Tommasi and Kathryn Ierulli (Cambridge: Cambridge University Press, 1995), 188, 193–94.

53. Ibid., 195.

54. See ibid; also see Sunstein, *Why Societies Need Dissent.*

55. See Lisa Anderson and Charles Holt, "Information Cascades in the Laboratory," *American Economic Review* 87 (1997): 847.

56. See Angela Hung and Charles Plott, "Information Cascades: Replication and an Extension to Majority Rule and Conformity-Rewarding Institutions," *American Economic Review* 91 (2001): 1508, 1515.

57. Thus, 72 percent of subjects followed Bayes's rule in Anderson and Holt, "Information Cascades in the Laboratory," 847, and 64 percent in Marc Willinger and Anthony Ziegelmeyet, "Are More Informed Agents Able to Shatter Information Cascades in the Lab?" in *The Economics of Networks: Interaction and Behaviours*, ed. Patrick Cohendet, Patrick Llerena, Hubert Stahn, and Gisèle Umbhauer (New York: Springer, 1998), 291, 304.

58. See Willinger and Ziegelmeyet, "Are More Informed Agents," 291.

59. See Anderson and Holt, "Information Cascades in the Laboratory," 847.

60. See Hung and Plott, "Information Cascades," 1515–17.

61. Ibid., 1516.

62. Roger Brown, *Social Psychology: The Second Edition* (New York, N.Y.: Free Press, 1986), 206–7.

63. Ibid., 204.

64. Ibid., 224.

65. Ibid.

66. Sunstein, Schkade, and Ellman, "Ideological Voting," 301.

67. See David Schkade, Cass R. Sunstein, and Daniel Kahneman, "Deliberating about Dollars: The Severity Shift," *Columbia Law Review* 100 (2000): 101.

68. Brown, *Social Psychology*, 200–45.

69. Ibid. It has similarly been suggested that majorities are especially potent because people do not want to incur the wrath, or lose the favor, of large numbers of others, and that when minorities have influence, it is because they produce genuine attitudinal change. See Baron et al., "Social Corroboration," 82.

70. Baron et al., "Social Corroboration," 537.

71. Ibid.

72. For valuable overviews, see Justin Wolfers and Eric Zitzewitz, "Prediction Markets," *Journal of Economic Perspectives* 18 (2004): 107; Michael Abramowicz, "Information Markets, Administrative Decisionmaking, and Predictive Cost-Benefit Analysis," *University of Chicago Law Review* 71 (2004): 933; Saul Levmore, "Simply Efficient Markets and the Role of Regulation," *Journal of Corporation Law* 28 (2003): 589.

73. Kay-Yut Chen and Charles Plott, "Information Aggregation Mechanisms: Concept, Design and Implementation for a Sales Forecasting Problem" (Working Paper 1131, Caltech Social Science, Pasadena, Calif., 2002).

74. See Abramowicz, "Information Markets," 933.

75. Ibid., 992. Of course, it would be necessary to specify a source that would produce, at the relevant time, an authoritative judgment about benefits—that is, a judgment that could be deemed authoritative by all sides.

76. See Abramowicz, "Information Markets," 990–92.

77. Ibid., 987–90.

78. Ibid., 988.

79. See Robert W. Hahn and Paul C. Tetlock, "Making Development Work: Using Markets to Improve Performance," *Policy Review* 132 (2005): 27–38.

80. Ibid.

81. As noted below, this is not inevitable. We could easily imagine a market in which cognitive problems are reflected in prices; indeed, this appears to happen with ordinary stock markets. See Robert Shiller, *Irrational Exuberance* (Princeton, N.J.: Princeton University Press, 2000). In information markets, it is entirely possible to imagine booms or crashes produced by cognitive errors in combination with social influences. My point is not that this is impossible, but that the track record of information markets, at least thus far, is exceptionally good.

82. A general overview is Andrei Shleifer, *Inefficient Markets: An Introduction to Behavioral Finance* (Oxford: Oxford University Press, 2000).

83. See, for example, ibid.; Hersh Shefrin, *Beyond Greed and Fear: Understanding Behavioral Finance and the Psychology of Investing* (Boston: Harvard Business School Press, 2000); Shiller, *Irrational Exuberance*; Richard Thaler, ed., *Advances in Behavioral Finance* (New York: Russell Sage Foundation, 1993).

84. For a good discussion, see Abramowicz, "Information Markets," 972–76.

85. Erica Klarreich, "Best Guess," *Science News Online*, http://www.sciencenews.org/articles/20031018/bob9.asp (accessed September 5, 2005).

86. For an overview, see Christine Jolls, "Behavioral Economics Analysis of Redistributive Legal Rules," *Vanderbilt Law Review* 51 (1998): 1653.

87. D. Granberg and Edward E. Brent, "When Prophecy Bends: The Preference-Expectation Link in U.S. Presidential Elections," *Journal of Personality and Social Psychology* 45 (1983): 477.

88. Wolfers and Zitzewitz, "Prediction Markets," 107.

89. Robert Forsythe, Thomas Rietz, and Thomas Ross, "Wishes, Expectations, and Actions: A Survey on Price Formation in Election Stock Markets," *Journal of Economic Behavior and Organization* 39 (1999): 83, 94.

90. Ibid.

91. Muzafer Sherif and Carl Hovland, *Social Judgment: Assimilation and Contrast Effects in Communication and Attitude Change* (New Haven, Conn.: Yale University Press, 1961).

92. Wolfers and Zitzewitz, "Prediction Markets," 107

93. Joyce Berg, Forrest Nelson, and Thomas Rietz, "Accuracy and Forecast Standard Error of Prediction Markets" (working draft, 2003), http://www.biz.uiowa.edu/faculty/trietz/papers/forecasting.pdf.

94. Forsythe, Rietz, and Ross, "Wishes, Expectations, and Actions," 100. The term "quasi-rational" comes from Richard Thaler, *Quasi-Rational Economics* (New York: Russell Sage Foundation, 1991).

95. Richard H. Thaler and William T. Ziemba, "Anomalies: Parimutuel Betting Markets: Racetracks and Lotteries," *Journal of Economic Perspectives* 2, no. 2 (Spring 1988): 161; Charles Manski, "Interpreting the Predictions of

Prediction Markets" (Working Paper 10359, National Bureau of Economic Research, 2004).

96. Justin Wolfers and Eric Zitzewitz, "Prediction Markets" (preliminary draft), http://faculty-gsb.stanford.edu/wolfers/Papers/Predictionmarkets.pdf.

97. The most important evidence can be found on TradeSports predictions, where highly unlikely outcomes were overpriced in a number of domains. See ibid.

98. See the notations on speculative bubbles in Wolfers and Zitzewitz, "Prediction Markets," *Journal of Economic Perspectives*.

99. See Shiller, *Irrational Exuberance*.

100. Compare ibid. (discussing such errors in the stock market).

101. Celeste Biever and Damian Carrington, "Pentagon Cancels Futures Market on Terror," *New Scientist Online*, http://www.newscientist.com/news/news.jsp?id=ns99994007 (accessed September 6, 2005).

102. Joseph E. Stiglitz, "Terrorism: There's No Futures in It," *Los Angeles Times*, July 31, 2003, http://www.commondreams.org/views03/0731-08.htm.

103. See Richard Posner, *Catastrophe: Risk and Response* (Oxford: Oxford University Press, 2004).

104. Recall the reaction to the Policy Analysis Market, outlined above.

105. Note, however, that "thin" markets have proved remarkably accurate, and that some small groups might encourage outsider investors. See Levmore, "Simply Efficient Markets," 589.

106. Abramowicz, "Information Markets," 933.

107. See Robert W. Hahn and Paul C. Tetlock, "Using Information Markets to Improve Public Decision Making," *Harvard Journal of Law and Public Policy* 29, no. 1 (Fall 2005): 213–89.

108. One complication here is that the market's prediction would be affected by the likelihood of government's response to that very prediction. If investors know, for example, that government is likely to respond if the market predicts a high number of fatalities from a natural disaster, then they should predict a lower number of fatalities, because government will by hypothesis be taking protective steps. This possibility might be handled by conditional markets. For example, the question might be: "How many deaths will come from earthquakes in the United States in a specified year if government does not take new steps to prevent those deaths?"

109. Abramowicz, "Information Markets," 933.

110. For this example, and for others, it would, of course, be necessary to identify some agreed-upon source for an answer to the predictive question.

5

Deliberative Information Markets for Small Groups

Michael Abramowicz

Information markets have proved to be effective tools for aggregating information into consensus predictions, particularly when they involve a large number of traders and have a large amount of information available to them. As currently designed, however, information markets offer traders only limited incentives to reveal new information unknown to other market participants or to explain their evaluations of existing information, aside from through their trading activity. A market that provides such incentives would be useful, however, and, especially in one in which only a small number of individuals are participating, might increase the accuracy of the market and decrease the redundant acquisition and analysis of information by different traders. Building on literature suggesting designs for such small markets, this chapter explains how they might be structured to encourage release of information and analysis. Rewards to predictors would be based, not on the ultimate value being predicted, but on the value of predictions at later points in the market. To succeed, a predictor would thus need not only to make an accurate prediction, but also to convince other participants of that accuracy.

Participants in information markets do not deliberate; they compete. Information markets give participants strong incentives to trade on information available to them and to consider what the trading patterns of others might reveal about their information. Their purpose has generally been seen as the aggregation of information, and, at least in markets with sufficiently high liquidity, they have proved able to offer relatively accurate predictions.[1] One might, however, imagine an additional aspiration for these markets: stimulation of the production and release of information and analysis.

Markets may already produce some incentives for releasing information. For example, someone who knows something positive about a stock might buy the stock and release that information to allow for quick profit on a sale. This release can be expensive, however, particularly when it is in the form of a subtle analysis not yet committed to writing in an accessible way. A market that could stimulate production of this kind of information beyond the level provided by existing markets could serve a useful social function. At the same time, it could improve the aggregation of information into a single price prediction by making clearer to each trader the information on which other traders are relying.

In a recent article, Cass Sunstein noted that, because information-market traders "stand to gain or lose from their investments, they have a strong incentive to use (and in that sense to disclose) whatever private information they hold."[2] As the parenthetical indicates, information-market participants generally disclose information indirectly, by trading on it, not by releasing the information itself. Sunstein sensibly concludes that these markets might serve as a "complement to or even a substitute for deliberation."[3] Although information markets sometimes might be so powerful that they make traditional deliberative institutions unnecessary, the functions served by the two will often be distinct. Deliberative institutions have the potential to produce arguments, analysis, and models, and information markets can, in turn, be used to convert these into concrete numerical predictions.

The question for this chapter is whether an information market itself can function as a deliberative institution that encourages traders to explain the reasons for their analysis. The first section explains why having such markets might be useful, particularly where they seek to assess questions on which there is relatively little public interest. In the second section I describe some general problems of designing information markets in which only a small number of traders are expected to participate, and in the third I describe and assess a mechanism to stimulate production and release of information by traders.

The Benefits of Information Revelation

Assuming it is possible to create one, an information market that provides incentives for traders to explain the basis of their decisions would be useful for three reasons. First, the production of such information might improve market accuracy. Second, there would be less redundant acquisition and analysis of information. Third, the information produced might be valuable in and of itself.

Improved Accuracy. Consider a mundane information market used to predict the proportion of red balls originally existing in an opaque urn containing red and blue balls, and assume that, a priori, every proportion of red balls from zero to one is equally likely. Suppose that each potential participant in the information market is allowed in secret to draw several balls from the urn without replacement. Though the ultimate question is empirical, one might imagine the market doing a fairly good job of estimating the proportion of balls in the urn nonetheless. Each trader would seek to estimate the price by considering not only the balls he had drawn, but also the actions of the other traders. If all act rationally, they might be able to develop over time quite accurate estimates of the number of balls from the trades entered into by others, as well as the bid and ask offers of other traders.[4]

There are at least two problems, however. The first is that a potential trader might hesitate to enter into a trade for fear that the person on the other end might have inside information. The second is that the Bayesian calculations may turn out to be quite complex. If some traders do not act perfectly rationally, the market might mispredict and converge to an incorrect value. It seems doubtful, then, that the market would be maximally accurate, in the sense that the market price would exactly equal the best estimation of the proportion of balls, given full information about each trader's draw. If each trader, however, had an incentive to reveal honestly the number of balls he had drawn and other traders then took the revealed number into account, then the market might be accurate in this sense.

A more complicated information market that produced incentives to reveal information might have an even greater advantage in terms of accuracy over one that did not. A trader who identifies a particular argument as relevant to pricing is not able to ascertain whether the information-market price already takes it into account. With the trader not knowing how aggressively to trade on this piece of information, it might end up over- or underweighted in the price. An argument, for example, will end up being overweighted when a trader underestimates the extent to which the market has taken it into account.

In theory, it might sometimes be possible for a trader to trade on some other information market, or even create a new market that will allow him to assess more precisely the extent to which it has incorporated the relevant argument. It may at times be too costly to do so, however, or too difficult to create a market that can disaggregate the relevant piece of information from other pieces of information being considered. Suppose, for example, that someone considering investing in a political candidate in an election market has done a complex psychological analysis indicating that the candidate will connect well with voters. Because it will be difficult even ex post to measure connection with voters, it is hard to see how this aspect of the problem can be separated from the overall task of predicting the result of the election. Moreover, although the sponsor of the market might have some incentive to create such a market if one were possible, an individual trader would not profit by doing so. Thus, we cannot expect the set of information markets to be complete.

These problems presumably have received little attention in the context of information markets, because while they are endemic to all securities markets, they apparently cause little harm. They are likely to be much more severe, however, in markets with very few active participants. In a sufficiently large and liquid market, a relatively large number of traders is likely to come across any relevant piece of public information or analysis of such information. In a very small market, the danger of misestimating the extent to which other traders will take information into account is greater. Even if a trader could accurately calculate the probability that any other trader would have the information, the actual proportion of traders might differ from the probability, and will tend to do so more, the smaller the group of traders. Some equity, bond, and derivative markets seem to function well with only a small number of traders, but as that number approaches zero, and as the possibility of asymmetric information increases, there is a greater danger of inaccurate pricing or of no trading at all.

Reduced Redundancy. An information market is thus likely to arrive at a more accurate answer, given the information available to traders, if traders have incentives to reveal the information they possess. Revealing information can, of course, be costly. Nonetheless, a market that induces disclosure would also reduce the redundant acquisition of information. Jack Hirshleifer recognized that, in conventional securities markets, there might be an excessive number of traders because the social gains to trading might be lower than the private gains.[5] The analysis conducted by these traders, moreover, might be redundant, with each reinventing the models used by the others to assess prices.

The problem will also exist when traders do not have incentives to reveal information. Suppose that the balls, instead of lying in an urn, are located behind each of one hundred bolted doors, and that it is costly to find the key for each door to open it and reveal the ball. Some traders might nonetheless seek to obtain an advantage by opening one or more of the doors, viewing the balls behind them, and then closing the doors again. The problem is that if we assume the traders cannot observe one another, different traders might well open the same doors. The result is not merely that the ball behind a single door might end up having disproportionate weight in the market estimate of the total proportion of balls, but also that the repetitive costly opening of the same door is inefficient. If traders instead had an incentive to reveal information, they might either reduce their expenses or use their funds to open other doors, thus further improving the market estimate.

External Uses. The two preceding considerations suggest that an information market in which participants have an incentive to reveal information might potentially be more efficient than a traditionally structured market. An additional reason markets that induce traders to reveal information might be useful is simply that information revelation might be inherently useful. The primary purpose of an information market is, of course, to produce a piece of information, a number that represents a prediction. In some contexts, however, a market that also produced explanations for the traders' assessments might be even more useful.

Suppose, for example, that a market was created to predict the outcomes of each of a large number of cases filed in a small-claims court.[6] The prices produced might be useful by themselves by serving, for example, as an objective form of mediation that might encourage parties to settle cases on the basis of market probability assessments. In addition, judges deciding cases might compare prices to their own initial assessments to identify cases that deserve further analysis, because they might have missed a relevant piece of information. But such a market would be considerably more useful if it actually encouraged the production and public release of the analysis of each case.

An information market that encouraged the production of analysis might provide a useful substitute for or complement to legal counsel. Though some traders might be lawyers (and thus implicitly demand reasonable compensation for their services), nonlawyers might well learn the pricing dynamics of certain types of small-claims cases. Such a market thus might be able to assess claims relatively cheaply and, just as important, serve as a substitute for law clerks. A market that produced only price information would provide a very weak substitute, the equivalent of a law clerk who, instead of writing a bench memo, offers only a summary assessment of the decision the court ought to reach. But a market that provided incentives to release information might produce the equivalent of a large number of bench memos, analyzing legal and factual issues relevant to each particular case.

If information markets provide a decentralized approach to evaluating information, then they might also provide such an approach to producing and analyzing it. Information markets provide a means of generating predictions without hiring a single expert or group of experts, along with some assurance that predictions will not be ideologically biased. Similarly, markets that induced information revelation would provide a means of generating information without hiring a specific analyst or group of analysts who might have their own limitations. Whatever the contexts in which it might or might not be useful, is it possible to create an information market that works in this way? That is our primary question, but before we can turn to it, we must address a more fundamental problem.

Small-Group Information Markets

Some information markets may be so esoteric that few individuals will want to participate. Only so many zero-sum games will be interesting enough to attract risk-takers. For information markets to be effective, they may need to attract at least a few individuals and be structurally altered to function effectively when only a small number of people participate. If information markets are to substitute for many existing institutions that depend on deliberation and involve relatively small numbers of participants, such as corporate boards and juries, such structural alterations will need to be made.

In the discussion that follows, I show, first, that it is indeed possible to design information markets that will work effectively in small-group settings, and that at least one existing simple proposal accomplishes this aim. Second, I point out that even though this design would allow information markets to function with small groups, we cannot be confident that participants would always have incentives to reveal information, and thus we cannot be sure that we will have created a truly deliberative institution.

Addressing the Liquidity Problem. Any solution to the dilemma of low liquidity in information markets with few participants must meet two criteria. First, the market design must provide a means by which someone can profit on information without finding a trading partner. In a market in which only a very small number of traders may participate, it may be sufficiently difficult to profit on inside information that no one will have the incentive to acquire the information in the first place. Each trader will recognize that others might have inside information and therefore be reluctant to trade. Second, the solution must provide some means by which a market can be subsidized, such as through the creation of a market-maker who provides liquidity.

In a 1999 article, I suggested combining an information market with a self-assessment mechanism.[7] In particular, I suggested that the government auction off one or more securities for a particular information market to the highest bidder. The highest bidder would be required to announce a valuation price, and other parties would be given a free put option (an option to sell an equivalent security) and a free call option (an option to purchase an equivalent security) at the announced valuation price.[8] As soon as any party exercised one of these options, it would, in turn, have to value it, and any other party would have a free put and a free call on it. The procedure would continue recursively. At any time, the latest valuation of a put or call option could be roughly translated into a valuation of the underlying security.

The key to this approach is that it ensures that a participant cannot simply passively own a security and refuse to sell it. I will not, however, develop this approach or defend it here because the central insight may be easier to understand if we abandon the market metaphor altogether. The operator of an information market can request a series of predictions of a variable of interest and then reward the predictors on the basis of their valuations.[9] A very simple approach to accomplishing this would be to select the initial predictor through an auction, as described above, and then allow each subsequent predictor to bet the prior one that the security value will be either higher or lower than that prediction.[10]

Robin Hanson has recently offered a variation on this approach.[11] Hanson notes that information markets are, effectively, sequential "scoring rules"—formulas that can be used as incentives for individual predictors to make accurate probability or other estimates.[12] For example, if the government wanted to predict some number, it could promise compensation to a predictor for making a prediction, with the amount of compensation dependent on its accuracy. Hanson suggests allowing a subsequent predictor to displace the one immediately prior by announcing a new prediction and promising to pay the prior predictor what he would have received from the government under the scoring rule. Hanson argues that this "market scoring rule" will function like a scoring rule when there is only one participant, and like an information market when there are many participants.

A potential limitation of this approach is that the government must specify a scoring rule that will induce sufficient participation in the market. Suppose, for example, that in the small-claims market described above, the government promises it will pay a total of $100, less $0.10 for each dollar by which the estimate is off. If the prediction were off by more than $1,000, then the predictor would owe money to the government, and if this were a sufficient danger, no one would be willing to be the predictor. This problem, however, has a straightforward solution, if, as suggested above, the market scoring rule is combined with an auction for the right or duty to be the first predictor.[13] As long as the high bidder can be the high bidder with the least negative bid, there should always be someone willing to serve.

I do not mean to imply that the market scoring rule approach is better than others. For example, David Pennock has recently described a dynamic variation on parimutuel betting which, he argues, has some advantages over Hanson's approach.[14] A full analysis comparing the market scoring rule with my approach, Pennock's, and others is beyond the scope of this chapter. Nonetheless, the elegant simplicity of the market scoring rule is useful because it establishes that an information market can be used to generate predictions even if only a small number of people, indeed even if only one or two people, study the dynamics underlying the market.

Assessing Incentives to Release and Withhold Information Underlying Predictions. Information and other markets provide some incentives to release information, and in some cases the benefits of release might exceed the costs. We know that securities traders do sometimes explain the bases, or at least the alleged bases, of their trading recommendations. For example, stock analysts commonly advocate and explain their clients' trading positions. Although they risk that such revelation might cause loss of a competitive advantage, analysts who release information presumably believe this disadvantage is outweighed by any publicity or public relations benefits associated with explaining strategy.

Another reason to release information in some markets is that it might allow the holder of a security to achieve a profit without waiting for the market to close. For example, an individual who has conducted an analysis of a stock suggesting it is underpriced might buy the stock, release the information, and then sell the stock once the market incorporates the new analysis. A trader may wish to take advantage of information without subjecting himself to the risk that other unrelated information might cause the stock price to fall.

We should not think, however, that all traders in information markets will always do this. Let us look at three general reasons for them not to reveal information before we consider why the problem is likely to be worse in small-group information markets employing the market scoring rule.

First, someone with inside information might keep it secret for the duration of the information market. A sensible strategy might be to trade on the new information, hoping that the prediction fails to take it into account and rebounds to its initial level. If that occurs, a trader could trade again on the information, and might be able to do so repeatedly.

Second, sometimes it is expensive to convey an analysis in a comprehensible manner. This point will be familiar to lawyers who, after reading relevant cases, recognize a critical legal argument but must spend some time writing it down in a persuasive way and answering objections before others can understand it. Thus, at least in some instances, the cost of releasing information may be high. The small-claims market described above provides a useful example. Some pieces of information might be expressed quite succinctly and powerfully in a few sentences. But other kinds of analyses, if they are to be absorbed and evaluated by other traders at low cost, take time to prepare.

Third, sometimes the benefits of having the market incorporate information are low. Consider, once again, the small-claims market. If a case is to be resolved within a few days anyway, someone who has made a prediction may not care much about receiving the benefit of that prediction immediately, rather than waiting for the close of the market and the end of the case.

There are at least four additional reasons behind particularly low incentives to release information in the context of small-group information markets, especially those operating according to the market scoring rule. First, the market scoring rule itself does not provide a mechanism by which individuals sell securities. Private parties could, in theory, enter into contracts in which they voluntarily transfer the risk they have assumed in a market scoring rule information market to others. The reason we need the market scoring rule is low liquidity, however, and low liquidity by definition means that it will be more difficult or expensive to transfer one's position to a third party.

Second, such sales may be difficult to effect because of the danger of adverse selection. A trader will be hesitant to buy out another trader's position because the seller may have specific information indicating that his position, in fact, is weak. The adverse-selection problem is a prominent reason that legal claims and defensive positions are difficult to alienate in markets, and some of the same dynamics are at work here.[15] Adverse selection contributes to bid-ask spreads in even high-liquidity markets, but bid-ask spreads are larger in markets with low liquidity.[16]

Third, in markets with many analysts, it may be rarer for a single trader's analysis to constitute unique information, and thus there may be less of a strategic disadvantage to releasing it. When playing against only a few other participants, traders may have a greater chance of possessing unique information and a greater incentive to hold onto it. Traders will be most likely to reveal information when the information, however valid and insightful, is economically useless.

Fourth, in small-group information markets, a participant with unique information may be less likely to reach his risk threshold immediately. Even someone who develops new information suggesting that Microsoft stock is underpriced by $10 might not keep buying it until the price rises by $10, either because of liquidity limitations or because a portfolio heavily invested in Microsoft stock might be risky. But in an information market operating on the basis of the market scoring rule and receiving a relatively small subsidy, a trader might well not reach the limits of his risk tolerance in announcing a prediction; the trader, for example, might want to double his bet, but be unable to do so.[17] The predictor thus might hope that someone else will be skeptical and push the prediction in the other direction, so that he can announce his prediction back and effectively double his bet. This would allow the trader to increase his profits from his information beyond the maximum possible with a single announcement of a prediction. But no one will challenge the original trader and push the prediction in the other direction if the original trader has released information unambiguously supporting his original prediction. As a result, hoping to be challenged, he may not release information that would allay skepticism.

My claim here is a limited one. I have no a priori reason to conclude that incentives to conceal information will always outweigh those to reveal it. But with a variety of incentives for both, the former may well outweigh the latter in some cases. There is reason to be skeptical that there will be more incentives to release information for small-scale information markets than for capital markets with relatively high liquidity. Thus, it may be desirable to explore mechanisms that might lead to release above what we otherwise would see in information markets.

There may, anyway, be a reason to seek greater revelation than naturally occurs in traditional capital markets. In a market in which prediction is simply a happy byproduct of trading, there may be little or no reason to induce disclosure of information underlying trades. Information markets, however, have no purpose other than to produce information. Thus, if the market mechanism itself can encourage release of the information and analysis underlying participants' predictions, that might itself be a benefit, particularly where they are complicated and costly both to produce and to release. Of course, some information markets, such as sports-betting markets, might produce information of dubious social utility; but if we accept the premise that the purpose is to produce information, then we may wish to design these markets to maximize its value, even if the costs of doing so might exceed the benefits for traditional securities markets.

Moreover, in hypothetical markets like the small-claims market described above, the revelation of underlying argument and information might be more socially useful than the aggregation of predictions into a single number.

Deliberative Information Markets

In the first section of this chapter, I showed that market designs may allow for predictions even when the total number of predictors is small, at least if the subsidy is sufficiently large, but that these designs provide only incomplete incentives to release information during the information market. This second section introduces a design mechanism that would add to these incentives. Here, I first introduce a simple insight that can serve as the basis of a strategy: If traders are rewarded based on the extent of their influence on subsequent traders, they will have incentives to release information. I then describe one way this insight might be implemented—that is, by rewarding predictors based on their success in predicting the market price at later points in the market. The second part of this section models the incentives to reveal information that this approach would produce, and the third part provides some additional analysis, identifying strengths and weaknesses of this market design.

Developing a Strategy for Inducing More Information Revelation. How might we stimulate the release of information underlying trades, beyond the level we ordinarily would see in a small-scale information market employing the market scoring rule? A strategy emerges from the recognition that once the market closes, a trader might have some incentive to release information. Suppose, for example, that a participant in the small-claims market recognizes a legal argument that provides a strong reason to bar any recovery by the plaintiff, and the trader trades on this information. The success of this trading strategy may depend in part on whether the small-claims court recognizes the argument.[18] If there is some risk that the judge might miss the argument, and if the trader would indeed fare better if the court recognizes it, the trader has some incentive to provide the information to the court. Doing so after the market closes, however, will do nothing either to improve the accuracy of the market itself or to reduce the redundancy of market activity. Ideally, a deliberative information market would encourage the release of information while the market is running so that the market can take the information into account, and traders can avoid unnecessarily duplicating one another's work.

The recognition of incentives to release information after an information market closes provides a basis for identifying a strategy to encourage release before the market closes. A trader will reveal information if the success of the trade depends on convincing others of the information's relevance. The key is thus to ensure that the trader's compensation depends not just on alerting some eventual decision-maker to the information (a strategy that anyway will work only where it is a subsequent decision that is being predicted) but also on whether other traders are convinced of the information's relevance. We must thus create an approach that results in payments being made to or from traders based not solely on the eventual result that is the focus of the information market but on the response of other traders to the information.

A simple way of implementing this insight would be to compensate traders on the basis of the market price at some point in time after the initial trade, a point that we may call the measurement point. For a market lasting a few months, for example, the measurement point might be one week after the time of the initial prediction. As the end of the market approached, the measurement time would be moved progressively closer to the prediction time. The formula compensating the predictors must meet the following criterion: The greater the extent to which a predictor could make his own alleged improvement over the prior prediction stick at the measurement point, the greater the predictor's compensation.

One approach would simply be to require a trader to liquidate his position at the measurement point. A virtue of this approach is that it could be implemented relatively easily in conjunction with traditional information market designs. It would, however, be less effective for small-group information markets because of their relatively low liquidity. The purpose of the market scoring rule is to allow someone to enter a prediction without finding someone else who wishes to enter into a transaction at the same time. Requiring liquidation of positions under a market scoring rule would mean, in effect, that someone entering a prediction would have to be confident that someone else will be willing to enter into a transaction at some point in the future. Conceivably, one might develop a formula by which an automated market-maker would allow liquidation of positions under a market scoring rule. Rather than determining an algorithm for a liquidation price, which presumably would depend on subsequent predictions preceding the measurement point, it might be simpler to tie compensation directly to the extent to which a predictor is able to convince others.

A simple approach, bearing a closer resemblance to the market scoring rule, would be to calculate for each participant the degree to which his prediction was closer to the most recent prediction at the measurement point than was the prior prediction. Participants whose predictions correctly anticipate the direction of the market between the time of the prediction and the measurement time would profit, and those whose predictions are contrary to that direction would be required to pay. This approach could be implemented with an algorithm no more complex than that underlying a traditional information market and would be only a bit more complex than the algorithm underlying the market scoring rule itself.

In a more straightforward implementation, the market sponsor announces a default prediction p_0 (perhaps 0), and, as described above, auctions off the right to be the first predictor. T_1 is the high bidder at the auction, in some cases by offering the negative bid that is lowest in absolute value terms. (If this bid were greater than the preestablished market subsidy, the market would have to be canceled.) Over the course of the information market, there are n predictions, p_1 through p_n. A measurement point is calculated for each prediction, and let m_i equal the most recent prediction at the time of the measurement point for p_i. Predictor T_i would receive compensation of d_i points, where $d_i = \text{Abs}(p_{i-1} - m_i) - \text{Abs}(p_i - m_i)$, where Abs represents the absolute value function.

Immediately following the close of the market, an additional prediction is solicited through a proper scoring rule or, better still, through a brief market scoring rule information market employing a proper scoring rule.[19] This provides a means of disciplining the last predictor, T_n, and m_n is set to this prediction. In the absence of this second phase, someone might have an incentive to enter a prediction in the last instant before the close of the market, before anyone else would have sufficient time to respond to it. Such a prediction might be used, for example, to validate the one immediately prior. One could profit by entering two predictions at the close of the market if there were no independent punishment for a bad final prediction.[20] There are other plausible means of disciplining the final predictor in the information market, but one virtue of this approach is that it reduces risk in the first-stage information market, because the success of predictions in that stage will not depend on any randomness associated with N.[21]

Suppose, for example, that for p_2, two subsequent predictions occurred before the measurement point, p_3 and p_4, and that no predictions occurred from this measurement point until the close of the market. Then, $m_2 = p_4$, and p_2's score would depend on the extent to which p_2 predicted p_4 better than p_1 did. Thus, p_2 would receive compensation in points $d_2 = \text{Abs}(p_1 - p_4) - \text{Abs}(p_2 - p_4)$. For example, suppose $p_1 = 10$. If $p_2 = 20$, and $p_4 = 30$, then $d_2 = 30 - 20 = 10$. If, however, $p_4 = 10$, then p_2's prediction did not stick, and $d_2 = 0 - 10 = -10$.

Once scores are assigned, the pot (that is, the market subsidy plus the amount of the high bid at the initial auction) can be distributed in proportion to the number of points. (Note that the pot might be specified for a single market or aggregated over a number of markets.) Let *pos* equal the total number of points by participants who have positive point totals, and let *neg* equal the total number of points by participants who have negative point totals. Then, each point is worth the amount of the pot divided by *pos* – *neg*. Of course, those with negative totals would pay money in, and those with positive totals would pay money out.

A Simple Model. Here we use a simple model to explain formally why making payment contingent on the predictions of subsequent predictors will increase the incentives of participants to release information. Let us assume that T_1 is making a prediction in a prediction market that works according to a market scoring rule. The sponsor of the market has specified a simple difference scoring rule.[22] Thus, the scoring rule will provide for some fixed reward, R, reduced proportionately to the difference between the final prediction, p_F, and the actual number, N, which will be revealed following the close of the market but will not depend on the activity of the market itself. Assume that the actual number N is normally distributed with a mean of 0. Thus, the final predictor will receive from the sponsor, $R - k \cdot \text{Abs}(p_F - N)$, where k is some constant converting the units of the prediction into dollars, and Abs represents the absolute value function. The predictor, however, will have to pay off the penultimate predictor according to the same formula, substituting the penultimate prediction for p_F.

Let us assume that the default market prediction, p_0, is 0 and that T_1 enters as his prediction, p_1, his best estimate, e_1. We will initially assume that everyone recognizes that $p_1 = e_1$, but we will return to that assumption shortly. This will allow us to focus initially on the possibility that other predictors are unsure of the precision of the first predictor's prediction before considering the case in which other predictors are unsure of whether the first predictor has made a false announcement. We assume that T_1 knows the information underlying the predictor's estimate and thus knows the precision of the estimate. Other predictors, however, cannot know the precision of the estimate unless T_1 reveals the information underlying the estimate. For simplicity, assume that there are two possible levels of precision: high precision (with mean 0 and variance $V > 0$) and low precision (with variance $2V$), and assume that all potential predictors recognize that there is an equal probability that the first predictor's prediction is based on information providing high precision, and that the prediction is based on information providing low precision.

Let us further assume that there would be a cost c to revealing the information and that all potential market participants know the value of c. (We will assume that any information revealed by T_1 can be costlessly verified by other market participants.) The variable c reflects both the direct monetary cost of releasing information as well as any loss of competitive advantage. Any benefits to information revelation, such as facilitating a sale of the first predictor's position to a third party or impressing potential client investors, are included negatively within c. We count in c only costs and benefits exogenous to the market mechanism; the endogenous incentives produced by the market mechanism are, of course, the object of ultimate interest. Let us assume for now that $c > 0$, but that c is very small, so that a predictor will be willing to release information if there is some positive endogenous benefit to doing so, that is, if release will improve market payoffs.

Under the traditional market scoring rule, T_1 would be willing to reveal information if and only if $c < 0$, that is, if and only if the exogenous benefits of information revelation exceed the exogenous costs. The receipts to T_1 from participation in the information market will be determined entirely by the scoring rule (more specifically, the difference applying the scoring rule to p_1 and to 0). The scoring rule is a function of N, and because we have assumed that predictions cannot affect N, the first predictor's payout will be invariant to subsequent predictions. Thus, the market scoring rule provides no endogenous incentives to reveal information.

Now, let us imagine that the compensation regime is as described above. We will assume that there will be one additional predictor, T_2, before the end of the market. (This assumption is without loss of generality. We would reach the same result if there was some probability that there would be no additional predictors or multiple additional predictors. The second-stage information market disciplines the last predictor, and each prior predictor ultimately anticipates the prediction announced by this last predictor.) The compensation in points for T_1 will equal $d_1 = \text{Abs}(p_0 - p_2) - \text{Abs}(p_1 - p_2)$, where p_2 is a prediction based on the market's consensus anticipation of the result of the second-stage information market, which itself may depend on any information provided by T_1 or any of the other market participants.

Let us assume that T_2 has an estimate e_2 of N independent of that of T_1, with a low-precision variance of $2V$. Let us first consider the case in which the second predictor, T_2, concludes that the first predictor's information was based on a high-precision estimate, for example because T_1 credibly releases the information showing the first predictor's estimate to be high precision. Then T_2 will announce $p_2 = (2/3) \cdot p_1 + (1/3) \cdot e_2$.[23] Thus, T_1 will receive in compensation $d_{\text{high}} = \text{Abs}((2/3) \cdot p_1 + (1/3) \cdot e_2) - \text{Abs}((1/3) \cdot p_1 - (1/3) \cdot e_2)$. If, on the other hand, T_2 concludes that the first predictor's prediction is based on a low-precision estimate, then T_2 will announce $p_2 = (p_1 + e_2)/2$, and T_1 will receive in compensation $d_{\text{low}} = \text{Abs}((1/2) \cdot p_1 + (1/2) \cdot e_2) - \text{Abs}((1/2) \cdot p_1 - (1/2) \cdot e_2)$. It follows that $d_{\text{high}} \geq d_{\text{low}}$.

That is, the amount of compensation that T_1 receives will be at least as great when T_2 concludes that T_1's prediction was based on a high-precision estimate as when T_2 concludes that the T_1's prediction was based on a low-precision estimate. Because we have assumed that c is small, T_1 will release the information underlying the prediction if in fact that information provided a high-precision estimate. T_2 recognizes this, so if T_1 does not release the information underlying the prediction, then T_2 will correctly conclude that the information provided a low-precision estimate. The mechanism, however, will not have led T_1 to have released the information itself.

But what happens if we relax the assumption that T_2 will necessarily believe that $p_1 = e_1$? The same dynamic that exists as to uncertainty about the precision of an estimate exists as to the validity of the estimate. Suppose there is some probability that T_1 is bluffing and has no information that would justify changing the estimate from p_0, and some probability that T_1 is not bluffing. T_2's announcement of p_2 will be closer to p_1, and T_1 will receive more compensation, if T_2 concludes that T_1 is not bluffing. Thus, T_1 will have an incentive to reveal the information underlying the estimate if he indeed is not bluffing as to the estimate. Thus, if T_1 can reveal information at low cost, then T_1 will do so if T_1 needs to establish either that T_1 is not bluffing as to the estimate or that the estimate is indeed of high precision.

Analysis. The model above is admittedly a simplification of the dynamics underlying the market. There is, for example, a possibility that T_1 may be exaggerating even if not bluffing, and a possibility that there might be a range of possible precision in estimates.[24] Perhaps the most significant assumption is that c is small relative to potential gains and losses from the market. The results above as to estimate precision will continue to hold as long as $0 < c < E(d_{high} - d_{low})$, where E() represents the expected value function, but for sufficiently high values of c, T_1 would not reveal information. A related critical assumption is that information released can be costlessly processed. There is no reason to incur costs to reveal information if other market participants will not be able to process the information once it is revealed.

The dynamics of a market in which information is costly to release and costly to assess are more complicated, and in such a market, we cannot be entirely confident that predictors will be able to distinguish predictions based on information from bluffs. A market participant who has no information may attempt to perform the equivalent of "pump and dump." If a market participant can convince others, as of the time of the measurement point, that some information justifies his announcement of a prediction deviating from the prior prediction, then he will be able to profit even if information later emerges indicating that the announcement was not based on any information at all. This conclusion should not be surprising. If we reward predictors based on the extent to which they convince others that their predictions are correct, then predictors may be able to earn money on the basis of falsely convincing others.

The existence of an incentive to profit on false information does not, however, necessarily doom a market design. In existing markets, such an incentive exists. The market scoring rule itself might produce some. A participant in the market scoring rule, for example, might have an incentive to release false information suggesting that the existing prediction is inaccurate, so that if another predictor announces a prediction incorporating the false information, the source of the false information can then bring the prediction back to its original level.

The usefulness of the information-revealing market thus may depend on the cost of releasing and processing information. If information costs are sufficiently low, it will be very difficult to fool other market participants, and the market will induce release of information. For intermediate levels of information costs, the market design described here might well induce more attempts to release false information than the market scoring rule. If information costs are sufficiently high, then no one will release or consider information. Predictors might try to convince one another by bonding themselves (for example, credibly offering to take large, contrary bets independent of the market mechanism), but the information-revealing market will have failed to achieve its goal of inducing the release of the underlying information.

The technique described here is thus unlikely to be useful for information markets with large numbers of participants and large amounts of information to be processed. Where traders must process a large amount of information, the contribution of any one trader's information or analysis may be so small as to have only a negligible effect on the market price. As a result, especially if it is expensive to reveal information, traders might simply choose to assess whatever information they have access to, especially public information, without revealing the private. Some traders may correctly anticipate that they can beat the market by doing a better job than other traders at assessing the public information, and the traders with the most confidence in their analyses will likely be those who will set market price. But information markets with large numbers of participants, such as the principal election markets on TradeSports, seem unlikely to encourage much information revelation beyond what is provided with the market scoring rule, because most individual pieces of new information will tend to have only very small effects on market prices.

Whether the information-revealing market should count as an improvement depends on the social costs of whatever level of false information would result and how great the social benefits are from inducing release of information underlying predictions. Recall from the first section that social benefits to inducing release of information underlying predictions might exist both because the release might itself be socially useful, and because it might increase the accuracy of the market. The model above is intended only to illustrate that information release can be induced, not that it will necessarily improve the accuracy of the market. Immediately after the announcement of T_2's prediction, the information-revealing information market would be more accurate than the market scoring rule, but this does not necessarily mean the market itself will be more accurate. Just as in the analysis in the first section, if all participants are rational, then the market might well converge to the precise correct number. With the market scoring rule, this might occur as a result of further iterated predictions by T_1 and T_2. Participants in a market scoring rule information market can convey the precision of their estimates by repeated betting, much as participants in a traditional information market might do so by altering the magnitude of a bet.

Nonetheless, the information released may be valuable in and of itself, and release can only help increase the accuracy of the market, for the reasons described in the first section. The model above obscures the benefits of information revelation to accuracy by assuming that T_2's information is necessarily independent of T_1's. When this is so, then, once T_2 is satisfied regarding the honesty and precision of T_1's estimate, T_2 need not worry about overweighting or underweighting T_1's prediction relative to T_2's estimate. But when T_2's information may not be entirely independent of T_1's, then there is a risk of overweighting or underweighting T_1's prediction, should there turn out to be more or less overlap in information than T_2 expects. If T_1 reveals the information underlying the prediction, then T_2 may be able to assess accurately the independence of the two participants' estimates.

The information-revealing market, in sum, will give predictors incentives to offer arguments and information supporting their predictions in cases in which they might not have sufficient incentives under a market scoring rule. Participants will have some incentive not only to consider the information initially available to them and the predictions announced by others, but also to evaluate the evidence offered by previous predictors and to assimilate all available information to make the best possible prediction. Participants will sometimes release false information if they think that, more likely than not, they can fool others. Market participants, however, will have an incentive to ferret out such false information.

Conclusion

Information markets have proved to be effective aggregators of information, but they have not been designed specifically with the aim of stimulating the revelation of information or analysis. Some information markets using previous designs might provide adequate, perhaps even excessive, incentives to reveal information. There remains, however, at least the theoretical possibility that a new information market design providing incentives for participants to reveal information might be useful in some contexts.

In this chapter I have suggested that two separate steps might contribute to information markets serving this function. First, the structure of these markets must be changed so that they produce reasonable predictions even when only small numbers of individuals participate. If an information market on average will be of interest to only a handful of people, each potential trader will have difficulty finding someone against whom to trade. This chapter has described Robin Hanson's approach to eliminating that problem by eliminating the need for consensual transactions, but there may be other approaches as well. Second, information market structure must be changed so that traders have incentives not only to predict accurately the eventual variable of interest, but also to sway other participants.

The modifications I have suggested remain only theoretical, and empirical testing is needed to assess whether they would have the desired effects.

Experiments should be easy to design, however. A very simple one might involve the balls in the urn, as described earlier. The same experiment might be run with several different market structures, including the two-stage or multistage approach described above. Ideally, participants in the experiment under any particular market design should have several trial runs to give them an opportunity to identify the best strategy over time. If the analysis here is correct, the information-revealing market will lead participants to share more information with one another and should produce more accurate results over a large number of iterations of the experiment. If the experiment confirms this result, then information markets may function not merely as information aggregators but also as deliberative institutions.

Notes

1. In a prior article, however, I argued that the greatest virtue of information markets for public policy purposes is not their ability to aggregate information per se, but rather their ability to do so in a relatively objective way. See Michael Abramowicz, "Information Markets, Administrative Decisionmaking, and Predictive Cost-Benefit Analysis," *University of Chicago Law Review* 71 (2004): 933.

2. Cass R. Sunstein, "Group Judgments: Deliberation, Statistical Means, and Information Markets" (Working Paper 219, University of Chicago John M. Olin School of Law and Economics, August 2004), 56.

3. Ibid.

4. Richard D. McKelvey and Talbot Page, "Public and Private Information: An Experimental Study of Information Pooling," *Econometrica* 58 (1990): 1321 (showing how rational Bayesian updating can incorporate information held by an arbitrary number of people).

5. Jack Hirshleifer, "The Private and Social Value of Information and the Reward to Inventive Activity," *American Economic Review* 61 (1977): 561.

6. In a separate article, I explain how an information market might be used to perform the task of adjudication. See Michael Abramowicz, "Trial by Market" (unpublished manuscript, 2004). Here, I assume that adjudication will be performed eventually by the court, with the information market simply predicting how the court (or parties in settlement) will resolve each case.

7. See Michael Abramowicz, "The Law-and-Markets Movement," *American University Law Review* 49 (1999): 327.

8. See ibid., 370.

9. Rather than offer an alternative term, I will use the term "information market" to describe even approaches that abandon the market metaphor.

10. See Abramowicz, "Information Markets," 958, 960–61.

11. Robin D. Hanson, "Combinatorial Information Market Design," *Information Systems Frontiers* 5 (2003): 107.

12. See, for example, Robert L. Winkler, "Scoring Rules and the Evaluation of Probability Assessors," *Journal of the American Statistical Association* 64 (1969): 1073 (discussing scoring rules).

13. I have previously suggested combining Hanson's approach with an auction for the right to be first predictor. See Abramowicz, "Information Markets," 961.

14. David M. Pennock, "A Dynamic Pari-Mutuel Market for Hedging, Wagering, and Information Aggregation" (ACM Conference on Electronic Commerce, New York, N.Y., May 2004).

15. See Michael Abramowicz, "On the Alienability of Legal Claims," *Yale Law Journal* 114 (2005): 697.

16. The size of bid-ask spreads is generally proportional to expectations about the amount of inside information in a market, as traders will be more hesitant to

trade when they worry that the party on the other side of a transaction may have inside information. See, for example, James Harlan Koenig, "The Basics of Disclosure: The Market for Information in the Market for Corporate Control," *University of Miami Law Review* 43, no. 47 (1989): 1021, 1030. Even as the market awaited exit poll data and official vote tabulations in the 2004 presidential election, bid-ask spreads rarely exceeded two percentage points, indicating that market participants were relatively unconcerned about inside information.

17. There is a flipside problem, that someone who has information might not participate in the market scoring rule because the risk is too great. A possible solution to this would be to allow partial predictions. For example, one might imagine running one hundred market scoring rule information markets on the same issue at the same time, so a participant with low tolerance for risk could make a prediction on just some of these markets. It seems quite plausible, however, that this may not be necessary for most information markets, where many traders may wish to exploit their information to the maximum extent possible.

18. If settlement is permitted while the market is running, then traders might have similar incentives to present information to the negotiating litigants before the close of the market. But they might well condition the provision of such information on an agreement that the litigants and their lawyers not share the information with the market as a whole.

19. For a description and analysis of proper and strictly proper scoring rules, see Tilmann Gneiting and Adrian E. Raftery, "Strictly Proper Scoring Rules, Prediction, and Estimation" (Technical Report no. 463, University of Washington, Department of Statistics, September 2004).

20. It would be necessary, of course, to prevent predictors from taking small losses on this second-phase information market in order to achieve gains in the first-phase information market. Even if the second market has a relatively small subsidy, that could be avoided by making its precise end stochastic. That way, if a predictor were to enter an unrealistic prediction, others would have the incentive to counter it with new predictions. Someone committed to manipulating the second information market would have to be willing to take an unlimited number of bets on the prediction entered, and losses from doing so could easily exceed any gains.

21. Consider, for example, the small-claims market information market. It may be that once all available information is analyzed, predictors will anticipate a 0.5 probability that a case will be resolved in a particular way. Because the judge resolving the case is fickle, there may be no information that would move this probability estimate toward 0 or 1. The last predictor in the first stage of the information market will not bear the risk associated with the judge's fickleness, because the second-stage market presumably should also end with a prediction of 0.5. Of course, the predictors in the second-stage market may bear some risk, but its stakes could be smaller, reducing the total risk that market participants must bear.

22. The same results would be reached with a strictly proper scoring rule. The difference scoring rule is used for ease of exposition.

23. Two independent estimates *Y* and *Z* from a normal distribution can be combined into a single estimate $(V_z / (V_y + V_z)) \cdot Y + (V_y / (V_y + V_z)) \cdot Z$, where V_y and V_z represent the variances of estimates *Y* and *Z*.

24. Some models, however, show that when third parties might conclude that information is weaker than represented, those possessing information may have strong incentives to reveal it. See Paul Milgrom and John Roberts, "Relying on the Information of Interested Parties," *Rand Journal of Economics* 17 (1986): 18; Chris William Sanchirico, "Relying on the Information of Interested—and Potentially Dishonest—Parties" (Legal Studies Working Paper 00-12, University of Virginia Law School, 2001). The insight is essentially that adverse selection forces revelation of information. The parties with the best information will reveal it to distinguish themselves from those with weaker information, but then of the remaining parties who have not released information, the ones with the best information will have an incentive to release it. Under certain conditions, all parties may end up revealing their information.

6

Foul Play in Information Markets

Robin Hanson

People have long noticed that speculative markets, though created for other purposes, also do a great job of aggregating relevant information. In fact, it is hard to find information not embodied by such market prices. This is, in part, because anyone who finds such neglected information can profit by trading on it, thereby reducing the neglect.[1]

So far, speculative markets have done well in every known head-to-head field comparison with other forecasting institutions. Orange juice futures improved on National Weather Service forecasts,[2] horse race markets beat horse race experts,[3] Oscar markets beat columnist forecasts,[4] gas-demand markets beat gas-demand experts,[5] stock markets beat the official NASA panel at fingering the guilty company in the Challenger accident,[6] election markets beat national opinion polls,[7] and corporate sales markets beat official corporate forecasts.[8]

Recently, some have considered creating new markets specifically to take advantage of these effects. Called prediction markets,[9] information markets, virtual stock markets,[10] artificial markets,[11] or idea futures,[12] such markets are now beginning to estimate such things as product sales, project completion dates, and election outcomes.

Many observers have expressed concerns that such markets might induce various forms of foul play. For example, during the recent furor

---

For their comments, I thank Robert Hahn and the participants of the 2004 AEI–Brookings conference on information markets. I thank the Center for Study of Public Choice, the Mercatus Center, and the International Foundation for Research in Experimental Economics for financial support.

over the Policy Analysis Market (PAM) of the Defense Advance Research Projects Agency (DARPA), otherwise known as terrorism futures, critics complained that PAM might have allowed bets on the details of individual terrorist attacks.[13] In particular, critics feared that bad guys might do more bad things in order to win bets about those bad events, or might intentionally lose bets in order to reduce market information.[14]

In addition, others have expressed concerns that such markets might induce more people to lie, that markets inside organizations might misdirect resources, perhaps maliciously, and that threats of retribution might limit their effectiveness. In this chapter, I review what we know about these possible forms of foul play, and I suggest some new approaches to dealing with them.

Evaluation Standards

Let us begin by considering what standard we should apply when evaluating possible foul play. Information markets are created so that their price estimates can inform the policy choices of a for-profit, nonprofit, or government organization. Those creating such markets would naturally seek the most accurate possible prices on the most valuable topics at the lowest possible costs in terms of time, money, and other relevant resources, including the disruption to existing cultures and practices.

The existence of some estimate error or some resource cost, however, should not by itself be much of a criticism. The relevant benchmark should not be an infeasible perfection, but the accuracy and costs of other social institutions that perform a similar function with similar inputs. In particular, the most relevant benchmark is set by currently used forecasting institutions, such as in-house experts, ad hoc expert committees, independent forecasting agencies, and opinion polls.

Regarding each possible form of foul play, a key question is the degree to which a similar form occurs in competing social institutions. Do information markets pose special concerns?

Limiting Participation

Before discussing specific forms of foul play, let us consider a generic mitigation strategy: limiting participation. Foul play is always committed by someone. Thus, we might hope to limit it in any social institution by limiting who can participate in that institution.

The effectiveness of this strategy depends on our ability either to find indicators of who will engage in foul play or to detect acts of foul play directly. Effectiveness also depends on the rate at which institutional performance degrades with reduced participation.

Information markets can be used to aggregate information from any given set of participants. (Even having just one participant can work.[15]) Although most of the impressive track record of speculative market accuracy has come from markets that are open to all participants, some recent successes, such as some internal markets at Hewlett-Packard, have also come from markets with closed participation.[16] Even so, to the extent that information markets seem especially attractive due to their ability to allow and take advantage of wider participation than other institutions, a special concern must be the additional opportunities for foul play that wider participation might induce.

Let us now review the various forms of foul play: lying, manipulation, sabotage, embezzlement, and retribution.

Lying

The participants of a forecasting institution are those who make direct contributions to the forecast. There are also advisors who offer to make suggestions to the participants, and participants may advise other participants. Perhaps the simplest form of foul play is that committed by advisors who lie to, or mislead, the participants. Stock analysts, for example, are often accused of being paid by certain companies to give overly optimistic advice about their company stock.

Misleading advice is a familiar issue with all known existing social institutions, including speculative markets.[17] In general, participants should think skeptically about advice, taking into account any clues they have about advisor track records and incentives. The institutional process that combines participant contributions into forecasts seems largely irrelevant to this skeptical evaluation of advice. If so, all forecasting institutions should have similar levels of this sort of foul play.

Forecasting institutions, however, might vary in the clues they offer to detect lies, or in the incentives they give advisors. If, without information markets, one could get good advice from people who are trustworthy because of their neutral or transparent interests, allowing such advisors to trade could be a problem if doing so would obscure their interests. Advisors who could acquire hidden trading positions might become less trustworthy.

A sufficient way of addressing this problem would be to allow traders to reveal credibly their relevant holdings to those whom they advise. Advisors who chose not to reveal, and not to arrange for neutral holdings, would be treated more skeptically. Revelation should include not only an advisor's direct asset holdings but also any strong shared interests with others who may have such holdings. This is a familiar approach to dealing with conflicts of interests in other areas. Secret accounts, trader anonymity, and complex shared interests, however, might conspire to make it difficult for advisors to reveal credibly their relevant holdings.

Another approach is to expect advisors to reveal their relevant information directly, as participants, rather than indirectly, as advisors. Trading might well be a more effective way for them to reveal their information. If neither of these approaches were sufficient, one might prohibit certain groups of potential advisors from trading.

Manipulation

Another possible form of foul play occurs when participants who want to influence policy decisions directly distort their contributions to the institution forecasts. This is a familiar issue with existing institutions, such as ad hoc expert committees and supposedly independent forecasting agencies. In information markets, this foul play would take the form of people making trades that lose money in order to change prices and hence policy. Even if such trades lost money on average, those losses might be outweighed by gains from more favorable policy.

Even if successful, this sort of manipulation would mainly just reduce the accuracy of information-market prices.[18] As long as decision-makers knew roughly the level of forecast error in prices, such prices could be still useful inputs into decisions. And if such manipulators could similarly bias other forecasting institutions, this would not be a special concern about information markets.

Information markets seem especially hard to manipulate, however. We know of only one apparently successful attempt,[19] and many people have reported failed attempts to manipulate speculative market prices with trades historically,[20] in the field,[21] and in the laboratory.[22] A recent review article concludes that none of these attempts at manipulation had much of a discernible effect on prices, except during a short transition phase.[23] How can this be?

The key thing to understand is that all known speculative markets have a lot of "noise trades," that is, trades made because of mental mistakes, for insurance purposes, or for other noninformational reasons. Furthermore, a manipulator is just another kind of noise trader.

In theory, perfectly rational informed traders could use a subsidized market to aggregate their information and exactly reveal their common estimate.[24] Real markets, however, are full of fools, hedgers, and others whose trades are prompted by factors other than the information they hold. In fact, the opportunity to trade, and win, against noise traders is usually the main profit incentive informed traders have to participate.

If we hold other trading behavior constant, adding more noise trading must increase price errors. But when other traders expect more noise trading, they change their behavior in two important ways.

First, they eagerly scale up the amount they trade for any given amount of information they might hold, as this increases their expected profits. In the limit where the amounts traded are small compared to traders' aggregate risk tolerance, this should fully compensate for the increased noise, leaving the price error exactly the same. That is, as long as there are a few participants with deep enough pockets, or enough participants with shallow pockets, there will be enough people willing to accept the noise traders on average losing bets.[25]

Now, it may well be true that financial market traders do not fully correct for increases in aggregate noise trading in the world economy, at least along the handful of dimensions that command risk premiums. Irrational traders who underestimate the risk they are taking on can create aggregate risks that rational traders cannot afford to eliminate.[26] But this does not seem very relevant for most information markets, which do not estimate aggregate risks.

The second change in behavior is that the increased profit opportunity from more noise traders increases the effort by other traders to obtain relevant information. So, on net, more noise trading should increase price accuracy.[27] And, in fact, empirically it seems that financial and information markets with more noise trading, and hence a larger trading volume, tend to be more accurate, all else being equal.[28]

Models of financial market microstructure have considered several types of noise traders, including fools who act randomly, traders with immediate liquidity needs, traders who seek to manipulate a closing price in order to raise their futures-market settlement,[29] and, more generally, traders with quadratic preferences over the market price.[30]

These models verify that manipulators are just another kind of noise trader. A manipulator has hidden information about his bias—that is, how much and in what direction he wants to bias the price. (This includes the possibility of zero bias—that is, of not being a manipulator.) Other traders can respond only to the average expected bias. When the hidden bias is exactly equal to the average bias, it is as if there is no manipulator. When the bias is higher or lower than expected, the price will be higher or lower than expected. But competition among speculators ensures that on average the price is right, and that average price error is reduced when manipulators have larger biases.

Even if manipulators reduce price error on average, however, they might still increase the harm from price errors. Imagine that the harm from a price error depended not just on the magnitude of the error, but also on some additional state that was positively correlated with the hidden manipulator bias. For example, in a market estimating the chance of a terrorist attack, terrorists might perhaps arrange for the size of the attack to be correlated with the forecast error. The market might then become more accurate in estimating whether an attack would occur, but it would also miss the big attacks more often. In such a case, the expected harm from price errors could increase with more manipulation, even as the expected error decreased.

One approach to mitigating this problem is via the parameters that markets estimate. The closer those parameters are to the actual decision parameters of interest, the less likely should be the existence of hidden states that modulate the magnitude of the harm from estimation errors and that are correlated with some manipulator bias. For example, it would be better for a terrorist-attack market to estimate the harm caused by the attack and not just whether an attack occurs.

Sabotage

A potentially very serious form of foul play is where people cause harm to gain trading profits. For example, some people suspected that the September 11, 2001, terrorist attacks on the New York World Trade Center were funded in part by trades of airline stock options. Similarly, some feared that the 1982 Tylenol poisonings were done to profit from short sales on the Tylenol stock. Airline stock prices did fall on September 11, as did the Tylenol stock with the 1982 poisonings. And a study has found that Israeli stock and currency prices respond to Israeli suicide bombings.[31] Thus, it is not crazy to think that terrorists might use financial markets to profit from their acts. Nevertheless, we know of no examples of anyone using financial markets to profit from such sabotage. A thorough study of the September 11 attacks found nothing suspicious, and no trades were ever linked to the Tylenol poisonings.[32] The closest example I can find is the case of Roger Duronio, a well-paid PaineWebber employee who, in 2002, set off a logic bomb in one thousand company computers after investing $20,000 in options betting that the stock price would fall. The damage totaled $3 million, but system redundancy prevented any loss of data, the stock price did not fall, and Duronio was soon caught.[33]

We do, however, know of examples of murder committed to gain life insurance, where the insurance was purchased with this plan in mind. Thus, speculation on sabotage is possible when one person can acquire a large enough stake in an asset whose value he can influence directly enough. We also have examples of extortion of large corporations by people who first demonstrate their ability to cause large amounts of damage. Compared to speculating on sabotage, the extortion strategy runs a greater risk of detection but requires less capital to implement.

A simple interpretation of these facts is that the need for secrecy makes it very hard for skilled labor and willing capital to find each other to implement the strategy of speculating on sabotage. Because relevant prices move for other reasons, one needs a large portfolio of sabotage acts to be reasonably confident of a net profit. But those who are well-positioned to commit a single act of sabotage are usually not well-positioned to commit a stream of such acts. A willing source of capital would thus have to find many skilled saboteurs and would risk detection with each new potential saboteur contacted.

Information markets are typically very thin compared with most financial markets, with relatively little money changing hands. All else being equal, this makes them poor places to speculate on sabotage. Nonetheless, financial markets are also typically tied to large economic aggregates, which are difficult for individuals to influence reliably. If information markets are created to estimate smaller-scale social processes that individuals could more directly influence, speculating on sabotage might be more of an issue. For example, a company might create a market on whether a certain project will meet its deadline, and many individual employees might have the ability to sabotage the project and delay its completion.[34]

One can try to deal with this problem by only estimating large aggregates, by limiting participation,[35] or by allowing investigators of suspicious events to see who made what trades.[36] Another approach, however, is to set limits on trading positions. For each class of traders, one might limit how far asset holdings could move in dangerous directions. For example, regarding the corporate project completion market, the company might estimate bounds on the current implicit stake and minimum acceptable stake for different classes of people. Each employee working on the project might be expected to gain at least $200 worth in professional reputation should the project be completed on time, while a benefit of $100 would be considered sufficient to ensure that he did not harm the project.

Given these assumptions, such an employee could safely trade until he reached a position where he would gain $100 via bets if the project were not completed on time. That is, if he started with no bets, he could be allowed to pay $50 for the asset, "Pays $100 if project misses deadline." At that point he would still be set to gain at least $100 if the project were completed on time, and so he would not be tempted to sabotage the project.

What if some employees were already at their asset limits, such as having a zero initial stake, where any negative stake is considered dangerous? Well, being that close to a dangerous boundary seems unwise. The company should probably give them all an explicit bonus contingent on project completion and then allow them to trade this down to zero or up to infinity. To make this approach work, one might have to worry about whether people could trade via multiple accounts and whether they had shared interests with others whose stakes should be limited.

Embezzlement

Many observers are concerned that information markets inside organizations could misdirect time, money, and credit, perhaps maliciously. If one creates real-money markets on company-related events, where employees can bet large sums, they may shirk on other tasks to play the market. But if one creates play-money markets, or real-money markets where only small sums can be bet, they may not see why they should bother to participate. How can markets induce enough, but not too much, effort?

Those who choose market topics might do so in part to reward their friends. For example, creating a market on future sales might reward those who have first access to relevant organizational data on sales. Also, team members may withhold insights from team production in order to gain more cash in the markets privately.

These sorts of difficulties with creating explicit monetary reward schemes are ubiquitous in most organizations. Consequently, most employees are not given direct financial rewards on most tasks. Instead, they are usually rewarded on the basis of overall performance evaluations. Such evaluations consider many relevant indicators, but usually no commitment is made to any particular formula for combining those indicators. This allows managers more flexibility to notice and correct for the sort of foul play that direct and formulaic monetary rewards might induce.

A similar performance evaluation approach can be used to deal with foul play in information markets. A standard salient entry in an employee evaluation is that the employee, alone or with some group, initiated a change that was estimated to have added so many dollars to the organization's bottom line. I suggest that we design internal organization information markets to facilitate similar statements by introducing a new color of money. Creating different colors of money, with limits on their convertibility, is a standard accounting technique for dealing with complex incentive problems in organizations.

Instead of betting cash or play-money, we could enable bets of information-money. Initial holdings of info-money would be distributed not only to groups and individuals, but also to automated market-makers on chosen trading topics. Some specialists would estimate the value of more accurate information on each trading topic, and then each topic's market-makers would be subsidized at a level corresponding to the estimated value of information on that topic.[37]

Given such subsidies, traders would, on average, increase their holdings of info-money as they made market prices more accurate, and the total increased holdings would correspond to the estimated total value of the information produced. Employees or groups who could show they had consistently increased their info-money holdings could then claim credit on their evaluations. They would claim the amount of their increased holdings as a dollar-valued contribution to the organization's bottom line. This approach would give managers a reasonable basis for allocating the efforts of their subordinates among various tasks, including various info-production tasks.

Statistical analyses of the history of each person's or group's trades would be needed to distinguish consistent increases from mere random fluctuations. Those people with consistent decreases could be encouraged to change something or stop. Those with large but inconsistent fluctuations could be encouraged to keep their fluctuations small until they learned how to make consistent contributions. And those who were afraid to make any trades for fear of losses could be encouraged to make only small trades, where losses need not be stigmatized, while they learned how to make consistent contributions.

To discourage individuals from embezzling team information, one might have the team account trade first on any new team information and only afterward allow individual team members to trade on their own accounts. This could allow individual team members to write dissenting minority reports while avoiding embezzlement of team information.

In cases where there is concern that members might withhold their insights from the team, the team might be given the right of first refusal on member trades, so that a trade would be an individual trade only if the team did not want to make it as a team trade. This approach, however, would make it difficult to allow for anonymous dissenting opinions.

One would want to avoid wasteful contests by different groups to be the first to arrive at the market with easily collected information that is not especially time-critical. This might be done by creating standard processes that trade on such information. Only after this standard trading were done would one let others trade on the information, to express any different beliefs they might have about how exactly such information should be incorporated. One might also slowly raise the subsidy level on a topic from zero, to entice the cheapest possible info supplier to supply it first.

Retribution

Existing forecasts are often inaccurate because someone wants them to be so. For example, a salesman may want to create low expectations about future sales so that his efforts will look good by comparison. Or someone proposing a new project may want to create high expectations so that his project will be approved. Such people often distort the information they present to others in order to create inaccurate forecasts.

If only a few insiders knew that these forecasts were inaccurate, and if information markets threatened to entice those insiders to rat on the deceptive forecasts, then those who preferred the deception might threaten retribution against anyone who contradicted them in the markets. For example, a project leader might punish anyone on his project team who disputed his rosy forecast.

Because similar processes exist in other forecasting institutions, this approach does not appear to create a special concern for information markets. In fact, information markets can substantially reduce this problem via anonymous trading. Anonymous trades can avoid retribution, at least if the leader is not willing to punish all team members whenever the market goes against him. This approach can, however, require a lot of routine anonymous trading to take place so that the mere fact that one is trading anonymously does not make one a target of retribution. Anonymity can also conflict with giving teams a right of first refusal on team member trades.

Anonymous trading can be consistent with allowing managers to oversee their employees' allocation of effort. Even if managers are not able to see individual trades, they might see the time that their subordinates spend trading, along with statistics on their overall trading performance.

Conclusion

The impressive accuracy of information markets, relative to competing forecasting institutions, is encouraging their wider application, but many people have expressed concerns that such markets might encourage various forms of foul play, including lying, manipulation, sabotage, embezzlement, and retribution. I have reviewed each of these forms and provided strategies for mitigating them.

The standard for evaluation should be how information markets compare to competing forecasting institutions, and limiting participation is a generic but crude strategy for limiting foul play.

Inducing lies is only a special concern of information markets when such markets have wider participation than other institutions. Reasonable solutions include having advisors trading instead of talking, or giving them the ability to show their neutral trading position.

Manipulation seems a much weaker concern for information markets than for competing institutions, as manipulative trading should usually improve price accuracy. Manipulation should be a potential problem only when all traders are very risk-averse, or when the harm from price errors correlates in unusual ways with those errors.

Sabotage is not a concern when markets estimate large social aggregates that are hard for individuals to influence, or when the trading stakes are too small to pay for any substantial sabotage efforts. When the events are small enough relative to the trading stakes for sabotage to be a concern, one can limit participation, reveal trades to investigators, or place bounds on individual trading stakes.

To discourage the embezzlement of time, money, and credit within organizations, internal markets could trade a new color of money. When trading topics are subsidized at their value of information, those with consistent trading gains can take credit for adding so many dollars to the organization's bottom line. Standard information sources should have special processes that trade on them before others, and teams should trade on team information before team members do.

Retribution does not seem a special concern of information markets, and anonymous trading can greatly reduce the ability to suppress information through threats of retribution.

Overall, none of these forms of foul play seems worse in information markets when one holds constant who can participate in the forecasting institutions. Allowing information markets to have broader participation than other institutions can bring in more people who may engage in foul play, but many approaches are available for limiting this problem to tolerable levels.

Notes

1. Andrew Lo, "Finance: A Selective Survey," *Journal of the American Statistical Association* 95, no. 45 (2000): 629–35; Koleman S. Strumpf and Paul W. Rhode, "Historical Presidential Betting Markets," *Journal of Economic Perspectives* 18, no. 2 (2004): 127–41.

2. Richard Roll, "Orange Juice and Weather," *American Economic Review* 74, no. 5 (1984): 861–80.

3. Stephen Figlewski, "Subjective Information and Market Efficiency in a Betting Market," *Journal of Political Economy* 87, no. 1 (1979): 75–88.

4. David M. Pennock, C. Lee Giles, and Finn A. Nielsen, "The Real Power of Artificial Markets," *Science* 291 (2001): 987–88.

5. Jakab Spencer, "New ICAP–Nymex Derivatives Have U.S. Gas Market's Number," *Wall Street Journal*, August 4, 2004.

6. Michael T. Maloney and J. Harold Mulherin, "The Complexity of Price Discovery in an Efficient Market: The Stock Market Reaction to the Challenger Crash," *Journal of Corporate Finance* 9, no. 4 (2003): 453–79.

7. Joyce Berg, Forrest Nelson, and Thomas Rietz, "Accuracy and Forecast Standard Error of Prediction Markets" (technical report, University of Iowa, College of Business Administration, 2001).

8. Kay-Yut Chen and Charles R. Plott, "Prediction Markets and Information Aggregation Mechanisms: Experiments and Application" (technical report, California Institute of Technology, 1998).

9. Berg, Nelson, and Rietz, "Accuracy and Forecast Standard Error of Prediction Markets"; Justin Wolfers and Eric Zitzewitz, "Prediction Markets," *Journal of Economic Perspectives* 18, no. 2 (2004): 107–26.

10. Martin Spann and Bernd Skiera, "Internet-Based Virtual Stock Markets for Business Forecasting," *Management Science* 49, no. 10 (2003): 1310–26.

11. Pennock, Giles, and Nielsen, "Real Power of Artificial Markets," 987–88.

12. Robin Hanson, "Market-Based Foresight—A Proposal," *Foresight Update* 10 (1990): 1, 3, 4; Robin Hanson, "Could Gambling Save Science? Encouraging an Honest Consensus," *Social Epistemology* 9, no. 1 (1995): 333; Robin Hanson, "Idea Futures," *Wired* 3, no. 9 (1995): 125.

13. Actually, PAM would have focused on aggregate geopolitical trends, such as how the chances of political unrest in Saudi Arabia depend on whether U.S. troops leave there. See Charles Polk, Robin Hanson, John Ledyard, and Takashi Ishikida, "The Policy Analysis Market: An Electronic Commerce Application of a Combinatorial Information Market," *Proceedings of the ACM Conference on Electronic Commerce* (Association for Computing Machinery, New York, 2003), 272–73.

14. Senators, reporters, and economists complained. For example, U.S. senators Ron Wyden and Bryon Dorgan said, "Terrorists themselves could drive up the market for an event they are planning and profit from an attack, or even make

false bets to mislead intelligence authorities" (R. Wyden and B. Dorgan, press release, July 28, 2003). Steven Pearlstein argued that "would-be assassins and terrorists could easily use disinformation and clever trading strategies to profit from their planned misdeeds while distracting attention from their real target" (Steven Pearlstein, "Misplacing Trust in the Markets," *Washington Post*, July 30, 2003, E1). Joseph Stiglitz said that "trading . . . could be subject to manipulation, particularly if the market has few participants providing a false sense of security or . . . alarm. . . . The lack of intellectual foundation or a firm grasp of economic principles—or the pursuit of other agendas—has led to a proposal that almost seems a mockery of itself." (Joseph Stiglitz, "Terrorism: There's No Futures in It," *Los Angeles Times*, July 31, 2003).

15. Robin Hanson, "Combinatorial Information Market Design," *Information Systems Frontier* 5, no. 1 (2003): 105–19.

16. Chen and Plott, "Prediction Markets and Information Aggregation Mechanisms."

17. Franklin Allen and Douglas Gale, "Stock-Price Manipulation," *Review of Financial Studies* 5, no. 3 (1992): 503–29.

18. Other sorts of manipulation are less of a concern, such as strategic contrary trading by an informed trader to control the rate at which his information is revealed. See Archishman Chakrabortya and Bilge Ylmaz, "Manipulation in Market Order Models," *Journal of Financial Markets* 7, no. 2 (2004): 187–206.

19. Jan Hansen, Carsten Schmidt, and Martin Strobel, "Manipulation in Political Stock Markets—Preconditions and Evidence," *Applied Economics Letters* 11, no. 7 (2004): 459–63.

20. Koleman S. Strumpf and Paul W. Rhode, "Historical Presidential Betting Markets," *Journal of Economic Perspectives* 18, no. 2 (2004): 127–41.

21. Colin Camerer, "Can Asset Markets Be Manipulated? A Field Experiment with Racetrack Betting," *Journal of Political Economy* 106 (1998): 457–82.

22. Robin Hanson, Ryan Oprea, and David Porter, "Information Aggregation and Manipulation in an Experimental Market," *Journal of Economic Behavior and Organization* (forthcoming, 2006).

23. Wolfers and Zitzewitz, "Prediction Markets," 107–26.

24. Hanson, "Combinatorial Information Market Design," 105–19.

25. Note that if aggregate noise trading risk is a problem, then increases in potential participation can reduce this sort of foul-play problem by increasing total pocket depth relative to noise trading.

26. J. Bradford De Long, Andrei Shleifer, Lawrence H. Summers, and Robert J. Waldmann, "Noise Trader Risk in Financial Markets," *Journal of Political Economy* 98, no. 4 (1990): 703–38.

27. Albert S. Kyle, "Informed Speculation with Imperfect Competition," *Review of Economic Studies* 56, no. 3 (1989): 317–55; Matthew Spiegel and Avanidhar Subrahmanyam, "Informed Speculation and Hedging in a Noncompetitive Securities Market," *Review of Financial Studies* 5, no. 2 (1992): 307–29.

28. Joyce Berg, Robert Forsythe, and Thomas Rietz, "What Makes Markets Predict Well? Evidence from the Iowa Electronic Markets," in *Understanding Strategic Interaction: Essays in Honor of Reinhard Selten*, ed. Wulf Albers, Werner Guth, Peter Hammerstein, Benny Moldovanu, Eric van Damme, Martin Strobel, and Reinhard Selten (New York: Springer, 1996), 444–63.

29. Praveen Kumar and Duane J. Seppi, "Futures Manipulation with Cash Settlement," *Journal of Finance* 47, no. 4 (1992): 1485–1502; Pierre Hillion and Matti Suominen, "The Manipulation of Closing Prices," *Journal of Financial Markets* 7, no. 4 (2004): 351–75.

30. Hanson, Oprea, and Porter, "Information Aggregation and Manipulation."

31. Rafi Eldor and Rafi Melnick, "Financial Markets and Terrorism," *European Journal of Political Economy* 20, no. 2 (2004): 367–86.

32. Thomas H. Kean, Lee H. Hamilton, Richard Ben-Veniste, Bob Kerrey, Fred F. Fielding, John F. Lehman, Jamie S. Gorelick, Timothy J. Roemer, Slade Gorton, and James R. Thompson, *The 9-11 Commission Report*, http://www.9-11commission.gov/report/911Report.pdf (accessed July 2004).

33. Andy Geller, "Pained Webber: Geek Tried to Sink Stock with Cyber Bomb," *New York Post*, December 18, 2002.

34. A perhaps bigger problem with such project deadline markets is that managers often manipulate employee overconfidence and uncertainty about deadlines in order to get more work out of them. See Magne Jorgensen, Karl H. Teigen, and Kjetil Molokken, "Better Sure Than Safe? Overconfidence in Judgment Based Software Development Effort Prediction," *Journal of Systems and Software* 70, no. 1–2 (2004): 79–83. Such managers would resist the introduction of these markets.

35. Limiting participation for this reason is analogous to having regulations requiring that one have an "insurable interest" to buy insurance.

36. Tad Hogg and Bernardo A. Huberman, "Avoiding Moral Hazards in Organizational Forecasting," Hewlett-Packard Labs, http://www.hpl.hp.com/research/idl/papers/moral/moral.pdf (accessed June 2004).

37. Hanson, "Combinatorial Information Market Design," 105–19.

7

The Iowa Electronic Markets: Stylized Facts and Open Issues

Joyce E. Berg and Thomas A. Rietz

Prediction markets, markets in which contracts are specifically designed so that prices forecast particular future events, appear poised for acceptance as alternatives to more conventional forecasting methods.[1] One frequently mentioned reason to believe such markets could be successful forecasting tools is the predictive accuracy of the presidential-election markets conducted by the Iowa Electronic Markets (IEM). To our knowledge, these are the longest-running, real-money prediction markets to date. Created in 1988, they continue to be used as a research and teaching tool as well as a more practical forecasting tool. In this chapter, we examine what has been learned from these markets and, more important, what is still to be learned.

Although the Iowa Electronic Markets have proved quite accurate in forecasting through the years, they do not behave in ways one might expect from efficient markets populated by rational traders. Large market volumes stand in contrast to Milgrom and Stokey's 1982 no-trade theorem.[2] IEM traders exhibit biases and lack self-insight.[3] Some traders claim attempts to manipulate IEM prices.[4] Nor are these markets simply polls. IEM traders are clearly not a representative sample of the population.[5]

With all of these issues, how could one expect that prediction markets like the IEM would aggregate information and make efficient forecasts? Yet IEM prices respond quickly to information, are accurate in both a relative and absolute sense immediately before the event and well in advance, and appear to exhibit little bias.[6] Empirically, prediction markets "work." As Nobel laureate Vernon Smith writes, "Things sometimes work better than we had a right to expect from our abstract interpretations of theory."[7] He encourages us to pursue the "exciting implications" of this conundrum. This chapter follows in that vein. We investigate some intriguing results from the Iowa Electronic Markets, using the 2004 election markets as our primary examples, and examine the potential for future research.

IEM Overview

The IEM is a real-money, small-scale futures market that focuses on the information-revelation and aggregation roles of market prices rather than on their role in determining allocations. Though the IEM is best known for its U.S. and worldwide election markets, it has also conducted markets on political appointments, outcomes of legislative processes, international relationships, economic indicators, movie box office receipts, market capitalizations after an initial public offering (IPO), corporate earnings forecasts, corporate stock price returns, and the incidence of influenza.[8]

IEM contracts take several payoff forms. The primary forms are linear payoff contracts (called "vote-share" contracts when used in elections), binary payoff contracts (called "winner-takes-all" contracts), and conditional contracts (generally a linear payoff form that will be implemented only if some second event happens).[9] Contract payoff form determines the interpretation of market prices.

Linear contracts are so named because their liquidation values are a linear function of the associated event.[10] For example, the 2004 KERR contract's liquidation value was specified as $1 times John F. Kerry's share of the two-party popular vote. Because the expected value of a linear contract is a multiple of the expected value of the associated event, contract prices should reflect expected values of events (for instance, in the case of KERR, Kerry's expected two-party vote share).

Winner-takes-all contracts have binary payouts: The contract is liquidated for a fixed positive amount (for instance, $1) if the associated event happens, and $0 otherwise. For example, the 2004 DEM04_G52 contract's liquidation value was $1 if the Democrats received more than 52 percent of the two-party popular vote, and $0 otherwise. Because the expected value of a winner-takes-all contract is the probability that the associated event will happen, contract prices should reflect each event's probability.

Finally, conditional contracts are based on combinations of events and, as a result, give information about potential combinations of events. For example, before the Democratic nominee was known for the 2004 U.S. presidential election, the IEM traded contracts tied to the vote shares each potential nominee would receive in a race against George W. Bush if that nominee were actually to become the Democratic candidate for president. In this market, the contract GEPH was associated with Dick Gephardt; and had Gephardt actually become the nominee, the contract would have liquidated at $1 times the vote share he received in the election. An associated contract, BU|GEPH, would have liquidated at $1 times the vote share received by Bush if Gephardt had become the nominee. Because Gephardt did not become the nominee, both contracts liquidated at $0. The contracts KERR and BU|KERR (associated with John Kerry as the nominee), however, did have positive liquidation values because Kerry became the Democratic nominee. These two contracts became the sole vote-share contracts after the Democratic convention and were liquidated at the relative vote shares received by Kerry and Bush after the election. Because the values of conditional contracts are tied to combinations of events, prices reflect expectations about the combination of events (in this case, the relative vote shares received by the candidates, conditional on the nomination).[11]

IEM traders are voluntary participants who invest between $5 and $500.[12] Though the 1988 IEM traders were all University of Iowa affiliates (students, faculty, and staff), current IEM political market traders include both academic and nonacademic traders from around the world.[13] The percentage of nonacademic traders in political markets has increased greatly as the Internet, and therefore the markets, have become more accessible. In the IEM 2004 presidential-election markets, nonacademic traders represented 44 percent of traders in the vote-share market and 64 percent in the winner-takes-all market.[14] Typically, between twenty-five and fifteen hundred traders are active in any one market.

IEM contracts are traded in a continuous double-auction market. No fees are charged for trading or liquidating contracts. The trading is anonymous, with the trader's market information set consisting of the current best feasible offer to buy (called the "best bid"), current best feasible offer to sell (called the "best ask"), and last trade price. This information is updated every fifteen to thirty seconds, with traders having the option of refreshing their information more often. Traders also have access to a daily price history that reports daily quantity and dollar volumes and high, low, average, and last (before midnight) prices. They can also see historical graphs of the daily last prices at any time. Finally, they know their own cash and contract holdings and can access historical records pertaining to their own offers to buy (bids), offers to sell (asks), and trades.

As part of the market structure, the IEM issues contracts in sets called fixed-price bundles. Each fixed-price bundle consists of a set of contracts guaranteed to have a fixed total payout. For instance, after Kerry was determined to be the Democratic nominee, the 2004 U.S. presidential vote-share market bundle consisted of two contracts: KERR and BU|KERR (that is, Bush in a match against Kerry), where the liquidation value for each contract was the associated candidate's share of the two-party vote.[15] Because, as defined, total vote share is always 100 percent, holding one of each of the contracts (a contract bundle) to liquidation always results in receiving \$1. At any time and at no cost, traders can exchange dollars for bundles, increasing the market supply of contracts, or exchange bundles for dollars, decreasing the market supply of contracts. This creates instantaneous and intertemporal arbitrage relationships that restrict the risk-free rate to zero in these markets.[16] Furthermore, because there is no need to bear risk (traders could hold riskless bundles), there is no reward for risk-sharing. No short sales or margin purchases are permitted. Traders can always replicate short positions synthetically, however, by purchasing bundles (which are equivalent to cash in this market) and selling individual contracts.[17] The bundle and short-sale features replace the need for a banking/credit function that would guarantee traders' promises to pay.

Stylized Facts from IEM Markets

IEM markets conducted across years and across events have several consistent characteristics. These "stylized facts" are discussed next, using IEM 2004 election market results as the primary source of examples.

Traders Are Not a Random Sample of the Voting Population. IEM traders are typically more educated, richer, and "more male" than both the average U.S. citizen and the average U.S. voter. Among IEM 2004 election-market traders responding to a voluntary survey, 95 percent reported that they planned to vote, 90 percent that they were male, 90 percent that they were white, 89 percent that they had college degrees, and 60 percent that they had household incomes greater than $75,000.[18] In apparent contrast to previous IEM election markets, traders' self-reports classified nearly equal proportions as Democrat and Republican (37.5 percent and 35.5 percent respectively; previous IEM markets reported that traders were overwhelmingly Republican).

Although these "nonrepresentative" features would invalidate a poll, they do not necessarily present a problem for prediction markets. Polls typically ask traders how they would vote if the election were held today and rely on random sampling for the validity of the prediction. In contrast, to profit in the IEM, traders need to forecast how the entire population will vote in the election, independent of how they feel about the candidates themselves. Market action, rather than statistical averaging, determines IEM prices and predictions.

Traders Are Biased. IEM traders do not appear to be fully rational. Their reported beliefs are biased by their preferences, and this bias appears to be reflected in their portfolio choices.[19] In addition, traders frequently "leave money on the table," trading in ways that do not take advantage of the best available prices.[20]

Survey results from 2004 also indicate that traders' beliefs are skewed by their preferences. In response to the question, "Regardless of your preferences, who do you think will receive the most popular votes in the upcoming U.S. presidential election?" 68 percent of self-reported Democrats reported that they believed Kerry would win the election. Among self-reported Republicans, only 5 percent reported that they believed Kerry would win. Similar biases were also present in IEM traders' reported beliefs about which candidate "won" the 2004 presidential debates, as well as who "rightfully" won the 2000 presidential election. These biases are comparable to those reported in Granberg and Brent.[21]

Further evidence that traders lack self-insight appears in traders' responses to the question, "Relative to other traders, how informed do you believe you were about the 2004 presidential election?" Some 89 percent of traders responding to the survey said they believed they were more informed than other traders in the market. This "Lake Wobegon" characteristic accords with Svenson's observation that by and large, we all think we are more skilled than our peers.[22]

Some Traders Are Robots. Although there may have always been robot traders in the IEM election markets, 2000 and 2004 were the first elections in which their presence was obvious to us.[23] In the 2004 election markets, fewer than a dozen traders appeared to be robots. But these robot traders were involved in a large percentage of the trades. For instance, in the 2004 winner-takes-all presidential market, a single robot trader was involved in 21 percent of the 1,106,722 units traded (or 20 percent of the $327,385 total trade volume as measured in dollars). A similar, though smaller, effect was seen in the 2004 vote-share market.

Our preliminary investigations indicate that these robots executed one of two strategies. Some appeared to be designed to take advantage of arbitrage opportunities; others appeared to rely on price-movement strategies. Robots that took advantage of arbitrage opportunities appear to make positive profits. The single robot trader referred to above earned an average of $0.002 per unit traded. That trading on arbitrage opportunities can be profitable is consistent with data reported in Oliven and Rietz using the 1992 presidential markets[24] and data reported by Rietz in laboratory markets.[25] We have not yet completed our analysis of the other robot traders' behavior.

Large Orders to Trade Can Move Prices. As with any market, changes in demand and supply will have an impact on prices. Large orders to buy (sell) may result in upward (downward) price movements. In finance, this is known as the adverse price effect of the order. Due to the particular market mechanism implemented by the IEM, however, not all large orders affect prices.

In IEM markets, large market orders (orders to sell or buy at the best currently available bid or ask) will have very little impact on prices because market orders are canceled after clearing the quantity available at the top of the opposing queue. For example, if the current best ask is $0.520 for ten shares of a contract and a trader puts in an order to purchase ten shares, ten contracts will trade, and the new best ask will be the next ask in the queue, say, $0.525. If the trader puts in an order to purchase twenty or one hundred or even one thousand shares, the same thing happens: Ten contracts will trade, and the new best ask will be the next in the queue. The rest of the trader's order is canceled.

Furthermore, in IEM markets, large limit orders (bids and asks) that do not cross the opposing queue will not affect prices at all—they simply create a new best bid or new best ask. For a trade to occur and hence a price to be recorded, the new bid or ask must be accepted by a trader submitting a market order. The market order will trade only the smaller of the quantity of the order or, as discussed above, the quantity available at the top of the opposing queue. Thus, the net effect of large limit orders that do not cross the opposing queue is to *prevent* prices from moving past that specified in the order.

One type of large order can affect prices in IEM markets: large bids or asks that cross the opposing queue. For example, if the current best ask is $0.520 for ten shares of a contract and a trader puts in a bid to purchase one hundred shares at $0.600, ten contracts will trade at $0.520. Then, the next best ask, provided it is lower than $0.600, will trade against the bid order, and so on, until the order is filled or no compatible asks remain in the queue. Thus, depending on the depth of the opposing queue, a large order that crosses the opposing queue could move prices substantially.

There are several reasons one might submit an order that crosses the opposing queue. First, it might be a mistake. Communications from traders suggest that this does happen from time to time. When mistakes are the cause, we should see queues recover quickly and prices reverse. Second, crossing the queue is a much faster and more efficient way to make informed trades than submitting a series of market orders to clear each opposing bid or ask. For example, suppose a trader has advance information that a particular candidate will lose the Iowa caucus and, hence, lose the Democratic nomination. The most efficient way for that trader to make the maximum profit from that information is to cross the candidate's associated bid queue with a large ask at a price of $0.000 before other traders have a chance to withdraw their bids. If the information proves valid, prices will remain at their new levels or, potentially, drift even further in the same direction. If not, prices may reverse. Similarly, suppose someone wants to manipulate the market. The fastest and most efficient way to move prices is to act in exactly the same manner. If the manipulation is successful, prices will stay at the new values, and the trader can unwind his position at a profit. If not, we will see prices reverse. We will discuss manipulation in more detail later. Here, we simply document the price impact of queue-crossing orders.

Though relatively rare, large bids that cross the ask queue and large asks that cross the bid queue do exist in IEM markets. The immediate effect of these orders depends on the depth of the opposing queue. In the 2004 winner-takes-all presidential market prior to the election,[26] 2,147 bids or asks crossed the opposing queue (less than 1.2 percent of the 179,930 total submitted bids and asks). The largest price movement from a crossed ask queue was a $0.110 increase resulting from a bid for one hundred contracts.[27] Most of this price change ($0.105) reversed within an hour, and it more than completely reversed within two hours. The largest price movement resulting from a crossed bid queue was $0.038, resulting from an ask for 530 contracts.[28] This price movement completely reversed within one minute. Because of the reversals, neither movement appeared in histories of closing prices.

Some price movements that reverse do appear in closing-price data because of the timing of the trading activity. For example, Kerry's price in the 2004 vote-share market was at $0.488 at 9:00 p.m. central daylight time (CDT) on October 7. With a sequence of small trades, two different traders drove the price up to $0.700 by 9:06 p.m. CDT. Another small trade occurred at $0.650 at 9:56 p.m. CDT. Although no other trade occurred before midnight, the best ask had fallen back to $0.482 by 10:18 p.m. CDT. At 1:36 CDT the next morning, another trade occurred at $0.480. In this case, the reversal in the price series took three and one-half hours, and the recording time for closing prices happened to occur before the reversal. Note that the reversal in asks had occurred well before this, even though no trade had yet occurred. In the final analysis, it appears that large orders are not significant factors in IEM prices.

IEM Prices Are Accurate, Both Relative to the Next Best Alternative (Polls) and Absolutely. Our most straightforward measure of IEM accuracy comes from the linear markets, because prices there predict vote share (an externally verifiable measure) rather than probability. As reported in many papers, IEM vote-share prices appear to be accurate both in an absolute sense (that is, relative to what actually happens) and relative to polls. Figure 7-1 is an expanded (to include the 2004 election results) version of a figure similar to one by Berg, Forsythe, Nelson, and Rietz.[29] It shows the accuracy of IEM election-eve contract prices for all IEM election vote-share markets conducted since 1988. The average absolute percentage error for presidential-election-eve contracts is 1.33 percent. Although we have not completed our analysis of poll performance for 2004, previous analyses of IEM accuracy relative to polls (for elections prior to 2004) indicate that final projection poll errors average 2 percent.[30]

IEM prices also appear to outperform polls in advance of the election. Figure 7-2 shows Bush's relative vote-share margin as reported in 2004 IEM prices and major national polls (all vote shares and poll shares have been normalized to sum to one; Bush's vote-share margin is calculated as Bush's normalized vote share less Kerry's normalized vote share). IEM prices were more stable than polls, respond less to transient events than polls, and were closer to election outcomes than the average poll when the election was more than one week away. Previous elections show strikingly similar results. Berg, Nelson, and Rietz report that when polls are compared to corresponding IEM prices over the course of the election, IEM prices are closer to the actual election vote share than polls in 76 percent of the cases.[31]

Our results about the accuracy of IEM winner-takes-all prices are mixed. When both linear and winner-takes-all markets are focused on the same event, the price distribution and its central tendency extracted from winner-takes-all market prices are consistent with the prediction implied by the linear market prices. By extension, then, prices in the IEM winner-takes-all prices would seem to have the same accuracy characteristics as the linear markets.[32] But we are also able to document some bias in winner-takes-all markets.

Berg and Rietz report that prices in a large sample of IEM computer-returns markets do not exhibit the same long-shot bias (in which the probabilities of low-frequency events are overestimated) documented in the betting literature.[33] For short horizons—that is, horizons of less than one day—these IEM markets appeared to be unbiased. For most horizons longer than one day, however, the same markets exhibited the reverse of the long-shot bias: Prices for events that actually happened with low frequency are too low, and prices for events that actually happened with high frequency were too high. Berg and Rietz interpret this as an overconfidence bias and document the potential gains to trade available by trading against this bias.[34]

FIGURE 7-1
IEM ELECTION EVE PREDICTIONS VERSUS ACTUAL VOTE-SHARE OUTCOMES

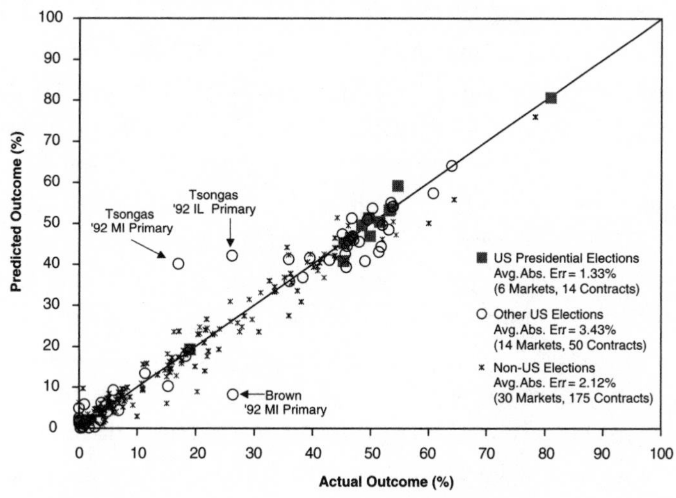

SOURCE: Authors' calculations.

FIGURE 7-2
BUSH VOTE-SHARE MARGIN IN THE IEM AND POLLS, 2004
(poll results are indicated by x's)

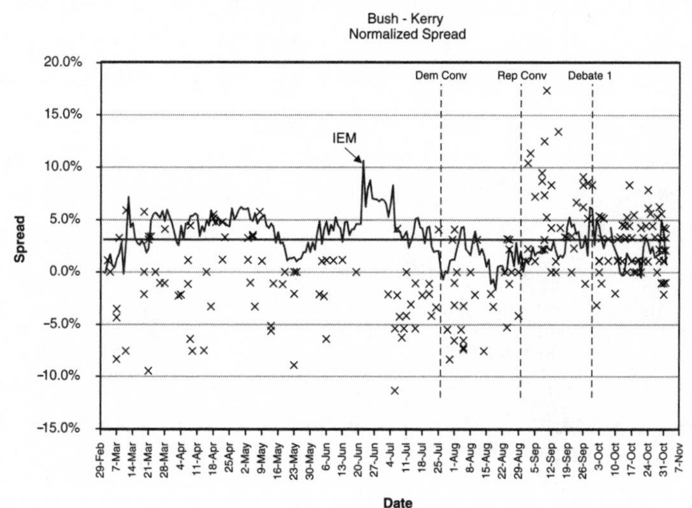

SOURCE: Authors' calculations.

IEM Prices Respond Quickly to News. IEM market prices appear to respond quickly to news, sometimes well in advance of the official public announcement. A most striking example occurred in the 1996 Powell Nomination Market, an IEM market focusing on whether Colin Powell's name would be placed in nomination at the 1996 Republican National Convention. During the fall of 1995, speculation was high that Powell would be nominated. IEM prices reflected that speculation, with the price of the P.YES contract (a contract that would pay $1 if Powell's name was placed in nomination at the convention in August 1996 and $0 otherwise), growing to more than $0.60 by November 7, 1995. On November 8, 1995, at 8:10 a.m. CST, Powell announced that he would be holding a press conference later that afternoon. As shown in figure 7-3, prices reacted immediately to that announcement even though it contained no explicit information about the content of the upcoming press conference. Within minutes, the IEM price dropped from above $0.60 to almost zero, correctly forecasting the content of the announcement that was not made until more than seven hours later. Apparently, traders put together the announcement that there would be "news" later in the day with the fact that there were few rumors about a campaign committee, to conclude that there would be no campaign.

A similar permanent effect of news can be seen in the response to the January 19, 2004, Iowa caucuses. Surprising both pollsters and the IEM, Dean lost the Iowa caucuses badly. Late in the evening, he made a speech that some say was the death knell of his campaign. As figure 7-4 shows, the IEM 2004 Democratic Nomination Market actually portended this fall. Though Dean was the most likely nominee according to IEM prices before the Iowa caucuses, his price had already fallen from a high of $0.76 on December 9, 2003, to $0.51 on January 18, 2004, the day before the caucus (a drop of $0.25). In contrast, he fell by only $0.16 (to $0.35) on the day of the caucus.

Some "announcement effects" are not permanent. Some of these events appear to be related to information that, if proved correct, would have a large effect, but is later proved incorrect. One such event occurred in the 2004 Democratic Nomination Market. As shown in figure 7-4, on February 11, 2004, Kerry's price in the IEM Democratic Nomination Market stood at $0.95. On February 12, 2004, at 10:45 a.m. CST, the *Drudge Report* posted a "world exclusive" claiming that several news agencies were about to release information that John Kerry had had an affair with an intern.

FIGURE 7-3
IEM PRICE RESPONSE TO ANNOUNCEMENT THAT POWELL WOULD HOLD A PRESS CONFERENCE LATER IN THE AFTERNOON

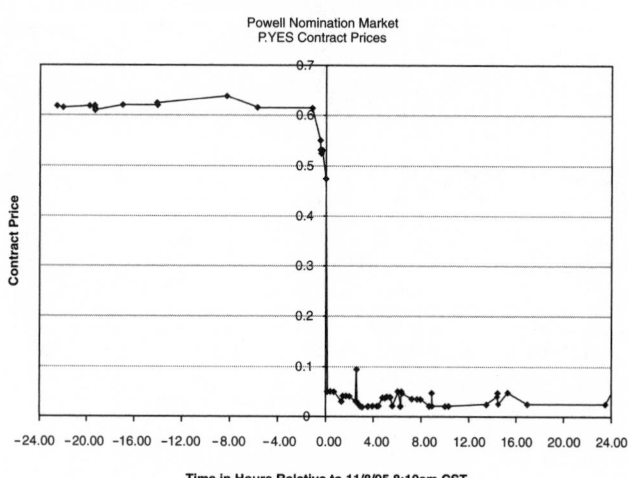

SOURCE: Authors' calculations.

FIGURE 7-4
2004 DEMOCRATIC CONVENTION MARKET PRICES

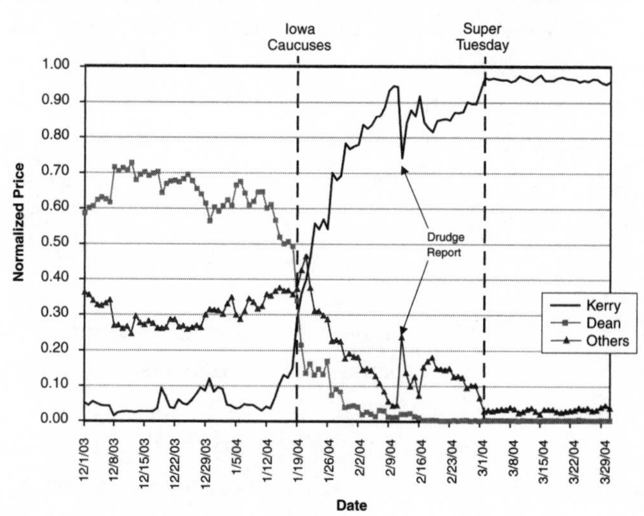

SOURCE: Authors' calculations.

FIGURE 7-5
IEM WINNER-TAKES-ALL PRICE RESPONSE TO ELECTION DAY 2004 NEWS

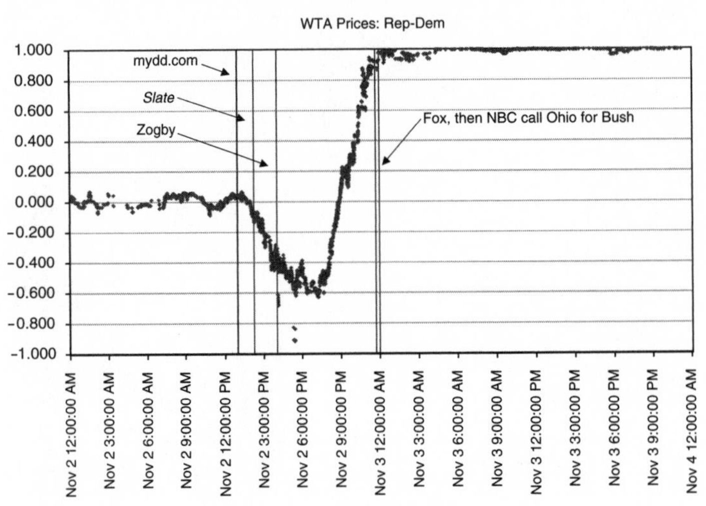

SOURCE: Authors' calculations.

Seconds later, sell orders began to flood the market. Within ten minutes, Kerry's price dropped to $0.75. Had Drudge's claim been true, it surely would have hurt Kerry's chances of nomination. This was reflected in market prices. Drudge's report remained unconfirmed, however, and within two days, Kerry's price returned to $0.86.

Election Day 2004 also provided an interesting view of IEM price response. Early election exit poll results were leaked on mydd.com (a political blog) at 12:58 p.m. CST. At 2:15 p.m. CST, *Slate* posted additional exit poll results. At 4:00 p.m. CST, Zogby posted its prediction that Kerry would take 311 electoral votes.

Figure 7-5 shows the IEM winner-takes-all price responses to these news events. For clarity, the graph collapses all four contracts in that market into a single statistic: the spread between the probability that Bush would get the most-popular vote and the probability that Kerry would get it.[35]

Though there was some price reaction to the mydd.com report, most of the reaction occurred after the *Slate* report and the Zogby forecast, possibly indicating sensitivity to both the tentative nature of exit polls and the quality of the news source. This downward trend began to reverse at 7:45 p.m. CST as actual poll results from the East Coast and Midwest began to be reported on the national news. By 11:00 p.m. CST, a full hour in advance of when national networks began to call Ohio for Bush, IEM prices reflected a 90 percent probability that Bush would win the most-popular vote.

Although IEM prices appear to respond quickly to news, whether they move by the "correct" amount in response to any particular news is difficult to document because there is no contemporaneous, externally accurate, and verifiable measure of expectations. In fact, it is difficult to imagine a nonmarket measure that could move with the speed of the market.

Open Issues

Theoretical Model. That IEM prices are efficient aggregators of information is generally motivated by a simple Arrow-Debreu asset-pricing model. In an Arrow-Debreu world, with rational, common expectations, it is easy to show that general equilibrium IEM contract prices should equal expected future values, weighted by marginal utilities of wealth across various states. That is, IEM contracts should conform to the familiar Arrow-Debreu asset-pricing relationship with no time-value-of-money factor (which drops out because of the arbitrage-induced zero risk-free rate discussed above). In this weighted sense, prices will always reflect expectations. Under the right conditions, however, this model yields prices that actually equal expected values. For expected value-pricing to hold, the marginal trader must have equal expected marginal utilities across the state outcomes. When might this be the case? There are several possible answers:

- If marginal traders are risk-neutral, the marginal utility of wealth is always 1.
- If marginal traders' wealth levels are largely unaffected by or uncorrelated with the state outcomes, marginal utility for even risk-averse traders will vary little across states.[36]
- If the market is the entire source of wealth risk and can be modeled by a representative trader, then market-clearing

implies that the trader holds equal numbers of contracts (because of the bundle structure) and faces no risk. As a result, the traders' wealth and, hence, marginal utility are constant across outcomes.

- If the market is the entire source of wealth risk in the economy, and traders are risk-averse, then Borch,[37] Caspi,[38] and Malinvaud[39] all show that the Pareto optimal, competitive equilibrium distribution of contracts implies that all traders hold only complete bundles. This also implies that traders face no wealth risk and, hence, marginal utility does not vary across states.

The latter two possibilities are what would result from the Capital Asset Pricing Model (CAPM) or Arbitrage Pricing Theory (APT) with no aggregate risk premium and zero time value of money.

Several other authors have also proposed agent-based models to explain IEM prices, with many of the models omitting the rational-expectations assumptions. All these models typically omit features of the IEM market structure that appear empirically to be important. In IEM markets, contract supply can expand and decrease as traders exchange dollars for contract bundles (which creates instantaneous arbitrage restrictions on prices); traders' market power is limited by a $500 investment cap (which may create binding budget constraints, but limits market power); and traders appear to be differentially informed (which may create differential expectations). Because trader information may contain different pieces of the puzzle, it is not clear how prices should be related, if at all, to average trader beliefs.

Trader survey responses may also provide some insights valuable to theoreticians. As we noted above, most traders believe they are more informed than other traders. This provides a possible reason for trade to occur even when the Milgrom and Stokey no-trade intuition appears applicable.[40] Our 2004 survey results also indicated that traders differ in their trading strategies. Only 76 percent of the respondents reported that more than half of their trades were based on information. Furthermore, in response to a question about trading strategy, it is clear that different traders used different strategies: 50 percent reported that they primarily followed buy-and-hold strategies, 21 percent that they primarily acted as speculators (defined in the survey as trading with the intent of reversing the trade before the election was over), and 18 percent that they primarily acted as arbitrageurs (defined in the survey as taking advantage of short-term inconsistencies in price).[41] Interestingly, traders did seem to have some insight into their own trading strategies. At the close of the 2004 presidential-election markets, 47 percent held more than one hundred contracts in inventory (consistent with a buy-and-hold strategy), 18 percent held small inventories (twenty or fewer contracts), and 19 percent held zero contracts (consistent with a short-term arbitrage strategy).[42]

Bundles and arbitrage may also play an important part in a theory of IEM prices. The costless, instantaneous conversions of cash into bundles and bundles into cash create arbitrage relationships that restrict the risk-free rate to zero. Conversions also allow synthetic short sales. But they may have an additional effect. Rietz documents that Arrow-Debreu contracts are consistently overpriced in markets similar to the IEM with contract bundles, but without the unlimited instantaneous conversion feature.[43] Nevertheless, *relative* prices in those markets do appear to be accurate: Normalizing prices (dividing each absolute price by the sum of all contract prices) results in prices that reflect true-state probabilities. Because bundles facilitate arbitrage and drive the sum of contract prices toward $1, the IEM markets create largely endogenous normalization of prices. Thus, the ability to trade fixed-price bundles costlessly and limitlessly may be at least partly responsible for the observed accuracy of IEM prices.

Manipulation. Whether prices can be manipulated may affect the predictive ability of the market. If successful price manipulation results in long-run price distortions, then the fact that IEM prices appear to be accurate suggests that they are not manipulated successfully. Nevertheless, this does not rule out the possibility of short-term manipulation.

To determine whether manipulation is a factor, one must ask a series of questions. First, is manipulation of prices possible? Second, if manipulation is possible, why would traders want to do it (that is, what are the benefits of manipulating prices)? Third, if manipulation is possible and traders want to do it, how costly would it be? And, finally, if manipulation is undertaken, can it be detected?

Is price manipulation possible? As we discussed, large orders can, at least temporarily, move prices by moving through the opposing queue. And there is ad hoc evidence that IEM observers believe prices can be manipulated. During the 1996 Republican primaries, Pat Buchanan's website listed trading on the IEM among the ways that supporters could "help Pat." During the 2000 election markets, Strumpf, as reported by Wolfers and Zitzewitz, attempted to manipulate IEM prices by issuing random large orders (but they claim the attempt had only limited success).[44] During the 2004 election markets, several political blogs posted claims that IEM prices were being manipulated,[45] and several individuals sent e-mail to the IEM office claiming that George Soros was manipulating IEM prices.[46] Evidence suggests, however, that prices recover quickly after large trades that do not correspond to actual changes in the prospects of candidates (see the evidence on large orders discussed above).

Why would traders want to manipulate prices? Answering this question helps pinpoint the benefits of manipulation. One commonly cited reason for price manipulation on commercial exchanges is personal (wealth) gain. Political blogs offer another reason, suggesting that price manipulation in the IEM could represent attempts to affect election outcomes. It is not clear that traders can create bandwagon effects in prices and profit by strategies such as pushing prices up by buying and later selling. The rapid reversals after large trades (discussed above) are evidence against this. Nor is it clear how voters respond to perceived relative strengths of candidates. For example, if a candidate is perceived to be too far ahead in an election, turnout among that candidate's supporters might actually fall, hurting that candidate's prospects. One might manipulate prices for "bragging rights" (to claim that one caused a price move). But because trading is anonymous, any bragging is cheap talk: Traders can always claim responsibility for price movements after the fact, and all know that no such claim can be verified. Thus, clear reasons for manipulation are not obvious to us.

Assuming that manipulation is possible and that there is a reason for it, how costly would it be? Manipulating prices in the IEM is costly and complex. As an example, consider the trades of an individual trader that appeared to be responsible for the transient price movement on February 27, 1996, in the 1996 Republican National Convention Market. That trader's actions contributed to a $0.04 increase in Buchanan's price. But the actions were also costly, at least in the short run. The trader spent $348 purchasing Buchanan contracts while later in the day selling at least some of those contracts for $98 (Buchanan contracts that were held to maturity expired worthless). Furthermore, because contracts are tied together through bundles, successful overall manipulation of this type would require the manipulator to move prices in other contracts as well (that is, a manipulator cannot just move up the price of one candidate; he has to force down the prices of the other candidates, too). This generates a need for additional trading and adds to the complexity and cost of executing a manipulation strategy. An obvious question is whether IEM price manipulation is the most effective way to achieve the desired effect.

Assuming that manipulation does take place, how can it be detected? In particular, can it be distinguished from either informed trading (trades based on new information relevant to a contract's value) or noise trading (trades based on something other than new information, for instance, a need for cash or even a mistake)? Our initial investigations suggest that detecting manipulation is difficult at best. We discuss three types of potential manipulation: attempting to affect prices through fraudulent information (the usual definition of manipulation from traditional markets); undertaking market activity that attempts to create short-run distortions in prices; and undertaking market activity that attempts to create long-run distortions in prices.

First, consider manipulation defined as circulating information with an intent to move price fraudulently. To detect this we would need a way, first, to identify fraudulent releases of information; second, to show that the release was made by one of our traders; third, to show that the trader took a position surrounding the release that benefited him; and fourth, to show that all this was done with intent. As the *Drudge Report* example above shows, information released on the Internet can affect prices. However, the anonymity associated with much of the information on the Internet often makes it impossible for us to associate such releases with our traders. Furthermore, taking positions with respect to news, as a manipulator would, might also be the optimal response of an astute trader. (Who wouldn't sell on rumors of an "intern problem" if there were some chance that the rumors were true?) So, identifying this type of manipulation is extremely difficult at best.

Next, consider market activity that attempts to distort prices in the short run. Such behavior consists of traders' actions in the market (which we observe) that are at odds with traders' private beliefs (which we cannot observe). We have not had traders announce in advance that they plan to manipulate prices, though we have seen a blog entry laying claim to an IEM Kerry price run-up and subsequent reversal on the first day of the 2004 Republican National Convention. As other bloggers were quick to point out, such claims are cheap talk after the luxury of observing the price sequence.

Finally, consider attempts to distort prices in the long run. Because IEM contracts are tied to events that are actually observed, successful manipulation permanently distorting prices would be detected in the accuracy tests of IEM prices. We do not detect such effects. That the IEM is accurate supports the argument that even attempts at permanent manipulation, if they exist, must be short-lived. This suggests that one feasible way to identify manipulation attempts is to look for price reversals. Such examinations are hampered by not knowing the time horizon over which to look. Because election cycles are characterized by many news events, price changes over relatively long horizons are not unusual, making it difficult to tell whether individual traders are engaged in market manipulation (trades or offers at odds with their beliefs) or simply have changed their beliefs on the basis of new information.

This leaves us looking for short-term price reversals as signals of manipulation. But short-term price reversals indicate failed attempts to manipulate the market. Furthermore, these reversals could be reactions to rumors and subsequent corrections, as occurred in the 2004 election day trades. Short-term price reversals could also indicate trader error or incorporation of information that later changes. For instance, our investigation of Buchanan prices during the 1996 primary revealed a second price run-up of about $0.04 that was reversed later in the day. This price change was caused by several new traders placing large orders for Buchanan contracts. Was it a manipulation attempt? Several factors confound this observation: Because the traders were new, they were also the participants most likely to make errors, and the trades occurred the same Tuesday as the Republican primaries in Arizona, North Dakota, and South Dakota. We cannot distinguish whether the trades were the result of trader error, an attempt to manipulate market prices, or reaction to early but erroneous exit polls.

An examination of trades that occurred on the first day of the 2004 Republican National Convention reveals a similarly ambiguous result.

Beginning at about 10:00 p.m. CDT, the spread between Democratic and Republican winner-takes-all contracts started to shrink. By midnight CDT, the contracts were equally priced.[47] By 2:00 a.m. CDT, prices returned to their previous levels, with Republicans leading Democrats. An investigation showed that many traders were involved in the trades that took place, eliminating the "single manipulator" explanation. So, what caused the price change—a manipulation conspiracy, a temporary adverse reaction to something that happened during the convention (for example, Senator Zell Miller's speech or the Bush daughters' presentation), or some Internet rumor?

Screening for large orders is similarly unproductive. For example, Strumpf (as reported by Wolfers and Zitzewitz) claimed he attempted to manipulate the IEM 2000 presidential election market prices by placing "random" large orders.[48] In this market, 685 large (500 or more unit) orders were submitted by 113 different traders (including Strumpf). Increasing the minimum order size to 750 units reduces the number of flagged orders to 522 orders by eighty-eight different traders, but also eliminates Strumpf from the trader set.

Structural features of IEM markets may also limit the possibility of price manipulation. Recall that individual trader investments are limited to $500 so that each trader represents only a small part of the funds invested in the IEM (the total dollar amount invested in the 2004 IEM markets was about $360,000). In addition, the IEM's fixed-price bundles allow supplies to expand or contract and provide the opportunity for low-cost arbitrage of contract mispricing. Information features of the election may also limit price manipulation by limiting the informational advantage held by particular traders. No single individual or small group of individuals controls the actual election outcome, so none will have perfect private information.

In summary, we do not find strong evidence of successful price manipulation in the IEM. In fact, we cannot differentiate between large orders placed in error and failed attempts at manipulation. Nor can we differentiate between the results of informed trading and successful manipulation in the short run. The long-run accuracy of the IEM suggests that long-run manipulation does not occur or succeed. Nevertheless, because the benefits, costs, and ease of manipulation are likely to vary across prediction-market settings, insights from the IEM may have limited generalizability to other prediction-market settings. The extent to which the prediction market can be manipulated and the circumstances under which traders may attempt and, possibly, succeed in manipulation are important open questions that require further study.

Why/When Are Prices Accurate? In order for prediction markets to be valuable forecasting tools, users need to know when they are likely to be accurate in both absolute and relative terms. For example, if the role of markets is simply to find the average of traders' beliefs, incentive-compatible survey techniques could be just as accurate. Gruca, Berg, and Cipriano report the results of movie box office receipt markets conducted by the IEM.[49] In many of those markets, traders were also required to prepare individual forecasts before participating in them. Predictions constructed from market prices and the average forecast of traders were generally not statistically different. But the variance of the market predictions was much smaller than that of trader forecasts. One limitation in interpreting these results is that forecasts were all prepared before market prices were observed, so the reduction in variance could be attributable to more public information being available before the market opened.

Berg and Rietz propose a more systematic investigation of the factors influencing the relative accuracy of prediction-market prices in a series of experiments designed to compare individual forecasts, Delphi forecasts, and market forecasts.[50] Because both Delphi techniques and markets allow traders to revise their beliefs, these experiments enable the experimenters to isolate the effects of incentives, feedback, and underlying information structure. Note that all three of these factors are confounded in traditional IEM markets: Prices provide both feedback and incentives, and the underlying information structure is not controlled by (and often unknown to) the experimenter.

Berg and Rietz posit that information structure will be an important determinant of whether markets outperform simple averages of individual forecasts, Delphi forecasts, or both.[51] Three information structures are examined: public information where each trader interprets the public information with noise, private information where a subset of traders has perfect information, and private information where traders have different pieces of information. Results from these experiments are not yet available.

What Are the Characteristics of the "Marginal Trader"? Forsythe, Nelson, Neumann, and Wright,[52] Forsythe, Rietz, and Ross,[53] and Oliven and Rietz[54] document that "marginal traders," or "market-making traders," appear to be responsible for the accuracy of IEM prices. But who these traders are and exactly why they drive market efficiency remains largely a mystery. Identifying the characteristics of traders who appear to be crucial to market accuracy should enable market administrators to create prediction-market trader pools more likely to result in accurate prices. But Forsythe, Nelson, Neumann, and Wright can say only that all their marginal traders are men.[55] Because most traders in the 1988 IEM markets were men, this result could be coincidence. Oliven and Rietz document that even more market-makers tend to be men, that they tend to be more highly educated than the already overwhelmingly male and highly educated trader population, and that they tend to be more experienced than average traders. Nevertheless, they also document a "low power to discriminate" between who will take on the role of market-maker—it is simply hard to tell who will be a market-maker.[56]

Barrick, Berg, Rietz, and Stewart take a different approach, investigating whether psychological and behavioral factors that appear to influence job performance also influence trading performance. In their study, IEM traders complete surveys that are traditionally used in job performance research. Traders' personality profiles are then compared to trading performance. The study is still in progress and has not yet reported results.[57]

Conclusion

What do we know about prediction markets? They appear to "work." Prices seem intertemporally efficient and forecast well both just before an event and well in advance of the event, both in absolute and in relative terms. Prices respond extremely quickly to news. But exactly how prediction markets become efficient is something of a mystery. Traders are biased and mistake-prone and are a nonrepresentative sample of the population. Some are not even human—they are robots that trade according to what must be technical rules. Price efficiency seems to be driven by marginal traders who are somehow more rational than average, but identifying such traders in advance is problematic.

Our state of knowledge today leaves many open questions about prediction markets and when they are likely to be most accurate. To date, no theoretical model exists that incorporates the features of the IEM that seem crucial to its accuracy and is consistent with observed trader behavior in these markets. Although we do not see strong evidence of manipulation, and the efficiency of prices argues against widespread long-run manipulation, we cannot rule it out. It seems difficult to detect in context. Nevertheless, as the use of prediction markets becomes more widespread, especially in the formulation of policy, the questions of whether they can be manipulated and how manipulation can be detected become important. We also think a more systematic investigation of accuracy is needed as prediction markets are used for wider ranges of applications. In particular, although marginal traders appear to drive results in IEM election markets, will they continue to do so in smaller markets?

In summary, the IEM markets continue to provide a rich institutional and informational environment in which to study the behavior of prediction markets. Understanding these markets has benefited by both theory and laboratory experiments, and future theory and experiments will undoubtedly benefit by information learned in the IEM.

Notes

1. For reviews, see Joyce Berg, Robert Forsythe, Forrest Nelson, and Thomas Rietz, "Results from a Dozen Years of Election Futures Markets Research," in *Handbook of Experimental Economics Results*, ed. Charles Plott and Vernon Smith (Elsevier, forthcoming); Justin Wolfers and Eric Zitzewitz, "Prediction Markets," *Journal of Economic Perspectives* 18, no. 2 (2004): 107–26.

2. Paul Milgrom and Nancy Stokey, "Information, Trade, and Common Knowledge," *Journal of Economic Theory* 26 (1982): 17–27.

3. Robert Forsythe, Forrest D. Nelson, George R. Neumann, and Jack Wright, "Anatomy of an Experimental Political Stock Market," *American Economic Review* 82 (1992): 1142–61; Robert Forsythe, Thomas Rietz, and Thomas Ross, "Wishes, Expectations, and Actions: A Survey on Price Formation in Election Stock Markets," *Journal of Economic Behavior and Organization* 39, no. 1 (1999): 83–110; Kenneth Oliven and Thomas Rietz, "Suckers Are Born, but Markets Are Made: Individual Rationality, Arbitrage and Market Efficiency on an Electronic Futures Market," *Management Science* 50, no. 3 (2004): 336–51.

4. BoCowgill.com, http://bocowgill.com/2004/08/prediction-market-pump and-dump.html (accessed August 18, 2004); Wolfers and Zitzewitz, "Prediction Markets," 107–26.

5. Joyce Berg, Forrest D. Nelson, and Thomas A. Rietz, "Accuracy and Forecast Standard Error of Prediction Markets" (working paper, University of Iowa, Iowa City, Iowa, 2003).

6. Ibid.

7. Vernon L. Smith, "Experimental Economics: Behavioral Lessons for Microeconomic Theory and Policy" (Nancy L. Schwartz Memorial Lecture, J. L. Kellogg Graduate School of Management, Northwestern University, Evanston, Ill., 1990), 2–3.

8. The IEM began conducting earnings forecast, corporate stock returns, and economic indicator markets in 1993. Movie markets based on individual movie four-week box office receipts were begun in 1995. Since that time, commercial exchanges have created similar event markets. See as examples the Goldman Sachs Economic Derivatives markets, the HedgeStreet markets (which incorporate the IEM innovation of using bundles), the Hollywood Stock Exchange (HSX) markets (a "fake-money" market trading IEM-like contracts on box office receipts as well as other contracts), and TradeSports (an online betting operation that has incorporated IEM-like contracts on political events, sometimes even duplicating IEM contracts).

9. The IEM first introduced conditional contracts in the 1996 presidential-election vote-share market. Berg and Rietz describe how prices from these conditional contracts consistently indicated that Dole was a poor choice to run against Clinton (in Joyce Berg and Thomas Rietz, "Prediction Markets as Decision

Support Systems," *Information Systems Frontiers* 5, no. 1 (2003): 79–93). This information could have been used to inform the choice of Republican nominee.

10. There is no theoretical reason the functional form needs to be restricted to one that is linear. Any function that will give an understandable, known, unique relationship between outcomes and payments and that bounds payments appropriately would do. In fact, in many cases the payoff functions used by the IEM are "flat" (bounded at 0 or 1) when the associated event measure is outside a prespecified range. For example, the IPO_UP contract in the Google IPO Market Capitalization Linear Market had a payoff specified as $0 if the IPO did not take place by March 31, 2005 (market cap in billions)/(100 billion), if the market cap was above $0 billion but less than or equal to $100 billion, and $1 if the market cap was above $100 billion. Such contract forms complicate the interpretation of prices. The IEM typically uses linear contracts because their payoff function is simple to explain to traders and because the informational interpretation of price is straightforward.

11. Later we will argue that, under the right conditions, prices will do more than reflect expectations; they will equal expected values.

12. In some markets used primarily for classroom purposes, students may be required to trade as part of their class assignments.

13. Some markets are open to academic traders only. Though developed primarily for classroom purposes, those markets also provide data for prediction-market research.

14. Though there is a higher percentage of nonacademic traders in the winner-takes-all markets, the percentages of dollar volume traded by trader type do not differ much between the two 2004 election markets. In the winner-takes-all market, 71 percent of purchases and 58 percent of sales were by nonacademic traders. In the vote-share market, 73 percent of purchases and 64 percent of sales were by nonacademic traders. The asymmetry in purchases versus sales reflects the fact that when trades involve one academic trader and one nonacademic trader, the academic trader is more likely to be on the sell side of the transaction.

15. As discussed above, prior to the determination of Kerry as the nominee, additional contracts corresponding to different potential nominees traded in this market.

16. Because cash in the traders' accounts does not earn interest, the return to holding the riskless asset is zero.

17. In essence, this is simply short-selling with a margin account in which cash covers the trader's position to the worst possible outcome.

18. Berg, Nelson, and Rietz, in "Accuracy and Forecast," document this "nonrandom sample" phenomenon for U.S. election markets prior to the 2004 election.

19. Forsythe, Nelson, Neumann, and Wright, "Anatomy of an Experimental Political Stock Market"; Forsythe, Rietz, and Ross, "Wishes, Expectations, and Actions."

20. Oliven and Rietz, "Suckers Are Born."

21. Donald Granberg and Edward Brent, "When Prophecy Bends: The Preference-Expectation Link in U.S. Presidential Elections," *Journal of Personality and Social Psychology* 45 (1983): 477–91.

22. Ola Svenson, "Are We All Less Risky and More Skillful than Our Fellow Drivers?" *ACTA Psychologica* 47, no. 2 (1981): 143–48.

23. A robot trader is a computer program that executes trades according to a predefined set of rules (a type of trading sometimes referred to as "programmed trading" in markets such as the New York Stock Exchange). We have three primary means to identify robot traders. First, they are sometimes revealed by their creators' asking whether there is a rule against robot traders (to date there is not). Second, they frequently use their own interface for accessing our markets rather than using our web pages. Reading our Internet server logs allows us to detect these differences. Finally, robot traders can process trades more quickly than human traders because they do not need to type their requests. So, we can detect robots by examining the speed and frequency with which orders are submitted to the markets.

24. Oliven and Rietz, "Suckers Are Born."

25. Thomas A. Rietz, "Behavioral Mispricing and Arbitrage in Experimental Asset Markets" (working paper, University of Iowa, Iowa City, June 2005).

26. We count only orders entered before midnight, November 1. On election day, we would expect and do observe orders crossing the queues in order to take advantage of the arrival of new, definitive information about the outcome of the election.

27. This was on the contract that would pay off $1 if Bush took more than 50 and less than 52 percent of the popular vote. The price moved from $0.223 to $0.333 on September 28 at 9:54 p.m. CDT. Prices fell back to $0.227 at 10:55 p.m. CDT, and the contract closed at $0.210 at midnight CDT.

28. This was on the contract that would pay off $1 if Bush took more than 52 percent of the popular vote. The price moved from $0.461 to $0.423 on September 30 at 5:24 p.m. CDT. The price had gone back up to $0.468 at 5:25 p.m. CDT and closed at $0.485 at midnight CDT.

29. Berg, Forsythe, Nelson, and Rietz, "Results from a Dozen Years."

30. Ibid.

31. Berg, Nelson, and Rietz, in "Accuracy and Forecast," analyze 596 national polls conducted while the 1988, 1992, 1996, and 2000 IEM election markets were open. Compared to contemporaneous IEM prices, 76 percent of the polls examined were less accurate in forecasting election outcomes than IEM prices.

32. Most IEM winner-takes-all markets do not have linear markets associated with the same event. Thus, it is not clear from IEM data alone what role is played by conducting both markets simultaneously.

33. Joyce Berg and Thomas Rietz, "Longshots, Overconfidence, and Efficiency on the Iowa Electronic Market" (working paper, University of Iowa, Tippie College of Business, Iowa City, January 2002).

34. Ibid.

35. Note that when market prices assess the probability of a Republican getting the most-popular vote at 90 percent (and therefore the corresponding probability of a Democratic getting the most-popular vote at 10 percent), the spread statistic will be measured as 0.80 percentage points. Note also that the traders are forecasting popular-vote share and not electoral votes, so they must translate state-by-state announcements into a popular-vote forecast.

36. The evidence on trading activity from Forsythe, Nelson, Neumann, and Wright, "Anatomy of an Experimental Political Stock Market," and from Forsythe, Rietz, and Ross, "Wishes, Expectations, and Actions," is consistent with this. Traders who seem to have a vested interest in the election hold all-or-nothing positions in contracts. The remaining price-setting traders are less likely to have significant marginal utility differences across states.

37. Karl Borch, "The Safety Loading of Reinsurance Premiums," *Skandinavisk Aktuarietidskrift* 43 (1960): 163–84.

38. Yaffa Caspi, "Optimum Allocation of Risk in a Market with Many Traders," in *Allocation under Uncertainty: Equilibrium and Optimality*, ed. Jacques H. Dréze (London: Macmillan Press, 1974), 89–97.

39. Edmond Malinvaud, "The Allocation of Individual Risks in Large Markets," in *Allocation under Uncertainty: Equilibrium and Optimality*, ed. Jacques H. Dréze (London: Macmillan Press, 1974), 110–25.

40. Milgrom and Stokey, "Information, Trade, and Common Knowledge."

41. The remaining 11 percent reported some other strategy. These survey results are preliminary. The survey was administered after the close of the 2004 election markets. As a result, our response rate is low relative to our other survey response rates. We are trying to increase sample size by sending traders e-mail requests to complete the survey.

42. We use twenty and one hundred contracts as cutoffs because the average trader investment is about $200. Holding twenty contracts represents putting about $10 (5 percent of the investment) at risk, and holding one hundred contracts represents putting about $50 (25 percent of the investment) at risk.

43. Rietz, "Behavioral Mispricing and Arbitrage." Unlike the IEM, which has instantaneous conversions of cash and bundles, Rietz had a fixed supply of bundles trading in a separate market. In contrast to the IEM, this resulted in many arbitrage opportunities between cash and bundles. There were few arbitrage opportunities between bundles and contracts in the laboratory markets, however.

44. Wolfers and Zitzewitz, "Prediction Markets."

45. For examples, see "Trading Manipulation at TradeSports and IEM," October 28, 2004, http://www.freerepublic.com/focus/f-chat/1259678/posts (accessed January 31, 2006), and "More on Manipulated Markets," October 18, 2004, http://www.chicagoboyz.net/archives/002497.html (accessed January 31, 2006).

46. In fact, our response to one individual was subsequently posted on a political blog. See "The Iowa Electronic Markets," September 2, 2004, http://www.freerepublic.com/focus/f-news/1205670/posts (accessed January 31, 2006).

47. It was this price change that caused observers to write to the IEM office claiming that prices were being manipulated.

48. Wolfers and Zitzewitz, "Prediction Markets." One can question whether "random" orders can be considered manipulation attempts. Such orders seem more akin to noise trading (generally a desirable feature in markets) than deliberate manipulation.

49. Thomas Gruca, Joyce Berg, and Michael Cipriano, "Consensus and Differences of Opinion in Electronic Prediction Markets," *Electronic Markets* 15, no. 1 (February 2005): 13–22.

50. Joyce Berg and Thomas Rietz, "Aggregating Information: A Comparison of Prediction Markets and Delphi Techniques" (University of Iowa, Iowa City, 2004).

51. Ibid.

52. Forsythe, Nelson, Neumann, and Wright, "Anatomy of an Experimental Political Stock Market."

53. Forsythe, Rietz, and Ross, "Wishes, Expectations, and Actions."

54. Oliven and Rietz, "Suckers Are Born."

55. Forsythe, Nelson, Neumann, and Wright, "Anatomy of an Experimental Political Stock Market."

56. Oliven and Rietz, "Suckers Are Born."

57. Murray Barrick, Joyce Berg, Thomas Rietz, and Gregory Stewart, "Personality and Trading" (University of Iowa, Tippie College of Business, Iowa City, 2004).

8

A New Tool for Promoting Economic Development

Robert W. Hahn and Paul C. Tetlock

"Our Dream is a World Free of Poverty" reads the sign at the entrance of World Bank headquarters. How can we achieve that goal? The short answer is that no one is certain. But there is a way to improve substantially on the basic model for economic development—using a new kind of market combined with paying for performance.

Not too long ago, foreign aid was viewed as a path to economic growth for the developing world. In some quarters, most notably the development banks and the United Nations, it still is. But there is dissension among the ranks. Scholars have been chipping away at the aid-buys-growth paradigm for more than thirty years—with some going so far as to suggest that state aid could actually hurt the poorest of the poor.[1] Over the past decade, a revisionist view asserts that foreign aid can be helpful, but only if countries pursue good policies. So, if a country has good domestic economic policies and open trade, aid can help; but it does little in the presence of poor policies.[2] Some scholars have even questioned this view, noting that measuring the impact of foreign aid depends on the definitions of such terms as "aid," "policies," and "growth."[3]

Foreign aid consists of labor and capital that flow to particular countries. The real question is how to spend aid wisely. This is a difficult

The authors thank Katrina Kosec and Rohit Malik for research assistance. This chapter represents the views of the authors and does not necessarily represent the views of the institutions with which they are affiliated. The chapter expands on some ideas presented by the authors in "Making Development Work: Using Markets to Improve Performance," *Policy Review*, no. 132 (August and September 2005): 27–38.

question because it involves trying to get governments that may be near-sighted or corrupt to take a longer view and think about investing in such areas as education, health, and roads, instead of squandering resources on wasteful activities. One can point to several success stories in getting developing countries to clean up their acts, but failures are numerous.

The potentially perverse incentives of aid are well known.[4] Recipient governments that use aid productively may not receive any more. Aid bureaucracies that solve problems effectively could put themselves out of a job. These perverse incentives prevent policymakers from spending aid wisely. Furthermore, like many government programs that give out money, aid programs rarely evaluate how well the aid is actually spent. The Meltzer Commission notes, for example, that three to ten years after final disbursement, the World Bank reviews the broad policy impact of just 5 percent of its programs.[5]

To some extent, these problems can be overcome by setting up rules for giving out aid. One rule currently in vogue is that aid be given to really poor countries that promote good policies in general.[6] Another is to make sure that aid actually does what it is intended to do by paying the project implementers on the basis of actual results. While both may make sense, both have problems. By giving aid only to well-behaved, poor countries, donor countries may have to write off a large part of the developing world. Paying for performance sounds great in theory, but it may not be practical.

Still, the problems in developing countries are too important to be ignored. In 2000, an estimated 2.7 billion people were living on less than $2 a day.[7] These people could potentially benefit from aid from rich countries and international institutions. A key question is how to make the best use of it.

This chapter offers a new approach to economic development, which we call performance-based policy (PBP). The basic idea is to obtain better information to implement better development decisions. The approach combines the use of information markets with payments for performance. An information market is a market for a contract that yields a payment based on the outcome of an uncertain future event, such as the number of people who will be infected by HIV in Africa in 2010. We suggest using these markets to help provide real-time information on the likely benefits and costs of different development projects.

A New Development Model

Aid agencies want to spend their limited resources wisely, but they frequently fall short. To allocate resources to their most highly valued uses and get the maximum bang for each aid dollar spent, an agency needs to do two things: get reasonable information on the likely costs and benefits of different projects, and implement projects effectively.

Consider one example of how to implement a project effectively. Suppose an aid agency is interested in getting children vaccinated to prevent the outbreak of a disease in Malawi, and suppose that the recipient government or the agency decides the value is worth $5 for each child vaccinated.[8] The agency can then auction off the right to administer the vaccinations to the highest bidder. That bidder receives $5 for each child vaccinated, where the number of children vaccinated would be measured by a third-party auditor.[9]

This is an example of paying for performance. The government gives out the performance contract and waits to see if the winning bidder will deliver. The winning bidder gets paid on the basis of what he delivers.

While there is much to be said for paying for performance, there is even more to be said for paying for performance when all parties have a good sense of what they are likely to get *before* the project gets started. In particular, such information can help an aid agency allocate its limited resources to its most highly valued uses—no small feat if it can be accomplished. This is where information markets can help, by providing information on the likely benefits of a project before things get underway.

Let's say a trading exchange facilitates trading in a contract that pays $0.01 for each child who will be vaccinated under the vaccination program, and that the current price of that contract is $1.00. This price implies that market participants expect that one hundred children will be vaccinated if the program goes into effect (100 times $0.01 equals $1.00). The ultimate value of the contract is determined by the actual number of children vaccinated by the end of the program. So, if 110 children get vaccinated, then the final contract value is $1.10.

This is a simple example of an information market. These markets allow informed parties to trade contracts that yield payments on the basis of the outcome of an uncertain future event, such as the number of children who would be vaccinated if the vaccination program were auctioned off to the highest bidder.

Now, suppose the same exchange offers another contract, which pays \$0.01 for each child vaccinated if there is no vaccination program in place. Furthermore, suppose the price of that contract is \$0.10, which means the market expects that ten children will be vaccinated if the program does not go into effect.

Using this market pricing information, we can estimate the benefits of the vaccination program. The market estimates that one hundred children will get vaccinated with the program, and only ten will get vaccinated without it. So, the program is expected to vaccinate an additional ninety children. Valued at \$5 per child, the expected monetary benefits are \$450 in this example.[10]

Note that the information markets can provide a way of distinguishing total vaccinations from those that would likely have taken place anyway. This ability to distinguish is a valuable feature of these markets that was not available up to this point, except by relying on so-called experts. It permits the aid agency, the host government, or both to assess the incremental impact of a program by determining how many additional children the program is likely to vaccinate. Implicitly, we are assuming that the market prices of the information market contracts are not affected by the government's reliance on these prices in implementing its decisions. If traders anticipate the government's use of the prices, they will recognize that only programs with higher benefits will be implemented. This will alter their willingness to buy information market contracts on the basis of policy benefits, potentially biasing the resulting prices and the government's decision based on them.

In subsequent work, we propose a mechanism that deals with this concern by separating the information-collection and decision tasks. Specifically, if the information market contracts do not depend on the government's decision rule, then their prices will be unbiased measures of benefits that can be used by the government. The idea is to have the contract settlement depend on the benefits from a random decision, but commit to using this random decision rule only infrequently. Most of the time, the government can simply implement its preferred policy, using the unbiased prices as a guide.

To see the problem caused by this bias and how it can be solved, consider again the child vaccination example. The problem with the mechanism is that the vaccination program will be implemented only if an organization is willing to bid on the project. This will not happen if, for example, no organization anticipates being able to implement the project at a cost of $450 or lower. If traders know that no firm will implement the project, they will not bother trading the information market contract whose payoff depends on benefits that will never be realized.[11]

Traders will trade the contracts linked to project benefits only if they expect the project will probably be implemented. Unfortunately, however, the price might be biased. For example, if a trader has information that the project is overvalued at the current price, he may hesitate to bet against it to the extent that he otherwise might, for fear that the price of the contract would decline to the point where the project is not chosen. In that case, his contract would be worthless. Similar concerns apply to the information market for vaccinations that would occur even without the project.[12]

To avoid this bias, a decision-maker can commit to implementing the vaccination program with at least some probability, say 5 percent, regardless of what information is revealed by the market price. Because a trader's payoffs no longer depend on the decision-maker's choice, the bias described above will be eliminated. Most of the time (95 percent), the decision-maker can still choose whether to implement the vaccination program. The disadvantage is that the decision-maker must sometimes choose the vaccination program when this choice will not yield the highest expected net benefits. This situation would arise no more than 5 percent of the time, and it may be a price that the decision-maker is willing to pay for the ability to implement an informed and unbiased decision at least 95 percent of the time.

We now have an estimate of the benefits of the program, which could be useful for both the host country and the aid agency—but only if the numbers tell us something meaningful. What can we say about the quality of estimates that come from information markets? The short answer is that information markets appear to do better than experts in a number of settings. For example, Las Vegas odds and point spreads have predicted the outcomes of sporting events better than sports experts. The prices in Iowa political markets were more accurate than the polls in forecasting elections 451 out of 596 times. Information markets at Hewlett-Packard Labs beat official forecasts of printer sales fifteen out of sixteen times. Even

Hollywood play-money markets have performed better than four out of five columnists in predicting the Oscars.[13]

These markets work for several reasons. First, almost anyone can participate. Second, they allow a person to profit from trading contracts that accurately forecast the future; buying when the vaccination forecast is low and selling when the forecast is high can result in profits. Third, the profit motive encourages people, including speculators, to look for better information all the time. So, the market price reflects a lot of information from diverse sources, resulting in what James Surowiecki calls "the wisdom of crowds."[14]

Besides getting data on expected benefits, the aid agency would like to know the expected net benefits of the vaccination project. A measure of expected net benefits could be obtained by conducting a pay-for-performance auction in which contractors are invited to bid for the right to implement a program to increase vaccinations and to receive $5 for each additional child who was vaccinated. The baseline vaccination rate could be determined by the level predicted in the information market with no change in policy—ten children, in this example.[15]

Note that there would be no bids unless at least one bidder expected to be able to increase vaccinations at a cost of less than $5 per child. The auction price should represent the difference between what the winning firm gets from producing results, in this case social benefits, and the costs of producing those results. In other words, the auction price is an estimate of social benefits. Suppose the auction price is $300, and the agency has decided to award the contract to the highest bidder, so long as the bid suggests there are net benefits.

We now have a measure of expected benefits and expected net benefits. With these measures, we can also estimate the cost to the development agency or state footing the bill. The payout, on the basis of expected benefits, is $450. The expected net benefits based on the auction are $300. Taking the difference yields the expected cost of the project to the agency—$150.[16]

Now we have three pieces of information that we did not have before: an estimate of benefits from the vaccination program, an estimate of net benefits, and an estimate of costs to the agency. This information is critical for the agency in making a decision on whether to fund the project. And even if these estimates turn out to be imperfect, they are generally better than those of experts.

Furthermore, the information on the vaccination program is not just available to the agency or the host government. It is available to everyone. That means the government can use it to choose wisely; potential bidders can base their bids on better information; and others can use it to assess whether the government's proposed policy is likely to do what it claims. The information from these markets is likely to promote greater openness and accountability.

Information markets also have another advantage in the context of development. They can help the winning firm with project financing, thereby encouraging competition in an area where ventures are often very risky. If the winning bidder for the vaccination project sells some information contracts to raise money, it can both reduce its risk and cover some of the costs of the project.

The vaccination example was based on a classic model of aid that comes from a state-sponsored institution like the World Bank, the United Nations, or the U.S. Agency for International Development (USAID). In some cases, the cost of the project may be split between the recipient country and the aid donor. Note, however, that the example could just as easily be applied to the private sector or to foundations.

Suppose, for example, the Gates Foundation is considering offering a performance contract that gives $1,000 for each case of HIV infection that was avoided in sub-Saharan Africa before 2010. The foundation could go through exactly the same exercise as we did for vaccinations. This would yield information on the likely benefits from the project in terms of reduced infection rates, the cost to the foundation of paying for results, and the cost to the firm or nongovernmental organization of implementing the project. It could then decide whether this project is worth doing in comparison with other worthy social projects.[17]

We have just addressed two big problems that confront all decision-makers who want to give out aid. Information markets can provide the aid agency and the host government with information about the likely effects from decision alternatives. And performance-based contracts can ensure that the contractor is paid for what he actually delivers. Now, let us consider how these ideas can be applied to a broad range of development problems.

Setting Development Priorities: The Copenhagen Consensus

To illustrate the power of performance-based policy in setting priorities, consider the Copenhagen Consensus, a high-powered attempt at prioritizing solutions to the world's most pressing problems. In May 2004, a group of eight distinguished economists, including three Nobel laureates, assembled in Copenhagen to see whether they could achieve consensus on the best ways to meet the biggest challenges. To make the problem interesting, they assumed that governments had $50 billion to spend.[18]

The panel of economic experts considered thirty proposals that addressed ten great global challenges, and ranked them on the basis of economic costs and benefits.[19] The panel found that information for thirteen of the proposals was too sparse for a judgment to be made, and so excluded them from the ranking.

The economists were able to rank the remaining seventeen proposals from "bad" to "very good." The "very good" category included investments in controlling HIV/AIDS and malaria, reducing malnutrition, and promoting free trade. The "bad" category included investments in slowing climate change and employing workers in a guest-workers program.[20]

This precise categorization, although important, is not our focus. Instead, we wish to illustrate the potential power and limitations of using information markets for improving cost-benefit analysis, using the Copenhagen Consensus as a starting point.

The experts based their rankings on their estimates of economic and social net benefits from different projects. To develop these estimates, they relied on their collective wisdom, papers written by other experts, and criticisms of those papers written by yet other experts. There is nothing wrong with that approach. It may even be the best approach if one is forced to rely on experts.

But there are two critical problems with the expert model adopted by the Copenhagen Consensus, both of which could be addressed by properly designed information markets. First, the experts have access to only a subset of the information available to the potential traders in information markets. The likelihood of success for many of the proposed policy interventions depends on information privately held by consumers, businesses, nongovernmental organizations, and other interested parties. It is virtually impossible for a group of experts to replicate the information-aggregation abilities of market prices—a point Hayek made more than half a century ago in his critique of central planning.[21]

Second, the Copenhagen Consensus experts had no financial incentive to make accurate estimates. Although we do not dispute their motives, we caution against relying on experts for advice when it is costless for them to speak from their hearts and not from their heads, though they may not be conscious of doing so. There is considerable psychological evidence showing that experts' predictions are subject to cognitive biases, and that they perform poorly relative to simple statistical models.[22] By contrast, information markets offer powerful financial incentives to overcome such biases. Experts and others bold enough to bet on their personal beliefs or preferences would incur large costs from inaccuracy.[23]

We went through all the social policies ranked by the Copenhagen experts and found that information market contracts could help provide guidance on most of these policies. The results are summarized in table 8-1, which lists hypothetical information market contracts based on sixteen categories of policy interventions. Each intervention would involve issuing a pay-for-performance contract to the winning bidder of an auction. There are two information market contracts corresponding to each possible policy: one to estimate the benefits without the policy and one to estimate the benefits with it. The price of each set of contracts would aggregate important information about the expected incremental benefits from the proposed interventions.

For example, the price of the first set of contracts described in the table provides an estimate of the effect of issuing a performance contract designed to control the spread of HIV. Suppose the Gates Foundation intends to offer the winning bidder a payment of $1,000 per reduction in HIV infections below some baseline. Prior to the auction, the price of one information market contract (for example, $4.75, indicating that 4.75 million HIV infections are expected without the policy) would tell the foundation the appropriate baseline to use in its incentive contract. The price of the other contract (for example, $3.75, indicating that 3.75 million HIV infections are expected with the policy) would give the foundation and auction bidders an idea of the expected benefits if the auction takes place.

Suppose the foundation, after seeing the expected benefits from issuing the performance contract, decides to go ahead with the auction. Then the

TABLE 8-1
COPENHAGEN CONSENSUS CONTRACTS

Proposed Activity	**Payments for Both Contracts (with and without the policy)**	**Source for Verification**
Control HIV/AIDS	$1 for each one million infections reduced below status quo	World Health Organization: World Health Report; UNAIDS: AIDS Epidemic Update
Control malaria	$1 for each case reduced below status quo (and/or reduction in infant deaths below status quo)	World Health Organization: Global Burden of Disease Estimates 2002; UNICEF: State of the World's Children
Improve basic health services	$1 for each reduction in child deaths below status quo (and/or $1 per disease case below status quo)	World Health Organization: World Development Report; World Health Organization: The World Health Report
Reduce the prevalence of iodine deficiencies	$1 for each reduction in number of children with low iodine below status quo (and/or $1 per increase in population consuming salt with twenty parts per million potassium iodide above status quo)	UNICEF: The State of the World's Children; UNICEF: Low Birth Weight Database
Reduce the prevalence of vitamin A deficiencies	$1 for each reduction in number of diarrhea or measles cases below status quo	United Nations Food and Agriculture Organization: The State of Food Insecurity in the World
Reduce the prevalence of iron deficiencies/ provide deworming for children	$1 for each increase in the wages (when they grow up) of the cohort of children who receive iron supplements/deworming, relative to the wages of a baseline cohort (and/or $1 per case treated)	UNICEF: The State of the World's Children; UNICEF: Low Birth Weight Database

(continued on next page)

(Table 8-1 continued from previous page)

Proposed Activity	Payments for Both Contracts (with and without the policy)	Source for Verification
Disseminate modern agricultural technologies	$1 for each reduction in number of anemia cases below the status quo	United Nations Food and Agriculture Organization: The State of Food Insecurity in the World
Promote breastfeeding in hospitals	$1 for each reduction in infant deaths below the status quo (and/or $1 per breastfed child above the status quo)	UNICEF: The State of the World's Children; UNICEF: Low Birth Weight Database
Improve child nutrition and care	$1 for each reduction in malnutrition cases below the status quo (and/or $1 per one-inch increase in child height)	United Nations Food and Agriculture Organization: The State of Food Insecurity in the World; UNICEF: The State of the World's Children; UNICEF: Low Birth Weight Database
Provide dietary supplements and antibiotics to pregnant women and infants	$1 for each reduction in number of neonatal deaths below the status quo (and/or $1 for each reduction in hospitalization costs for low birth weight babies below status quo)	UNICEF: The State of the World's Children; UNICEF: Low Birth Weight Database
Improve irrigation technology	$1 for each increase in crop yields above the status quo (and/or $1 for each increase in farmer net income above the status quo)	Food and Agriculture Organization of the United States Statistical Databases
Provide a community-managed, low-cost water supply	$1 for each increase in number of people with access to safe water and/or sanitation above the status quo	United Nations Development Program, United Nations Environment Program, the World Bank, and the World Resources Institute: Report on World Resources

(continued on next page)

(*Table 8-1 continued from previous page*)

Proposed Activity	Payments for Both Contracts (with and without the policy)	Source for Verification
Fund research to optimize water usage in food production	$1 for each decrease in gallons of water used per unit food production below the status quo (holding type of food constant)	Food and Agriculture Organization of the United States Statistical Databases
Lower barriers to migration for skilled workers	$1 for each one million person increase in global migrants from low- to high-income countries above the status quo	United Nations/ Department of Economic and Social Affairs/Population Division—International Migration Report
Levy a carbon tax or use emissions credits	$1 for each degree Celsius (and/ or $1 per pollutant parts per million in the atmosphere) decrease below status quo	NASA Goddard Institute for Space Studies: Global Temperature Trends Report
Liberalize trade	$1 for each increase in exports/ imports above the status quo	Organization for Economic Cooperation and Development; Economic Report of the President

SOURCES: The sources in column three can be located at the following websites:
World Health Organization: World Health Report, http://www.who.int/whr/en/
UNAIDS: AIDS Epidemic Update, http://www.who.int/hiv/pub/epidemiology/epi2003/en/index.html
WHO: Global Burden of Disease Estimates 2002, http://www.who.int/healthinfo/bodestimates/en/index.html
UNICEF: State of the World's Children, http://www.unicef.org/sowc05/english/index.html
WHO: World Development Report, www.worldbank.org/wdr/
UNICEF: LBW database, http://www.childinfo.org/eddb/lbw/database.htm
FAO (United Nations Food and Agriculture Organization): The State of Food Insecurity in the World, http://www.fao.org/sof/sofi/index_en.htm
Food and Agriculture Organization of the United States/ Statistical Databases, http://www.fao.org/
UNDP, UNEP, the World Bank, and the World Resources Institute: Report on World Resources, http://biodiv.wri.org/pubs_description.cfm?PubID=3027
United Nations/Department of Economic and Social Affairs/Population Division, International Migration Report, http://www.un.org/esa/population/publications/ittmig2002/ittmigrep2002.htm
OECD, www.oecd.org; Economic Report of the President, http://www.gpoaccess.gov/eop/index.html
(All sources accessed December 16, 2005.)

NOTE: Each row in the table describes two contracts, one that is issued if the policy is implemented and the other that is issued if the policy is not implemented. Both contracts are "when-issued," meaning trades take place when and if the contract is issued. The status quo, described in the contract payments column, is an arbitrary baseline. Any baseline would work as long as it is the same in both when-issued contracts. See text for additional details on contract design.

winning bidder will receive $1,000 per reduction in HIV infections below 4.75 million. If HIV infections fall to 3.95 million, the foundation will pay $800 million to the winning bidder for the 800,000 infections prevented. If, instead, the winning bidder does a poor job, and HIV infections actually increase by 100,000, the winning bidder will pay the foundation $100 million.[24]

In most of the cases listed in the table, there appear to be reasonable proxy measures for benefits that can be used to design information market contracts. The table highlights the importance of having accurate, verifiable measures of net benefits. If a policy intervention does not meet these criteria, then it is difficult to construct information markets that elicit a reasonable estimate of net benefits.

It is crucial that the sources for the measures in table 8-1 come from objective, widely respected organizations with transparent data-collection and decision-making processes. For international information, sources such as the United Nations, the World Bank, the World Trade Organization, and the World Health Organization meet all or most of these criteria. For domestic information, sources such as the Census Bureau, the Internal Revenue Service, the Federal Reserve, the Centers for Disease Control and Prevention, and the official government regulatory agencies meet most of these criteria. Objectivity and transparency are critical to avoid settlement disputes between counterparties to a given transaction in an information market. Such legal disputes would hinder the ability of prices to function as appropriate signals for policymakers, because agents would anticipate legal difficulties, and this expectation would be included in current prices.[25]

Although we did not show it in the table, we think it would be desirable to use more than one proxy for benefits in different cases. This is especially true when there are multiple measures of benefits, none of which clearly dominates, or when the measures of benefits are particularly uncertain. For example, it is likely that unemployment numbers from both payroll statistics and household surveys convey useful information about the true state of the economy.

In most cases, policymakers will not choose whether to implement a policy in the table based solely on its predicted effects on efficiency. Some policies with negative expected net benefits will be implemented on the basis of the argument that they enhance equity, and other policies with positive expected benefits will be dismissed because they are perceived to harm equity. Information market contracts for equity would allow policymakers to make informed decisions about the tradeoff between equity and efficiency.

To demonstrate the ability of information markets to measure equity, let us analyze the impact of one policy intervention in the table that has the potential to affect segments of the population differentially. Consider the impact of permitting skilled workers to migrate freely across national boundaries. This policy would undoubtedly cause changes in the distribution of wages in different countries. For example, it is possible that skilled workers in high-income countries would receive lower wages as the supply of skilled labor in their countries expanded.

To assess this possibility, policymakers could establish an information-market contract with a payment that depends on the wages of skilled labor. The price of this contract would measure the expected change in the fortunes of skilled laborers who might be adversely affected by an increase in labor immigration.[26] If policymakers thought this policy would also have an impact on the wages of unskilled laborers, they could introduce additional information markets to measure this change. Equipped with such measures of a policy's distributional impacts, policymakers could choose either to forgo implementation of the policy or to offset its distributional impact through targeted taxes or expenditures.

This analysis of the Copenhagen Consensus suggests that there is a great deal of knowledge to be gained by using information markets to help experts reach decisions. Sunstein suggests using them as a way of eliciting information in small groups, such as the group of experts involved in achieving the Copenhagen Consensus.[27] Surowiecki makes a similar suggestion for getting information on corporate decisions.[28] Although we believe information markets could be helpful in such groups, we also think a project on the scale of the Copenhagen Consensus could benefit from the application of information markets to a group in which anyone can participate. In some cases, providing special incentives for particular experts to participate may also prove beneficial. Each expert could be given a sum of money but be required to take a position on an issue—for example, long or short—so that her payoff is contingent on taking a position.

We would suggest the following policy experiment. Let the heads of state of leading developed countries commit a modest amount of resources to making contingent payments for one or two problems designated by a select group. One possible role for experts would be to help monetize the benefits and design the contracts for the information markets. Following our framework, the governments could implement the markets and auction the rights to the benefits from specific policies.

The experiment could be evaluated by assessing how the prices of the information market contracts change over time as the policy proposals are implemented. If the markets are functioning well, prices will follow an unpredictable path, implying that the original estimates of benefits were unbiased. It will also be important to assess whether the firms implementing the projects realize excessive profits, in order to determine if the process of auctioning net benefits is effective. Finally, if the information markets do a good job of forecasting realized benefits, and the auctions raise sufficient revenue, then the governments should consider running the experiment on a larger scale.[29]

Rethinking Existing Development Efforts

In September 2000, the UN issued the "Millennium Declaration," which contained the Millennium Development Goals (MDG). The declaration identified eight broad social goals, including eradicating extreme poverty and hunger, reducing child mortality, promoting gender equality and empowering women, reducing rates of HIV and other diseases, and ensuring environmental sustainability.

The goals have received widespread support. All 191 current UN member states have agreed to try to achieve them by the year 2015, using 1990 as a reference year.[30] The World Bank has signed on and displays all the goals prominently in the lobby of its Washington, D.C., headquarters.[31]

Several organizations are allocating considerable resources to achieving the MDG. In 2003, the World Bank spent $18.5 billion and did work in more than one hundred developing countries.[32] In late 2002, USAID announced that it would begin "monitoring and tracking all of its development assessment through the lens of the Millennium Development Goals,"[33] and in 2003 provided $14.2 billion in assistance.[34]

One problem with the goals, recognized by the UN, is that they lack specificity. For example, what does it mean to eradicate extreme poverty? To make them operational, the UN published targets associated with each goal and indicators associated with each target. Eighteen targets provide verifiable measures of achievement, while forty-eight indicators measure progress toward the targets.[35] Under the goal of eradicating poverty, for example, there is a target of halving, between 1990 and 2015, the proportion of people who earn less than $1 per day. One of the indicators for this target is the proportion of the population earning below $1 per day, using an exchange rate based on purchasing power parity. The United Nations keeps data on how well individual countries are progressing on these indicators.

Although the UN's approach is ambitious, it has two big problems. First, very little attention has been given to setting feasible goals that could maximize net benefits. Second, very little attention has been given to implementing policies in the most effective manner.

It should come as no surprise, then, that even the agencies charged with helping to achieve the goals, such as the World Bank, suggest that the MDG may not be achieved unless considerably more resources are devoted to the task. A 2002 World Bank study estimated that the world would require an additional $40 billion to $70 billion of development assistance per year to meet the MDG by 2015.[36] And although progress has been made in some parts of the world, such as East Asia, sub-Saharan Africa is lagging far behind.[37]

At this point, the MDG represents little more than a wish list specifying what some well-intentioned practitioners would like to see happen. The goal-setters do not appear to have paid significant attention to the benefits and costs of different options, nor to real budget constraints, so that they could provide a realistic assessment of the feasibility of meeting the goals. And they do not appear to have given much serious thought to putting proper incentives in place to ensure that maximum benefits will be achieved for a given level of expenditure. Instead, hundreds of countries and organizations have signed on to support the goals, without any clear rewards if they are reached or penalties if they are not.

It is almost certain that the UN, or some other agency, will go through a similar goal-setting exercise in the near future. Thus, it is worth asking how the process could be improved, and in particular how performance-based policy could help. The answer is that PBP could help both in setting broad goals and in implementing them, provided there is some concrete way to measure progress.

At the top level, PBP could help with establishing priorities, in the same way that was suggested for the Copenhagen Consensus. It could provide information on the costs and benefits of different alternatives using information markets, specifically, estimates of the costs, benefits, and expected results of different development projects. For example, in the context of the vaccination example considered above, the agency might want to know the difference in the number of children vaccinated if it pays \$3 per vaccination instead of \$5. And the agency might want to compare the likely effectiveness of different programs, such as that of a program paying \$100 per reduction in infant mortality with one paying \$5 per vaccination.

Armed with such information, the UN or another agency could make reasonable decisions about allocating limited resources to their most highly valued uses. It would do so by comparing the effectiveness of different programs, basing its estimates on an assessment of their expected impact. So, the UN, or whichever organization decides to implement these programs, would get well-deserved credit (or blame) for actions that directly result from its interventions. In this way, PBP encourages accountability. It also encourages openness, because the information gained in evaluating the projects and paying for results could be made public.

The same kind of approach could be applied to domestic foreign aid programs. The United States is currently engaged in an exercise that could be tailor-made for PBP. In January 2004, Congress created the Millennium Challenge Account (MCA) as a vehicle to provide more targeted aid to developing countries. The aim of the MCA is to help developing countries that satisfy certain criteria to meet specific goals. Congress appropriated \$2.5 billion in 2004 and 2005, and President Bush's 2006 budget proposal included \$3 billion for the MCA.[38] The former head of this effort, Paul Applegarth, said the United States "will enter into a compact with MCA countries that defines responsibilities. Each compact will include clearly defined objectives, outcomes, and intermediate benchmarks. Monitoring and evaluation will be built in from the start and be ongoing throughout the program."[39]

Although the MCA's focus on performance is laudable, we are concerned that this effort could get bogged down in unnecessary paperwork and bureaucracy. Countries wishing to receive aid must submit detailed project proposals that explain the financing required and the mechanisms for evaluation. Unfortunately, a proposal may give policy-makers little information about a project's true costs and benefits. If projects cost more or yield fewer benefits than countries expect, the MCA will have wasted money.

One clear alternative to the MCA is to pay for results using PBP without introducing all the complexities of the country's eligibility requirements. For example, a country's eligibility for aid is based on whether it rules justly, invests in people, and encourages economic freedom. Yet many countries that fail to meet the requirements may need aid the most.

For example, suppose a PBP framework indicates that the net benefits of vaccinating 500,000 children in Ecuador are much greater than those from an irrigation project in Yugoslavia. In this case, the United States may want to give a contract to the vaccination company rather than the irrigation company, irrespective of which government meets the basic qualifications. Because PBP is somewhat insulated from government corruption and misuse, the MCA's complex qualification process would be unnecessary. PBP would allow the United States to aid countries with "bad policies" and still lead to good results. The key point is that PBP allows the donor to target aid to its highest valued uses without imposing conditionality, if that is what the donor wants.

Some experts in the development field argue that PBPs are not likely to be helpful because policymakers already know which projects are most valuable to society. These critics view the problem in terms of government corruption and political instability. Our view is that this is an empirical question that can only be answered by experimenting with the PBP mechanism. In any case, because the PBP framework increases accountability and transparency, it may prove to be part of the solution to the corruption problem as well.

We would argue that it is unclear in many situations which policies are best for developing nations. Thus, investing in mechanisms that provide better information up front could pay handsome dividends.

The Transition to a Performance-Based Development Paradigm

To move to a PBP paradigm for development, governments should reduce regulatory barriers to the use of information markets. Interested parties should build prototypes to determine what really works. Finally, more attention needs to be paid to how this new approach will affect various interest groups.

There is already a lot of activity in the area of information markets. Professors at the University of Iowa pioneered the use of these markets to help forecast elections in the late 1980s.[40] A website called TradeSports.com has information markets for sporting events, financial indices, political events, and legal outcomes, and Goldman Sachs supports an exchange that hosts auctions for derivatives on the basis of the value of economic indices. Furthermore, firms are approaching regulators in Washington to find out whether they can set up other markets. Hurdles have arisen because information markets are regulated under "Internet gambling" laws.

To encourage the use of information markets for improving policy, we strongly recommend that regulators distinguish between markets for gambling—such as poker—and information markets aimed at improving, say, economic development. Although there are clearly gray areas, regulators could use a number of criteria for deciding whether contracts should be allowed, including whether the contract provides useful information on a policy objective or whether it would allow interested parties to spread risk more efficiently. Thus, a market used to predict the number of vaccinations that would result from a vaccination program should be permitted without question.

The next step is to develop prototypes to learn where the approach works best. The approach we have suggested here may or may not work well in the field, but there are many alternatives. For example, Hanson has developed an automatic market-maker that has some useful properties;[41] Wolfers and Zitzewitz suggest using an approach that would take advantage of instrumental variables;[42] and we are developing an alternative mechanism that may provide better incentives for some participants to provide accurate information.

Support for basic research and the development of prototypes could be provided by foundations or international lending institutions.

Developing countries could participate in the design of prototypes. There is no magic formula for ushering in a new paradigm, but there may be some useful rules of thumb. We believe it is useful to start on a small scale to refine the model before deciding to ramp up. It will also be important to educate the public and interest groups on why this approach can lead to better decisions.

The limitations of information markets also need to be acknowledged. To work well, the PBP process needs to be relatively free of corruption. Although we recognize corruption is a serious problem in some developing countries, we think that its potential adverse impacts can be managed through a judicious choice of project and PBP design. If, for example, the host country limits parties that are eligible to implement the performance contract, this will raise the costs of implementing the project. PBP could still work in this case, but it would be more expensive than if the project were competitively bid.[43]

A second problem is that these markets require a reasonable number of motivated buyers and sellers. Liquidity cannot be assumed, and the government may want to explore ways of subsidizing liquidity if it is interested in addressing a particular problem. Moreover, it should consider focusing on projects that will have a substantial impact, after the approach has been tested.[44]

Performance-based policy also cannot work if the results of a development project cannot be defined or measured. Although some projects with unquantifiable benefits and costs may be worthwhile, we think it is important for agencies charged with development to work on finding better performance measures before they embark on large development initiatives using taxpayer dollars.

Finally, moving to a performance-based policy paradigm for development is likely to create winners and losers. This system is designed to produce results by paying for them. Some parts of the development community may be more comfortable with the status quo, precisely because they benefit from the current system and know how it works. To the extent that these groups can block change, they will need to be compensated in some way.

We have argued that combining information markets with paying for performance has the potential to improve how aid is delivered. In addition to providing economic benefits, the system will enable lawmakers to hold bureaucrats more accountable for results. And ultimately, voters will be able to hold their elected officials more accountable for expenditures on economic development. The approach is still very new, however, and more work is needed to determine its relevance to decision-making.

Notes

1. See Peter Bauer, *From Subsistence to Exchange and Other Essays* (Princeton, N.J.: Princeton University Press, 2000); and Harold Brumm, "Aid, Policies, and Growth: Bauer Was Right," *Cato Journal* 23, no. 2 (2003): 167–74.

2. Craig Burnside and David Dollar, "Aid, Policies, and Growth," *American Economic Review* 90, no. 4 (2000): 847–68.

3. See William Easterly, "Can Foreign Aid Buy Growth?" *Journal of Economic Perspectives* 17, no. 3 (2003): 23–48; Henrik Hansen and Finn Tarp, "Aid and Growth Regressions," *Journal of Development Economics* 64, no. 2 (2001): 547–70; Carl-Johan Dalgaard and Henrik Hansen, "On Aid, Growth and Good Policies," *Journal of Development Studies* 37, no. 6 (2001): 17–41; Patrick Guillamont and Lisa Chauvet, "Aid and Performance: A Reassessment," *Journal of Development Studies* 37, no. 6 (2001): 66–92; Paul Collier and Jan Dehn, "Aid, Shocks, and Growth" (Policy Research Working Paper, series 2688, World Bank, Washington, D.C., 2001); Robert Lensink and Howard White, "Are There Negative Returns to Aid?" *Journal of Development Studies* 37, no. 6 (2001): 42–65; and Paul Collier and David Dollar, "Aid Allocation and Poverty Reduction," *European Economic Review* 46, no. 8 (2002): 1475–1500.

4. Judith Tendler, *Inside Foreign Aid* (Baltimore: Johns Hopkins University Press, 1975).

5. International Financial Institution Advisory Commission, "General Principles and Recommendations for Reform," 2000, http://www.house.gov/jec/imf/meltzer.pdf (accessed December 5, 2005).

6. See World Bank/IBRD, *Assessing Aid: What Works, What Doesn't, and Why* (Oxford: Oxford University Press, 1998); World Bank, "Effective Implementation: Key to Development Impact" (World Bank Portfolio Management Task Force, July 24, 1992); and International Financial Institution Advisory Commission, "General Principles and Recommendations for Reform," http://www.house.gov/jec/imf/meltzer.pdf.

7. World Bank, "About Us: What is the World Bank?" http://web.worldbank.org/WBSITE/EXTERNAL/EXTABOUTUS/0,,contentMDK:20040558~menuPK:34559~pagePK:34542~piPK:36600,00.html (accessed December 5, 2005).

8. For an innovative vaccination proposal designed to pay for actual results, see Michael Kremer, "Making Vaccines Pay: Creative Incentives to Stop AIDS, Tuberculosis and Malaria," *Milken Institute Review* (First Quarter 2004): 42–53.

9. The International Financial Institution Advisory Commission notes that pay-for-performance contracts can also be used for building roads, increasing literacy, and improving the water supply. International Financial Institution Advisory Commission, "General Principles and Recommendations for Reform."

10. Only under certain conditions will these markets give expected values. For an illuminating discussion of this issue, see Justin Wolfers and Eric Zitzewitz,

"Prediction Markets," *Journal of Economic Perspectives* 18, no. 2 (2005): 107–26; and Charles F. Manski, "Interpreting the Predictions of Prediction Markets" (Working Paper 10359, National Bureau of Economic Research, 2004).

11. If acquiring information about project benefits is costly for traders, then this point is even more relevant.

12. Traders will not trade in this market if they anticipate the project will be implemented.

13. Charles R. Plott, "Markets and Information Gathering Tools," *Southern Economic Journal* 67, no. 1 (2000): 2–15; David M. Pennock, Finn Arup Nielsen, and C. Lee Giles, "Extracting Collective Probabilistic Forecasts from Web Games" (International Conference on Knowledge Discovery and Data Mining, San Francisco, Calif., August 26, 2001); Joyce Berg, Forrest Nelson, Robert Forsythe, and Thomas Rietz, "Results from a Dozen Years of Election Futures Markets Research" (working paper, University of Iowa, Iowa City, 2003); Robin Hanson, "Shall We Vote on Values, but Bet on Beliefs?" (working paper, George Mason University, Department of Economics, Fairfax, Va., 2003); Robert Shiller, *The New Financial Order: Risk in the 21st Century* (Princeton, N.J.: Princeton University Press, 2003); Michael Abramowicz, "Information Markets, Administrative Decision-Making, and Predictive Cost-Benefit Analysis," *University of Chicago Law Review* 71 (2004): 933–1015; James M. Pethokoukis, "All Seeing All Knowing," http://www.usnews.com/usnews/biztech/articles/040830/30forecast.htm 2004 (accessed December 5, 2005); Robert W. Hahn, "Using Information Markets to Improve Policy" (Working Paper 04-18, AEI–Brookings Joint Center, Washington, D.C., 2004); Wolfers and Zitzewitz, "Prediction Markets."

14. James Surowiecki, *The Wisdom of Crowds: Why the Many Are Smarter Than the Few and How Collective Wisdom Shapes Business, Economies, Societies and Nations* (New York: Doubleday, 2004).

15. If this information were not available, some other benchmark could be used to estimate the number of vaccinations under the status quo.

16. If the agency were constrained in what it could pay the contractor, it could set a reserve price in the auction.

17. The terms of the auction would need to be modified so that resources are allocated to those projects with the highest expected social return.

18. See "Copenhagen Consensus Results," http://www.copenhagenconsensus.com/Files/Filer/CC/Press/UK/copenhagen_consensus_result_FINAL.pdf. (accessed December 5, 2005).

19. The ten challenges, selected from a wider set of issues identified by the United Nations, were as follows: civil conflicts; climate change; communicable diseases; education; financial stability; governance; hunger and malnutrition; migration; trade reform; and water and sanitation.

20. See "Copenhagen Consensus Results," 1.

21. Freidrich A. Hayek, "The Use of Knowledge in Society," *American Economic Review* 35, no. 4 (1945): 519–30.

22. Paul Meehl, *Clinical versus Statistical Prediction: A Theoretical Analysis and Review of the Literature* (Minneapolis: University of Minnesota Press, 1954); and M. Granger Morgan and Max Henrion, *Uncertainty: A Guide to Dealing with Uncertainty in Quantitative Risk and Policy Analysis* (Cambridge: Cambridge University Press, 1990).

23. Still another problem is that the Copenhagen Consensus does not explicitly address equity issues. We discuss the potential for such markets to address equity in Hahn and Tetlock, "Using Information Markets to Improve Public Decision Making," *Harvard Journal of Law and Public Policy* (forthcoming).

24. If either the winning bidder or the Gates Foundation is concerned about an inability to fulfill its monetary obligations, it can engage in risk management strategies, such as purchasing insurance contracts.

25. If information markets become more widely used in policy decisions, then government and other entities producing data will want to take measures to avoid potential sources of corruption. The U.S. government already addresses this problem in a number of contexts because it routinely produces statistics on which markets rely.

26. In addition, the existence of a liquid market for the aggregate wages of skilled labor would allow skilled laborers to hedge the risk in the policy's uncertain impact on their wages (without posing any moral-hazard problems).

27. See Sunstein, "Group Judgments: Deliberation, Statistical Means, and Information Markets," *New York University Law Review* (forthcoming). From the abstract: "Because of their ability to aggregate privately held information, information markets [have] substantial advantages over group deliberation."

28. For an earlier suggestion that information markets can provide valuable corporate forecasts, see Surowiecki, *The Wisdom of Crowds*, and Kay-Yut Chen and Charles Plott, "Information Aggregation Mechanisms: Concept, Design, and Implementation for a Sales Forecasting Problem," unpublished, 2002, http://www.hpl .hp.com/personal/Kay-Yut_Chen/paper/ms020408.pdf (accessed January 12, 2006).

29. Alternatively, the governments may want to fund more experiments to get more information on the design of these markets.

30. United Nations Statistics Division, "Millennium Indicators Database," 2004, http://unstats.un.org/unsd/mi/mi.asp (accessed December 5, 2005); and the Third World Institute, "In Depth: The Millennium Development Goals," 2004, http://www.choike.org/nuevo_eng/informes/302.html (accessed December 5, 2005). For a list of all 191 countries, see United Nations, "List of Member States," http://www.un.org/Overview/unmember.html (accessed December 5, 2005).

31. World Bank, "About Us: What is the World Bank?"

32. Ibid.

33. InterAction, "Creating an Enabling Environment for Achieving the Millennium Development Goals," Washington, D.C., October 2, 2002, http://www.interaction.org/files.cgi/994_MDG_Symposium_Agenda.pdf (accessed December 5, 2005).

34. U.S. Agency for International Development, "Fiscal Year 2003 Performance and Accountability Report," Washington, D.C., 2003.

35. United Nations Statistics Division, "Millennium Indicators Database."

36. Devarajan Shantayanan, Margaret J. Miller, and Eric V. Swanson, "Goals for Development: History, Prospects, and Costs" (Policy Research Working Paper, series 2819, World Bank, Washington, D.C., 2002).

37. Jeffrey Sachs, "Doing the Sums on Africa," *Economist*, May 20, 2004, 19–21.

38. Brett D. Schaefer, "Congress Should Fund the Millennium Challenge Account," Executive Memorandum #963, The Heritage Foundation, http://www.heritage.org/Research/TradeandForeignAid/em963.cfm (accessed January 25, 2006).

39. Paul V. Applegarth, "Remarks by Paul V. Applegarth," World Bank Conference on Scaling Up Poverty Reduction (Washington, D.C.: World Bank, May 27, 2004).

40. Robert Forsythe, Forrest Nelson, George R. Neumann, and Jack Wright, "Anatomy of an Experimental Political Stock Market," *American Economic Review* 82, no. 5 (1992): 1142–61.

41. Hanson, "Shall We Vote on Values, but Bet on Beliefs?"

42. Wolfers and Zitzewitz, "Prediction Markets."

43. Of course, there could be collusion if the project were restricted to local bidders. This, again, would raise its cost. The funder, of course, could decide not to do the project if the cost were too high or if collusion were detected. For an excellent discussion of corruption issues, see Robert Klitgaard, *Controlling Corruption* (Berkeley and Los Angeles: University of California Press, 1988).

44. Another problem not directly addressed by our approach is the risk associated with political instability. Information markets are being developed that address these issues, however. In particular, Shiller, in *New Financial Order*, has suggested some novel approaches for hedging against variation in the growth of income across countries.

Index

About the Authors

Michael B. Abramowicz is an associate professor of law at The George Washington University Law School.

Joyce E. Berg is an associate professor of accounting at the University of Iowa, Tippie College of Business.

Robert W. Hahn is cofounder and executive director of the AEI–Brookings Joint Center for Regulatory Studies and a resident scholar at the American Enterprise Institute.

Robin D. Hanson is an associate professor of economics at George Mason University.

John O. Ledyard is the Alan and Lenabelle Davis Professor of Economics and Social Sciences at the California Institute of Technology.

Thomas A. Rietz is Hershberger Faculty Research Fellow and an associate professor of finance at the University of Iowa, Tippie College of Business.

Cass R. Sunstein is the Karl N. Llewellyn Distinguished Service Professor of Jurisprudence, Law School and Department of Political Science, University of Chicago.

Paul C. Tetlock is an assistant professor of finance at the University of Texas at Austin, McCombs School of Business.

Justin Wolfers is an assistant professor of business and public policy at the Wharton School, University of Pennsylvania.

Eric Zitzewitz is an assistant professor of economics at Stanford University's Graduate School of Business.

JOINT CENTER

AEI-BROOKINGS JOINT CENTER FOR REGULATORY STUDIES

In order to promote public understanding of the impact of regulations on consumers, business, and government, the American Enterprise Institute and the Brookings Institution established the AEI-Brookings Joint Center for Regulatory Studies. The Joint Center's primary purpose is to hold lawmakers and regulators more accountable by providing thoughtful, objective analysis of relevant laws and regulations. Over the past three decades, AEI and Brookings have generated an impressive body of research on regulation. The Joint Center builds on this solid foundation, evaluating the economic impact of laws and regulations and offering constructive suggestions for reforms to enhance productivity and welfare. The views expressed in Joint Center publications are those of the authors and do not necessarily reflect the views of the Joint Center.

COUNCIL OF ACADEMIC ADVISERS